FRIDAY NIGHT
BITES

**KICK OFF THE WEEKEND WITH FOOD
AND FUN FOR THE WHOLE FAMILY**

by Karen Berman

Photographs by Steve Legato

RUNNING PRESS
PHILADELPHIA · LONDON

9   8   7   6   5   4   3   2   1
Digit on the right indicates the number of this printing

Library of Congress Control Number: 2008944123

ISBN 978-0-7624-3641-5

Cover and interior design by Amanda Richmond
Edited by Kristen Green Wiewora
Special thanks to Joanne Slike, Maria Soriano-Person, and NY Loft, Philadelphia
Typography: Frutiger, Swingdancer, and Sassoon

Running Press Book Publishers
2300 Chestnut Street
Philadelphia, PA 19103-4371

Visit us on the web!
www.runningpress.com

To my sister Ellen,

without whom this book would not have been possible, for so many reasons.

. . . .

And to my daughter Jessica,

who makes Friday night—and every other night—so precious.

★ Table of Contents ★

★ Acknowledgements ★

THEY SAY IT TAKES A VILLAGE TO RAISE a child, and I've concluded that it also takes a village to produce a cookbook. I've been blessed with the most wonderful village. My deepest gratitude to:

My sister Ellen for testing most of the recipes in this book, brainstorming, baby-sitting, and offering encouragement at every turn;

My daughter Jessica, for helping create some of the recipes, tasting the finished dishes, enthusiastically testing the crafts and giving me her kid thumbs up for each chapter;

My niece Anna, for her enthusiastic tasting and testing of crafts, and serving as a general excitement barometer for the project;

My partner Oscar and my brother-in-law Paul, for fearless tasting and offering useful critiques whenever needed;

My brother Bob, for his expert help with baseball terminology, and my aunt Raye, for her wonderful insights on modern art.

To my friend, Cindi Kruth, baker extraordinaire, for developing several of the dessert recipes in this book and offering good advice on others;

My foodie friends JoAnn Englund, Helen Brody, Stephanie Browner, Joanne Pelton, Francine Fielding, and Anne Tack, for brainstorming ingredients and techniques when I was stuck, Joy Schmidt, for her authentically British insights into Toad in the Hole, graphic artist Eileen Curran for her expertise, and **Mary Goodbody, for her wise and generous counsel, as always;**

My pal John Burgeson, (a newspaper editor who doubles as a college science instructor) for reviewing the scientific information in the book and setting me straight when necessary.

Food stylist Maria Soriano-Person, photographer Steve Legato, and his assistant Andrea Monzo, for making my little recipes dance off the pages, and designer Amanda Richmond, who put it all together and created a beautiful package. To copy editor Joanne Slike, for her eagle-eyed review of the manuscript, and editor Diana von Glahn for offering me the lovely opportunity to do this book.

My wonderful editor Kristen Green Wiewora for her professional wisdom in shaping the book, her thoughtful line-editing, and her encouragement and kindness throughout the project. The adorable kids, Eva Connell, Mia Connell, Tamyra Jones, Jared Cabrera, Josh Gordon, Bryn McLaughlin, Eddie Keiner, Ethan Keiner, Jacob Hamilton, Justin Hamilton, Alexis Noble, their families, my own daughter Jessica, good-looking adults Wayne Noble, Frank Sipala, and Susan Van Horn, for serving as the super-models for the photographs in this book.

And a host of taster-advisers: Lori Mangano, Sharon Green-Levine, Randi and Seth Block, Marc and Andrea Patten, Jennifer and Bruce Wallis, Joan and Krista Lucas, and the Teddy Bear and Tiger's Den gangs. And to my young tasters and crafters: Sara Morgan and Erica Block, Sarah Dawson, Kaitlyn and Ethan Mangano, Stephen Paolini, Jolie Patten and Eva Wallis.

What a wonderful village I have!

★ Introduction ★

Friday night.

YOU CAN ALMOST HEAR the collective *"Aaaa-hhhh,"* as families all across the land prepare to kick back and enjoy an evening at home.

On this one night of the week, there's no soccer practice to run to, no religious school to be on time for, no gymnastics, tennis, piano, no French or Mandarin Chinese language class, no PTA meeting or School Playground Committee on the agenda. Even homework and household chores can wait. Friday night is our night to call a halt to all our running, and simply revel in the company of the people we love most.

Of course, there are Friday nights when all we want to do is clamber into jammies, order pizza, and declare movie night. But there are other Fridays, nights when we have a bit more energy left after the hectic week, when we've carved out some time to shop and prepare beforehand, nights when all our personal planets are in their proper alignment. These nights call for something more ambitious,

something that will engage children and adults alike, something to please both timid and adventurous palates, and spark conversation and imagination.

Friday Night Bites is a book for those nights. Here, you will find the blueprints for some 20 dinners, each one planned around a theme, with food and activities that will appeal to kids and (I hope) the kids who reside deep within the rest of us.

But let me begin at the beginning. When the very smart folks at Running Press approached me with the concept for this book, I was, as the mother of a seven-year-old, hooked immediately. If you're a parent or have children in your life, you've doubtless experienced moments of awe at the sheer loveliness of a child's imagination. If, on occasion, you get to take part in the imagining, you are lucky indeed. And if, at times, imaginative play leads to a chance to explore together a little about where things come from and how the world works, you've hit the parenting jackpot.

This book offers a venue—dinner—at

which families can engage in all of the above. It is primarily a cookbook, with each chapter devoted to a single themed dinner. The recipes relate to the night's theme, either by virtue of a traditional name given a new application (for example, floating islands cast as a tropical island for Dinnertime on a Pirate Ship); or a whimsical name of my own making (as with the appetizer in Ye Royal Dinner—the Princess and the Sugar Snap Peas), or the architecture or presentation of the food itself (as in the Microphone Cupcakes in the You Might Even Be a Pop Star dinner). In each chapter, too, you'll find a game plan for the evening, tips for short-cuts and do-aheads, ideas for activities and crafts, and little bits of trivia that I call Table Talk—questions on the evening's theme that a child might be curious about, and factoids that parents might like to have at the ready.

About the Kids

IN MANY CASES, your kids will be working with you as you cook; I've marked recipes that I think are especially conducive to group participation with this icon. But if you're working with a sharp knife or a hot pot, or if the kids just don't feel like cooking on a particular night, there's a simple craft that goes with each dinner. You can set it up before the meal, or if you prefer, save it for after. If you do the craft before dinner, I've found it useful to set up a separate space away from the food prep area; maybe you have a small kid-sized table you can bring into the kitchen for the night, or a spot in the family room where they can do the craft while you cook, or even a corner of the kitchen where you can lay out some newspapers on the floor. You'll figure out what works best in your house.

About the Food

MOST OF THE RECIPES in this book will yield four adult servings. Because kids' appetites vary at different ages and because families vary in their makeup (two parents and two kids? one parent and three kids? two parents, a grandparent, and one child?), I found that four adult servings was flexible enough to accommodate many, if not most, family configurations and appetites. Most recipes can easily be doubled as necessary.

The food in this book is not the typical "kid-friendly" fare of mac-and-cheese and chicken nuggets (though heaven knows, I've served those, and gratefully so). I suggest saving those trusty standbys for other nights. Friday Night Bites is about exploration, culinary as well as intellectual.

I can hear some parents protest, "My kid will never eat that!" To be honest, my own didn't eat everything in the book, but she did discover many things she hadn't eaten before and many she never would have imagined she would like. You just never know.

What I do know, though, is that it's a good thing to introduce your kids to new foods at dinner, both because variety is a part of good nutrition, and also because it's a way of learning about the world. At the same time, I also believe in respecting a child's food preferences. I realize that there are parents out there who still subscribe to the "eat-it-or-be-hungry" school, but I believe that sharing the evening meal should be a time of comfort and pleasure for all. So when something unfamiliar makes its way onto my table, I always offer it, praise the timid taster for trying it, and if the food is rejected, I move to Plan B.

With this in mind, I've tried to structure the dinners so that even the most selective eaters will find enough to eat. If the little ones don't care for the Shipwreck Seafood Salad in Cucumber Boats from the Under the Sea Dinner, by all means make it for the grown-ups and older kids, and toss together the kid-friendly Shipwreck Fruit Salad in Cantaloupe Boats. Do offer a taste of the Seafood Salad, with its sweet crabmeat, fresh fennel, and dilled tomato mayonnaise; your picky somebody might just like it. Similarly, if you're doing Dinner on the Moon, and you know your littles won't abide the sight of bits of basil in the Green Cheese Tortellini Alfredo, make up a serving of pasta and Alfredo sauce for them before you add the basil. They'll likely love the tasty pasta and gentle cream sauce, and you can offer a taste of fragrant basil-kissed pasta from your plate. For the everything cold Dinner at the North Pole, if your forecast says they won't like the dried cranberry and scallion that perk up the Ho-Ho-Ho Cream Cheese Spread on the Cold Roast Beef Sandwiches, offer a taste of the spread first, and if they don't care for it, make theirs with plain cream cheese. You might all be in for a surprise.

Words for the Cook

SOME OF THE FOOD in this book is quick and easy, but other dishes will require some time. If you can do some of the prep the night before, it can be fun to get the kids involved and excited about the dinner to come. However, as a full-time working mom, I'm well aware of the needs busy families. I love the idea that my recipes might inspire you to cook up something delicious from scratch—but I fully endorse shortcuts that will enable you to enjoy the evening with your kids—and get dinner on the table in a reasonable amount of time. For the nights when you can't cook the whole dinner, pick the recipes you'd like to try and follow my suggestions for doctoring prepared ingredients and filling in with store-bought items. Or by all means, come up with quick solutions of your own.

In case your kid is like mine, clamoring for something to eat before the whole meal is ready, I've incorporated a relatively quick and healthful appetizer into every dinner. I know parents who discourage pre-dinner munching on the grounds that kids won't eat the full meal when the time comes. In my house, I find that it's better to have something to calm the hunger pangs—and for us, most of the time, that something has no effect on the amount eaten later on. You know your kids and their appetites, so plan your own meal accordingly.

One thing you'll notice in these recipes is an abundance of fruits and vegetables. If I have a culinary religion, it is fresh produce. I think that teaching kids to eat fruits and vegetables is one of the most valuable gifts we can give them, one that will last all their lives. Public health studies strongly suggest that people whose diets are high in fruits and vegetables can reduce their risk of chronic diseases like cancer and heart disease. Similarly, you'll find lots of calcium-rich foods (dairy and dark green, leafy veggies) in this book, because proper calcium intake in the first decades of life builds healthy bones and can reduce the risk of osteoporosis later on. What I like about this approach is that the message is positive. As a society, we tend to demonize foods and emphasize what we shouldn't put into our mouths; it's nice to be able to celebrate the things we should eat instead.

You will find fat and carbs in this book— bad words for some, especially when the headlines tell of an epidemic of childhood obesity. To these folks, I offer a reminder that fat is necessary for the absorption of vital nutrients, and that this is especially important for growing bodies and brains. Likewise, carbs are necessary fuel for active kids. Beyond this, I'd like to see parents teach their children not to make particular foods into bad guys, but to learn how to balance all the different kinds of foods that we are lucky enough to be able to eat.

After all, Friday comes but once a week.

Please take these dinners and make them your own. Savor the good smells that come out of your kitchen—and the smiles and the silliness that are sure to erupt at the table. Enjoy each bite. *Aaahhhh*. It's Friday night.

⋆ Dinner on the Moon ⋆

SEEING THE MOON THROUGH MY CHILD'S EYES REAWAKENED me to the beauty and wonder of Earth's companion in the sky. And when I talked to other moms and dads, I found that I wasn't the only nutty parent driving blocks out of my way so that my child could get a better view. It's hard to say who gets more excited by the sight of a full moon—parent or child. This dinner builds on that excitement, with a little science and a lot of whimsy. You can fly to the moon for dinner and be back in time for bed!

Menu

Mozzy's Comet

Garlic Crescent Moon Rolls

Distant Star Salad

Green Cheese Tortellini Alfredo

Moon Rock Chocolate Chip Biscotti

Game Plan

★ Make (and nibble) Mozzy's Comet appetizer.

★ Prep the Garlic Crescent Moon Rolls and set aside.

★ Mix the Moon Rock Chocolate Chip Biscotti batter and bake for 20 minutes.

★ Meanwhile, get the kids started on the Phases of the Moon Centerpiece.

★ Bring a pot of water to boil and cook the tortellini. When it's done, drain and keep warm.

★ Meanwhile, make the Distant Star Salad, but do not toss with dressing.

★ Process the basil and grated cheese for the Green Cheese Tortellini Alfredo.

★ Remove the Moon Rock Chocolate Chip Biscotti from the oven and let cool.

★ Bake the Garlic Crescent Moon Rolls for 10 to 15 minutes.

★ Make the Green Cheese Alfredo Sauce.

★ Toss the Distant Star Salad with the vinaigrette.

★ Toss the tortellini with the Green Cheese Alfredo Sauce.

★ Remove the Garlic Crescent Rolls from the oven and let cool.

★ Houston, we have dinner!

★ Bake the Moon Rock Chocolate Chip Biscotti for 10 more minutes.

★ One small step to dessert!

DINNER PREP IN SMALL BITES:

If you have time the night before or earlier in the day, bake the biscotti.

FRIDAY NIGHT TIME-SAVER:

Use bagged salad and bottled vinaigrette. Serve store-bought biscotti.

Crafty Friday:

PHASES OF THE MOON CENTERPIECE

MAKE A SHIMMERING CENTERPIECE THAT'S EDUCATIONAL, TOO. You'll have a centerpiece that looks a little like a candelabra, with pipe cleaners instead of candles. Moons will wave wildly at the tips, and the glitter glue swirls behind them in the "night sky" look like distant stars. When it's all put together, you'll have a 3-D timeline that shows how the moon waxes and wanes over the course of a month. If you don't have white foam packing material for the base on hand, your local craft store or mailing shop should have some.

8 toothpicks

8 dark blue or black pipe cleaners

Safety scissors

1 sheet (8½ x 11 inches) white paper

Pencils

1 sheet (8 x 10 inches) dark blue
   or black construction paper

Transparent tape

Glitter glue

1 white foam rectangle
   (8 to 10 inches x 3 to 4 inches)

Starting about ½ inch from the sharp end, wrap each toothpick loosely with about one quarter of a pipe cleaner to make a sharp anchor for the pipe cleaner. You should have at least three quarters of the pipe cleaner above the wrapped toothpick.

Next, make the pictures of the phases of the moon. Cut the white paper into 8 equally sized pieces and distribute them to everyone. With a pencil, copy the phases of the moon designs (see following page), one on each piece, making the designs just under an inch tall. Cut them out.

Next, make starry backgrounds for your moons in the color of the night sky. Cut the construction paper into 8 equal pieces to make 8 rectangles. Fold each of the 8 construction paper rectangles in half to make a square. Tape the sides together, leaving the bottom edge open, like a pocket.

Cap each pipe cleaner with one of the squares by inserting the unwrapped end of each pipe cleaner into the pocket. If necessary, seal the square with a little more tape so that it stays on. Don't put tape across the center of the square, as it will keep the glue from sticking.

(continued on next page)

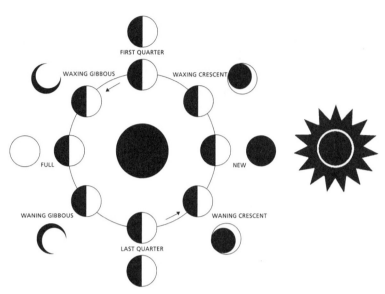

Swirl some glitter glue on both sides of each square in a random squiggle to make distant galaxies. Place a white "phase of the moon" in the center of each glue squiggle. If you wish, squiggle some glitter glue over the white foam base, too. Allow the moons and base to dry.

Mount your phases of the moon into your centerpiece. Stick the toothpicks into the foam base, from left to right, in the order that they appear during the month.

TABLE TALK

What are the phases of the moon?

WHEN YOU LOOK UP AT THE NIGHT SKY over the course of each month, the moon's shape looks like it's changing. These changes are called the phases of the moon. Actually, the moon's shape does not change at all. What we see when we look up at the moon each night is the light of the sun hitting it. It looks different from night to night because the moon moves around the Earth (in a path that takes a month to complete). As the moon moves, the amount of sunlight we can see on its surface changes. These changes have names: During the full moon phase, the entire moon is illuminated and we see a circle. As it travels, it appears to get smaller (this is known as *waning*) and bigger (known as *waxing*). The shape that looks a slice of cantaloupe turned sideways is called a *crescent moon*. The half circle is called a *quarter moon*. More than a half circle but less than a full circle is called a *gibbous moon*. When we can't see the moon at all, it's called the *new moon*.

Every month, the phases go like this: new moon, waxing crescent, first quarter, waxing gibbous, full moon, waning gibbous, last quarter, waning crescent, and new moon. Then the cycle starts all over again. If this is hard to understand, act it out after dinner. (See After-Dinner Fun, page 22)

MOZZY'S COMET

THESE LUMPY, BUMPY LITTLE TIDBITS WON'T FLY THROUGH SPACE, but they will fly into hungry mouths! They're a fast, easy appetizer that is full of protein and calcium for muscles and bones. By all means, buy pre-shelled pistachios to make the prep quick and easy. If someone at your table is allergic to nuts, use toasted sunflower or pumpkin seeds instead of pistachios.

MAKES 16 PIECES

4 sticks mozzarella string cheese, quartered or 16 small mozzarella balls, preferably low-fat

½ cup shelled pistachio nuts

Pour the nuts into a plastic bag and crush with a meat mallet or the bottom of a heavy pot. Pour the crushed nuts into a shallow bowl and roll all 16 pieces of mozzarella in it to coat.

TABLE TALK

What's a comet?

A COMET IS A ball of dust mixed with chemical gases and ice. Comets originate far from our planet Earth, but sometimes, as they move, their paths are disturbed and they get close enough for us to see. As they do this, the heat of the sun melts the ice a bit and it turns to vapor and dust. This process forms the comet's characteristic "tail," which arcs behind it as it flies. Comets are often named for the people who first discover them. Some comets fly in a set path that recurs over time. Halley's Comet, for example, comes into view every seventy-six years. Some people confuse comets with shooting stars. Shooting stars are tiny bits of rock that enter the earth's atmosphere and burn up after a second or two.

GARLIC CRESCENT MOON ROLLS

THIS IS A QUICK AND EASY ADDITION TO YOUR DINNER ON THE MOON. *If someone at your table doesn't care for garlic, leave a few of the rolls plain. If you've got garlic lovers in your midst, by all means, sprinkle on a little more!*

MAKES 8 ROLLS

2 cloves garlic, finely chopped

1/4 teaspoon salt

1 tablespoon unsalted butter or heart-healthy margarine

1 (8-roll) package crescent roll dough

Position an oven rack in the middle position and preheat the oven to 350° F.

Place the garlic in a small microwavable bowl and cover with the salt. Add the butter and microwave on high power for 30 to 45 seconds, or until the butter is melted. Let cool slightly. If you like a less intense garlic flavor, strain and discard the garlic pieces.

Separate the dough at the perforated lines and place the 8 triangles on a baking sheet. Brush some garlic butter on each, dividing it evenly among the triangles. Roll the triangles to form crescents, folding the wide side first.

When you are ready to bake, place them into the oven for 10 to 15 minutes, or until light golden-brown.

DISTANT STAR SALAD

THE NIGHT SKY IS FULL OF STARS—AND SO IS THIS SALAD! These stars will jazz up a bowl of healthful greens and introduce your kids to some tropical fruits that they might not be familiar with. Star fruit, or *carambola*, is a tropical fruit with an angled exterior that, when sliced crosswise, makes star-shaped slices; it isn't always available, but you can depend on finding kiwi, the fruit with the fuzzy brown exterior. Peel and slice the kiwi crosswise to reveal its brilliant green starburst seed pattern. Anyone who is brave enough to taste one or both fruits gets to make a wish on the star!

MAKES 4 TO 5 SERVINGS

Vinaigrette

2 tablespoons plus ½ teaspoon red wine vinegar

1 tablespoon Dijon mustard

6 tablespoons extra-virgin olive oil

Salt

Freshly ground black pepper

Salad

½ head red-leaf and ½ heart romaine lettuce, trimmed, washed, dried and torn (4 to 6 cups), or 1 bag mixed green- and red-lettuce salad, washed and dried

½ small Vidalia or other sweet onion, thinly sliced

2 kiwi fruit, peeled and sliced crosswise in rounds

2 star fruit (carambolas), trimmed and sliced crosswise into stars, if available (optional, see dietary caution in sidebar)

To make the vinaigrette, pour the vinegar and mustard into a small nonreactive container with a tight-fitting lid, cover and shake to mix. Add the olive oil; cover and shake again until thoroughly combined. Season to taste with salt and pepper, and set aside.

For the salad, toss the lettuces, onion, kiwi, and star fruit (if you are using them), in a salad bowl.

Just before serving, toss the salad with the dressing and portion it equally among 4 salad bowls. Pick out 1 kiwi slice and 1 star fruit slice and place them on top of each salad, so that the star pattern is visible.

A native of southern Asia, star fruit is a nutritious tropical fruit. Look for those that are shiny yellow or let green ones ripen. Avoid any that are shriveled with brown spots; they're overripe. To serve, trim the brown root end and edges, slice crosswise, and remove the seeds. Star fruit can be dangerous to people with kidney disease, and like grapefruit, can interfere with prescription drugs.

GREEN CHEESE TORTELLINI ALFREDO

LEGEND HAS IT THAT THE MOON IS MADE OF GREEN CHEESE. Science tells us that the moon's surface is covered with circular holes called craters. This dish imagines the tortellini as the craters of the moon, covered in tasty green cheese sauce.

If someone at your table doesn't like basil, toss his or her portion with the plain Alfredo sauce before adding the herb. And if you use the fat-free half-and-half, look for a brand without added corn syrup.

MAKES 4 SERVINGS

1 (16-ounce) package frozen cheese tortellini

1 cup fresh basil leaves, stems removed, washed and patted dry

¾ cup grated Parmesan cheese or Parmesan and Romano cheese blend, plus more for serving

2 ounces (½ stick) unsalted butter

1 cup light cream or fat-free half-and-half

¼ teaspoon salt, or to taste (optional)

Freshly ground black pepper (optional)

Cook the tortellini according to the package directions. When it's done, drain and keep warm.

Meanwhile, place the basil and grated cheese into a food processor or mini-chopper fitted with a metal blade and process just until the basil is finely chopped and thoroughly combined with the cheese.

Melt the butter in a large nonstick skillet set over medium-high heat. Add the cream and cook, stirring often, for about 4 minutes, or until the mixture is thick enough to coat a wooden spoon. Reduce the heat if necessary while you cook, to make sure the mixture does not burn. You can also remove the skillet from the heat for a minute, if necessary.

Add the basil-cheese mixture to the sauce in the skillet and stir gently to combine. Taste and season lightly with salt and pepper if you like. With a slotted spoon, transfer the remaining tortellini into the skillet and toss to coat. Spoon the tortellini into individual bowls and serve.

MOON ROCK CHOCOLATE CHIP BISCOTTI

BISCOTTI, THE TWICE-BAKED ITALIAN COOKIES MADE FOR DUNKING, are usually sliced into long strips and dunked into coffee. For our version, they're shaped into round "moon rock" cookies.

MAKES ABOUT 16 BISCOTTI

Nonstick cooking spray

2 cups all-purpose flour

¼ teaspoon salt

2 teaspoons baking powder

3 large eggs

1 teaspoon pure vanilla extract

¾ cup granulated sugar

¼ cup semisweet or milk chocolate chips

Milk, chocolate milk, or hot chocolate for dunking (See note, below)

Preheat the oven to 350°F. Spray 2 baking sheets with non-stick cooking spray.

In a medium bowl, combine the flour, salt, and baking powder.

In a large bowl, mix the eggs, vanilla, and sugar with a fork until the sugar is thoroughly dissolved. Add about a third of the flour mixture and, with an electric mixer set at medium speed, beat for 30 seconds, or until just combined. Add half the remaining flour mixture, beat again for 30 seconds or just until combined, then add the remaining flour mixture and beat for 1 minute, or until combined. Incorporate all the flour, but don't overbeat. Fold in the chocolate chips with a spatula.

Drop batter by heaping tablespoons onto the prepared baking sheets to make about 16 cookies, spacing them about 2 inches apart to allow them to expand. Bake for 20 to 25 minutes, or until light golden. Remove from the oven and let cool. When they have cooled, return them to the oven for 10 to 15 minutes, or until golden brown. Remove from the oven and let cool.

Biscotti are often served with coffee, but in Italy, they're also enjoyed with a sweet dessert wine called Vin Santo. Let the kids have milk or cocoa and, for a grown-up treat, parents can dip theirs into some Vin Santo or other dessert wine.

What's a moon rock?

Moon rocks are rocks that were brought back from the moon by various manned and unmanned space missions of the United States and what was then the USSR (now Russia). Scientists have studied moon rocks extensively to learn about what the moon is made of. (It's not green cheese!)

After-Dinner Fun: Moonwalk

AFTER DINNER, YOU CAN DEMONSTRATE THE PHASES OF THE MOON with members of your family. First read about the phases of the moon (see Table Talk, page 16). Then have one person take the part of the moon; one, the Earth; and one, the sun. The sun should stand in the center of the room holding a flashlight. Darken the room.

The Earth and the moon should walk together in a circle around the sun. The moon should also walk in a circle around the Earth while it is walking around the sun. The sun should shine the flashlight on both while they walk. (Go slowly to make sure nobody trips and falls!) Look at how the light falls on the moon as he or she walks around the Earth. Do you see the phases of the moon where the light touched the moon's body? (Walk in slow motion. You'll see the light on the moon's entire body, then progressively less light on his or her body, until you reach the new moon phase, when there should be no light touching the moon's body.)

Play Ball!

I HAVE TO ADMIT THAT I'M NOT MUCH OF A SPORTS FAN,
but I'm always moved and impressed when I see kids getting caught up in
sports like baseball; they're off on a love affair that will likely last a lifetime.
And there's so much learning that takes place off the field. Math is especially
important in baseball with all its statistics; good sportsmanship through
wins and losses is a lesson central to all sports—not to mention life.
Maybe most important is hope: There's always next year!

Menu
Popperjack
Chili Dawgs
Ballpark Nacho Salad (with Chili Dawg Chili)
Bat 'n' Ball Banana Split

Game Plan

I LIKE THIS DINNER BECAUSE IT GIVES YOU LOTS OF OPTIONS. So often parents end up eating what their kids prefer because they lack the time and energy to cook up two different meals. For this meal, the chili is the centerpiece; you can serve it in the form of Chili Dawgs or with the main-course Nacho Salad—or both. The chili recipe will yield enough for four servings of both recipes and you can refrigerate any leftovers for another meal (see the note at the end of the recipe). So if any of your small folks are salad-averse, it's easy to assemble the salads for those who'll eat them and throw a hot dog or two into the broiler; the hot-doggers will still get their veggie quotient from the chili and fresh condiments. Of course, if the grown-ups like hot dogs, too, you can make more of those and make the salads smaller—or skip them altogether. It's a parent/short-order cook's dream!

★ Make (and nibble) the Popperjack.

★ Get the kids started on the Ballpark Place Mats.

★ Cook the Chili Dawg Chili.

★ Cook the hot dogs and toast the buns, if serving, and keep warm.

★ If you are having the Nacho Salad, mix the cheese topping, but don't heat it yet.

★ Prep condiments for Chili Dawgs and/or Nacho Salad.

★ Prep the salad and assemble, leaving the heating of the cheese sauce and pouring it over the salad for last.

★ Get'cher ballpark dinner here!

★ Make the Bat 'n' Ball Banana Split. ✋

★ Batter up for dessert!

DINNER PREP IN SMALL BITES:

If you have time the night before or earlier in the day, you can make the chili and reheat it on the stovetop or in the microwave before serving.

FRIDAY NIGHT TIME-SAVER:

If time is short, buy the best-quality prepared chili you can find. Use packaged shredded Mexican blend or taco cheese instead of mixing the Cheddar and Monterey Jack for the nacho cheese sauce. Use bagged salad instead of tearing the lettuce yourself.

Crafty Friday:
BALLPARK PLACE MATS

MAKE YOUR DINNER TABLE INTO A BASEBALL DIAMOND. Tape is a better choice than glue for this project because you don't have to wait for it to dry before you put your dinnerware on top of it. If you like, you can use one big sheet of butcher paper to make a ballpark tablecloth, using the same concept as follows.

If your kids are too little to draw (or even understand) the concept of a baseball diamond, simplify the task by helping them write—or writing for them—the numbers 1, 2, and 3 and the letters H and P (for home plate and pitcher's mound) on the mats. Let them decorate as they wish.

White marker or white artist pastel

4 to 6 pieces (9 x 12-inch) brown construction paper

Green construction paper (9 x 12-inch) (optional), depending on the number of people at your table

Small team logos on paper, downloaded from the Internet or cut from a newspaper or magazine

Baseball cards

Transparent tape

Safety scissors

Crayons or markers (optional)

Using the white marker, draw home plate (in the shape of a house) and first, second, and third bases (squares) on separate pieces of brown construction paper.

If there are more than 4 people at your table, make more place mats using green construction paper for left field, right field, shortstop, center field, catcher, or base coaches for the other diners.

Draw the pitcher's mound on another sheet of brown paper. This will be a serving mat for the center of the table. You can also make a dugout, if you have the room!

Decorate your mats by taping on the team logos and baseball cards, using whole cards or pieces cut from them. If you like, you can position one team in the outfield and one team at bat and in the dugout. Or create a dream team and assign players to a team of your own choice.

The kids can also add details to any of the mats by drawing on them. Arrange the placemats and serving mats so they are in their proper positions on the table to make a baseball diamond.

POPPERJACK

TAKE ME OUT TO THE BALL GAME, TAKE ME OUT WITH THE CROWD! Try this lighter, less-sweet version of the ballpark favorite. If someone at your table is allergic to nuts, try breaking up honey-glazed sesame seed candy with a meat mallet or the bottom of a heavy pot (put the candy into a plastic bag first) and mixing pieces of it into the popcorn. You can make the servings as large or small as you like, and save any leftovers, sealed in an airtight container, for tomorrow.

MAKES 4 TO 8 SERVINGS

1 bag microwavable popcorn, preferably light

1 cup honey-roasted peanuts

¼ cup chopped dates

4 to 8 brown paper lunch bags or plastic sandwich bags

1 small plastic figure or 1 washable tattoo in its wrapper or other tiny prize per person (optional)

Pop the popcorn according to the package directions. When it is cool enough to handle, divide the popcorn between four brown lunch bags or plastic sandwich bags, picking out and discarding any unpopped kernels.

Divide the peanuts and dates between the bags. If you wish, throw a small prize into each. Close the bags and shake each one to mix. Serve.

TABLE TALK

CAN YOU SING "TAKE ME OUT TO THE BALL GAME" all the way through? Try singing it now.

CHILI DAWGS

IF BASEBALL IS AMERICA'S FAVORITE PASTIME, hot dogs are our favorite edible accompaniment to the game. This easy chili is a great addition to a hot dog and to another ballpark staple, nachos (try it with the Ballpark Nacho Salad, page 31). You can also use it to top baked potatoes, and it's might tasty on its own, with a slice of Sunshine Cornbread (see Teddy Bear Picnic, page 38). I like to use leaner ground turkey for this chili, but if you prefer beef or a mixture of the two, just drain some of the fat from the pan before adding the tomatoes and other ingredients. Dress with the condiments suggested or any others you might like; everyone knows that topping preferences are as personal as ball teams!

MAKES 4 TO 8 HOT DOGS

Chili

Nonstick cooking spray

1 small yellow or white onion, chopped

1 to 2 garlic cloves, finely chopped

1 to 1½ pounds ground turkey or ground beef

1 (28-ounce) can chopped tomatoes and juice and 1 (15-ounce) can chopped tomatoes and juice

1 cup amber-style beer (optional)

1¼ teaspoons chili powder, plus more to taste

1 teaspoon ground cumin

½ teaspoon salt, plus more to taste

Freshly ground black pepper to taste (optional)

Spray a large, heavy skillet with nonstick cooking spray. Set over medium-high heat, add the onion, and cook, stirring occasionally, for about 5 minutes, or until the onion is softened and golden in color. Add the garlic and cook, stirring occasionally, for about 30 seconds. Add the meat and cook, stirring and breaking up any large pieces with the side of a wooden spoon, for about 6 minutes, or until lightly browned.

Pour the tomatoes and their juice over the meat. Add the beer, if you are using it, chili powder, cumin, and salt and cook, stirring occasionally, for 20 to 25 minutes, or until the liquid has evaporated and there is no alcohol taste. Taste and season with salt, pepper, and more chili powder if you like, and stir to incorporate.

While the chili is cooking, prep the condiments and place them into individual serving bowls.

Preheat the boiler.

Hot Dogs

4 to 8 hot dogs

4 to 8 hot dog buns

Shredded Cheddar, for serving (optional)

Sour cream, for serving (optional)

Sliced scallions (white and green parts), for serving (optional)

Halved grape tomatoes, for serving (optional)

Sliced black olives, drained, for serving (optional)

Sliced pepperoncini peppers or small hot pickled peppers, drained, for serving (optional)

Mustard, relish or other hot dog toppings of your choice, for serving (optional)

Broil the hot dogs in a roasting pan in the toaster oven or the regular oven. Split and toast the buns.

When the chili is ready, place the dogs into their buns and top with $1/4$ to $1/3$ cup chili. (Use remaining chili for Ballpark Nacho Salad.) Let everybody dress their Dawgs with the condiments of their choice.

NOTE: This recipe will make enough chili to top both the hot dogs and the Ballpark Nacho Salad; if you are making one or the other, any leftovers will keep, covered, in the refrigerator, for 4 days.

 Instead of painstakingly peeling the garlic (and getting the pulp in your fingernails!) place the garlic clove on a cutting board. Press down on it with the flat (not the blade) of a large chef's knife. Press firmly but gently until the clove smashes. Alternatively, smash with the bottom of saucepan. Remove the papery skin and cut off the brown ends. Chop the garlic, if needed, and proceed.

What's the home team?

The home team is the team that is based in the city or ball field where the game is taking place. The other team is called the visiting team.

Ball Park Lingo

DID YOU KNOW THAT DINNER AND BASEBALL share some of the same language? Here are a few terms:

TABLE SETTER: The first or second batter in an inning; if one or both get on base, the table is set for the next batters to drive them in to home plate.

THE MEAT OF THE ORDER: The third or fourth batters in an inning; they are generally powerful hitters who can drive the table setters home to score.

GRAND SALAMI: A grand slam. When bases are loaded and the hitter hits a home run, the team scores four runs.

PICKLE: What a base runner is in when he or she is caught between two bases, with fielders on both bases throwing the ball back and forth overhead and the runner is forced to run back and forth until tagged out— or until one of the fielders makes a mistake.

JAM: A pitch that comes close to hitting the batter's body, so that he or she has a hard time batting the ball successfully.

MEATBALL: A pitch that is easy to hit.

CAN OF CORN: An easy outfield catch.

PLATE, DISH: Home plate.

BALLPARK NACHO CHILI SALAD

RE-CREATE YOUR FAVORITE BALLPARK NACHOS—and up the nutritional value with a good helping of fresh veggies and homemade chili. The resulting salad is fun, healthful, and delicious. If you use fat-free half-and-half for the cheese sauce, look for a brand with no added corn syrup. You can also make these as first-course or side salads; just reduce the quantities.

MAKES 4 MAIN-COURSE SALADS

Nacho Salad

4 cups Chili Dawg Chili, page 28

Nacho chips, for serving

8 cups torn iceberg, romaine or other crisp lettuce

20 grape tomatoes, halved

16 to 20 cucumber rounds

Cheese Topping

1 cup shredded Cheddar cheese

1 cup shredded Monterey Jack cheese

½ cup light cream or fat-free half-and-half

Condiments

Scallions, sliced, including white and green parts, for serving (optional)

Sliced black olives, drained, for serving (optional)

Sliced pepperoncini peppers or hot small hot pickled peppers, drained, for serving (optional)

Prepare the Chili Dawg Chili according to the directions on page 28. Check it frequently while you prep the rest of the meal, stirring to make sure it cooks evenly and that it does not burn. Reduce the heat if necessary and keep warm.

While it is cooking, place a handful of chips in each of 4 serving bowls. Divide the lettuce among them. Toss with the tomatoes and cucumbers. Top each with a generous handful of nacho chips.

Prep the condiments and place each into individual serving bowls.

Mix the shredded Cheddar, shredded Jack cheese, and cream or half-and-half in a microwavable bowl. Microwave on high power for 1 minute. Stir and microwave again for 1 minute, or until the mixture is smooth. Stir to be sure the cheeses are thoroughly incorporated.

Top each salad with a generous portion of chili and spoon some cheese sauce over the top. Serve hot. (If by chance the cheese sauce congeals before you can spoon it onto the salads, microwave it for about 45 more seconds and stir.) Let everybody dress their salads with the condiments at the table.

BAT 'N' BALL BANANA SPLIT

WITH THE BANANA AS A BAT AND A SCOOP OF VANILLA ICE CREAM AS THE BALL,
you've got a banana split for baseball fans. Heating the banana briefly and then drizzling it with caramel sauce gives it a little something extra, but if you prefer, you can serve the banana plain. Just don't forget the red licorice stitching or the chocolate chip autograph!

MAKES 4 SERVINGS

8 thin red peelable licorice strands (sometimes called "whips," not the thicker licorice twists)

½ cup mini semisweet or milk chocolate chips, or to taste

4 peeled bananas

Caramel sauce, for drizzling

1 large scoop vanilla ice cream per person

Place the licorice strands on a small serving plate and pour some chocolate chips into a small serving bowl. Set aside.

Place the bananas into 4 shallow microwavable soup bowls. Drizzle each with a little caramel sauce and, working with one at a time, microwave on high power for 30 to 45 seconds, or until the bananas are just softened.

When the bananas come out of the microwave, scoop a generous ball-shaped serving of ice cream into each bowl, centered on the banana. Work quickly so that the warm bananas do not melt the ice cream too much.

Bring the bowls to the table immediately and have each person decorate the ice cream: Bend the licorice strands to form "U" shapes and place two each onto the ice cream ball, facing in opposite directions, where the stitches would go. Spell out your name or your favorite player's name with chocolate chips—or just spell out the initials. Serve.

TABLE TALK

WHAT IS YOUR FAVORITE BASEBALL TEAM? Who is your favorite baseball player? Why? If you could assemble a team of your favorite baseball players from history or contemporary times, who would you pick to be on your team?

Teddy Bear Picnic

HERE'S A DINNER NAMED FOR AN OLD SONG, WHICH WAS, OF COURSE, inspired by everyone's favorite toy. Why is it that out of all the toys you had when you were a child, Ted D. Bear is one that you remember best? And why is it that a soft, huggable Teddy was one of the first toys you bought for your child? We connect with teddy bears—always have, always will.

Menu

Ants on a Log

Red Ants on a Snowy Log

Sunshine Cornbread

Honey-Kissed Pork Tenderloin

Blushin' Applesauce

Fruity Field O' Greens Salad

Baby Bear Claws

Game Plan

★ Make the marinade and marinate the pork in the refrigerator. (Or do this overnight.)

★ Make (and nibble) one or both of the Ants on a Log recipes. ✋

★ Make the Sunshine Cornbread and bake. ✋

★ Get the kids started on the Teddy Bear Bonnets and Boaters.

★ Take out the frozen puff pastry to thaw.

★ Prep the Blushin' Applesauce and microwave.

★ Remove the Sunshine Cornbread from the oven and put the pork in to roast for 10 minutes.

★ Prep the salad and mix the dressing, but do not dress the salad until just before serving.

★ Pour the marinade into the roasting pan with the meat. Roast the meat for 10 more minutes.

★ Prep the Baby Bear Claws. ✋

★ Remove the pork tenderloin from the oven and remove the pork from the pan. Deglaze the pan on the stovetop and make a sauce.

★ Toss the salad with the dressing.

★ Calling all bears to the table!

★ Finish prepping the Baby Bear Claws and bake.

★ Make tracks to a freshly baked dessert!

DINNER PREP IN SMALL BITES:

If you have time the night before or earlier in the day, any or all of these items—the Sunshine Cornbread, Blushin' Applesauce, Baby Bear Claws, and the marinating of the meat—can be done in advance.

FRIDAY NIGHT TIME-SAVER:

Buy cornbread, bear claws or both in your bakery, and use your favorite bottled salad dressing. You can also doctor jarred applesauce, but allow it some time in the fridge for the flavors to meld.

EVERY WELL-DRESSED TEDDY BEAR needs a bonnet or a snazzy boater hat. Make one or more for the bears in your house!

Safety scissors

1 paper plate for each hat (Use large or small plates depending on the size of the bear)

1 (2-foot) length of ribbon for each hat

More ribbon for decoration, including striped grosgrain if you are making boaters for boy bears

Small decorative flowers, fruits, birds, butterflies, colorful feathers, and buttons or other small decorations for bonnets

1 (2- to 3-inch wide) strip of oak tag (thin, flexible poster board) that is about 2 inches shorter in length than the circumference of your paper plate, for boater hats

Small buttons, feathers, birds, bugs, team logos, or other decorations, for boater hats

1 (5- to 6-inch wide) roll of tulle

Craft glue

Transparent or masking tape

If your paper plate has a design imprinted on it and you want it to be part of the hat, turn the plate "inside out" so that the design shows when you put the plate on the bear's head.

With the scissors, cut a slit in the plate about ¾ inch to 1 inch long; position it where the curved rim of the plate ends and the flat center begins, about an inch or so from the edge of the plate. Make another slit directly across from it, so that you can insert the 2-foot ribbon into the slits and tie the plate onto the bear's head.

To make a boater, take the strip of oak tag and make a ring to fit the circumference of the flat inside part of the plate. Trim excess cardboard and tape the strip together securely to make a ring. Tape the ring to the plate from the inside. Glue the grosgrain ribbon to the bottom of the ring, where it joins the plate. Finish the hat by gluing on feathers, buttons or other decorations. Let it dry.

To make a bonnet, cut a length of tulle and tie it into a bow, leaving 6 to 8 inches of tulle for each of the bow's "tails." Glue to the back of the bonnet. If you wish, cut a length of tulle to make a veil that will hang over the front of the bonnet and glue it on. Decorate the hat by gluing the flowers, fruit, birds, butterflies, feathers, and other decorations to it. Let it dry. Or use your imagination and decorate your bear's hat any way you wish.

ANTS ON A LOG

IT WOULDN'T BE A PICNIC WITHOUT ANTS. This classic snack for kids is a fast, easy starter for your picnic. If someone at your table doesn't like celery or can't eat peanut butter, substitute apples (the dish becomes Ants on a Rock) or low-fat cream cheese (Ants on a Snowy Log or Rock).

MAKES 12 TO 16 PIECES

4 celery stalks, trimmed and cut into 3½ - to 4-inch lengths (12 to 16 pieces)

Peanut butter, as needed

Raisins, as needed

Spread some peanut butter in the curve of each piece of celery, leaving about an inch at the end clear, so your log will be easy to pick up without getting peanut butter all over your hands.

Press 5 or 6 raisins on each—or as many "ants" as you like— and serve.

TABLE TALK

How did the teddy bear come to be?

IN 1902, THEODORE ROOSEVELT WAS THE PRESIDENT OF THE UNITED STATES. Roosevelt was known as a great supporter of nature, and he liked to hunt, so when he traveled to Mississippi for presidential business, he was invited to go on a bear hunt. After a few days of hiking in the woods, the hunters had not found any bears. The organizers of the hunt did not want the president to be disappointed, so they found an older bear, chased it until it was tired, tied it to a tree, and presented it to the President to shoot. Roosevelt refused, declaring that it would not be sportsmanlike to shoot an animal in that condition. The story made the news, and an artist named Clifford Berryman drew a newspaper cartoon showing Roosevelt refusing to shoot the bear. A man named Morris Michtom saw the cartoon and got an idea. His wife Rose sewed some toy bears and Mr. Michtom wrote to the President, whose nickname was Teddy, asking if he could call the bears by that name. More than 100 years later, teddy bears— in every color and size—are still a favorite of children and grown-ups, too.

RED ANTS ON A SNOWY LOG

HERE'S A VARIATION ON THE CLASSIC that will appeal to grown-ups and kids alike. The sweet-tart cherries contrast nicely with the creamy cheese and the tangy garlic. Be warned, though: the garlic flavor will intensify with time, so if, by chance, you make this ahead, use less garlic powder. And if you don't care for garlic, this recipe works just as well without it.

MAKES 8 PIECES

¼ cup (2 ounces) low-fat cream cheese, softened

½ teaspoon garlic powder (optional)

4 long breadsticks, cut in half, or 8 short breadsticks

½ cup dried cherries

Mix the cream cheese with the garlic powder, if using, in a small bowl and mash until the garlic is thoroughly incorporated into the cheese.

Spread some garlic-cream cheese on each breadstick, leaving about an inch at the end clear, so your log will be easy to pick up without getting the spread on your hands.

Press 5 or 6 dried cherries on each, and serve.

SUNSHINE CORNBREAD

SUNSHINE IS A KEY INGREDIENT FOR A PICNIC. This sweet-savory cornbread, baked in a circle, lets you bring your own sunshine to the table. A Bundt pan, with its wavy surface and hole in the middle, makes for an interesting presentation, but if you don't have one, use an 8-inch round cake pan or deep pie plate.

MAKES 1 ROUND LOAF

Nonstick cooking spray

¾ cup self-rising yellow cornmeal

¾ cup all-purpose flour

1 teaspoon salt

1 cup low-fat buttermilk

½ cup honey

1 large egg, lightly beaten

½ cup corn kernels (thawed if frozen, drained if canned, or cut off 1 ear of corn if fresh)

1 cup shredded Cheddar cheese (optional)

Place the oven rack in the middle position and preheat the oven to 450°F. Spray a Bundt pan with nonstick cooking spray.

Pour the cornmeal, flour, and salt into a mixing bowl and mix lightly to combine. Add the buttermilk and honey. Add the egg to the cornmeal mixture. Mix with a fork until the dry ingredients are thoroughly incorporated into the wet ingredients, scraping the sides and breaking up any floury lumps.

Add the corn kernels and cheese, if you like, and mix well.

Pour the batter into the prepared pan and bake for 20 to 25 minutes, or until a toothpick inserted into the cake comes out clean.

Remove the pan from the oven, and run a knife around the edges, including the center (if you are using a Bundt pan). Place a round serving plate face-down on top of the pan. With oven mitts on, grasp the pan from the bottom and the top, flip the cornbread onto the plate, and remove the pan. Serve warm or let cool. Wrap leftovers in foil; the cornbread will keep for several days.

Self-rising cornmeal has the baking powder already mixed in; if your brand also contains all-purpose flour, double the amount of cornmeal you use and eliminate the all-purpose flour called for in the recipe. If you can't find self-rising cornmeal, add 3 teaspoons of baking powder to the dry ingredients.

HONEY-KISSED PORK TENDERLOIN

WHAT'S A BEAR'S FAVORITE FLAVOR? Honey, of course. In this dish, honey is mixed with soy sauce and honey mustard to add a luscious sweet-savory dimension to the oh-so-tender tenderloin. The mixture begins as the marinade and ends up in the sauce. Just never use a marinade in which raw meat has been soaked as a sauce on cooked food; be sure to heat it to boiling once you remove the meat from it, or you run the risk of introducing food-borne bacteria to your cooked food. When you're shopping, look for a pork tenderloin that is not pre-marinated. You're making your own from scratch!

MAKES 4 TO 5 SERVINGS

2 to 4 garlic cloves, finely chopped (see page 29)

⅓ cup honey

3 tablespoons soy sauce

3 tablespoons honey mustard

2 tablespoons vegetable oil

1 (1 to 1½ -pounds) pork tenderloin

¾ cup beef stock

½ teaspoon arrowroot

Salt to taste (optional)

Feshly ground black pepper to taste (optional)

Preheat the oven to 475°F.

Place the garlic into a shallow nonreactive glass, ceramic or plastic container big enough to hold the tenderloin. Add the honey, soy sauce, honey mustard, and oil and mix until thoroughly combined.

Trim the pork tenderloin: With a sharp knife, peel off any silvery skin (it's called silverskin) and trim any fat. Place the trimmed tenderloin into the marinade and turn a few times to coat. Cover and refrigerate overnight or a few hours—or if time is short, while you prep the rest of the dinner.

When you are ready to cook, transfer the tenderloin to a roasting pan and roast for 10 minutes. Reserve the marinade, keeping it away from any raw food or utensils.

After 10 minutes, turn the tenderloin and carefully pour the marinade over it. Roast for 10 more minutes, or until an instant-read thermometer inserted into it reads 150 to 155°F and the tenderloin is nicely browned on the outside and just slightly pink in the center.

Remove the tenderloin from the pan and place on a serving
(continued on next page)

platter to rest. Deglaze the roasting pan by adding the beef stock and stirring to loosen any browned bits from the bottom. Pour the contents of the pan into a small saucepan, add the arrowroot, and cook over medium-high heat, stirring occasionally, for about 5 minutes, or until the sauce thickens and reduces in volume enough to coat a spoon lightly. Taste and season with salt and pepper if you like.

Cut the tenderloin into round medallions and pour some of the sauce over them. Pour the remaining sauce into a serving bowl or gravy boat and pass at the table.

TABLE TALK

Can you describe your favorite teddy bear?

EVERYBODY AT THE TABLE CAN TAKE TURNS telling about their favorite bears—their colors, sizes, any clothing or accessories, how old they were when they got their bears, how long they've had them, and why they are so special.

Can you sing all the words to "The Teddy Bears' Picnic?"

THE MUSIC TO THIS CLASSIC SONG WAS COMPOSED by John W. Bratton nearly 100 years ago. The words were added almost 30 years later by Jimmy Kennedy. If you can't remember all the words, you can find them on a number of Internet sites. Just search for "teddy bear picnic song."

BLUSHIN' APPLESAUCE

THIS HOMEMADE APPLESAUCE GETS ITS NAME AND ITS ROSY HUE from the dollop of black currant preserves that goes into the pot. The recipe came about by accident, when I was wondering what to do with an extra jar of preserves. The resulting flavor is as bright as the color. Use as many varieties of apples as you like, but be sure to include some sweet-tart ones.

MAKES 4 TO 6 SERVINGS

¾ cups (6 ounces) 100 percent apple juice or sweet cider

6 to 8 sweet-tart apples, such Royal Gala, Fuji, or Granny Smith

2 tablespoons black currant preserves

Pour the apple juice into a large microwavable bowl.

Peel and core the apples and cut them into wedges, placing the wedges into the juice as you go to keep them from turning brown.

Add the preserves and stir to dissolve and distribute them among the apples.

Cover loosely and microwave on high power for 15 to 25 minutes, or until the liquid has evaporated and the apples are soft enough to mash. (The time will depend on the apples you use.) Midway through the cooking, stir the apples and add a little more juice or water, if necessary. Be careful not to burn yourself, as the mixture will be hot.

Remove from the microwave and mash with a fork or potato masher. Serve warm or cold. Any leftover applesauce will keep, covered in the refrigerator, for 1 week.

NOTE: You can make this applesauce on the stovetop, too; just stir often and watch carefully to be sure it doesn't burn.

FRUITY FIELD SALAD WITH HONEY MUSTARD VINAIGRETTE

HERE'S A FRESH, FRUITY SALAD with a tangy-sweet vinaigrette that will please all the bears at your table, human and otherwise!

MAKES 4 SERVINGS

Honey Mustard Vinaigrette

¼ cup red wine vinegar

2 tablespoons honey mustard

½ cup extra-virgin olive oil

Salt to taste

Freshly ground black pepper to taste

Salad

1 apple, such as Royal Gala, Fuji or Granny Smith

1 (5- to 7-ounce) bag field greens or spring mix salad

½ pint blackberries

To make the vinaigrette, pour the vinegar into a nonreactive glass, ceramic, or plastic container with a tight-fitting lid. Add the mustard, cover, and shake to mix. Add the oil, cover, and shake until thoroughly combined. Taste and season with salt and pepper if you like.

Cut the apple in half and remove the core and seeds, leaving the peel on. Slice very thinly and place the slices into the vinaigrette as you go, to keep them from turning brown. Cover and set aside.

Just before you are ready to serve, place the greens in a bowl. Add the blackberries, apples, and vinaigrette and toss to coat the greens with the dressing.

BABY BEAR CLAWS

THIS DESSERT IS TYPICALLY EATEN AS A BREAKFAST PASTRY on the West Coast of the United States, but it's good anywhere, anytime—and just the thing for a Teddy Bear Picnic. The classic recipe calls for a dough made from scratch, but this quick and easy version makes use of frozen puff pastry. Bear claws are typically filled with almond paste and/or raisins; as a chocolate lover, I like to use chocolate-covered raisins. You should feel free to fill these pastries with any of these fillings or another of your choice.

MAKES 4 BEAR CLAWS

Nonstick cooking spray

1 sheet frozen puff pastry, thawed

½ cup chocolate-covered raisins, or more if needed

1 egg, lightly beaten with 2 tablespoons water, for egg wash

1 to 2 teaspoons granulated sugar for sprinkling

Place the oven rack in the middle position and preheat the oven to 400°F. Lightly spray a baking sheet with nonstick cooking spray.

Place the puff pastry on the baking sheet, cut it into four squares, and separate them.

Arrange 20 to 25 chocolate-covered raisins across 1 square in a single layer, so that you form a strip of raisins left to right in the center of the square.

Fold the top third of the pastry square down so that it covers about half the raisins. Fold the bottom third up so that it covers the rest of the raisins and overlaps the other flap of pastry by about half an inch and makes a pouch. Press to seal, and pinch the open edges together.

Hold a sharp knife at a 90-degree angle to one of the folded sides, and make 3 (1-inch) slashes. Fan the cut pastry out slightly to form the bear's "claws." On the other side, use your hands to taper the two corners inward a bit, to suggest a heel. Repeat with the remaining squares. Brush the egg wash over the top of the pastries. Sprinkle the claws with a little sugar. Bake for 15 to 20 minutes, or until golden in color. Remove from the oven and let cool a bit before serving.

After-Dinner Fun: Bookish Bears

GATHER YOUR FAVORITE TEDDY BEAR BOOKS and read them aloud. Don't forget *Winnie-the-Pooh, The Three Bears, Paddington Bear, Little Bear, Fozzie Bear, Corduroy*, the *Berenstain Bears, Smokey the Bear*, and all the rest.

Under the Sea

THERE'S NOTHING LIKE A RESTORATIVE DIP IN—OR EVEN A WALK BY—THE SEA.
The beautiful sea has always fascinated land-lubbing humans; we're lucky
to live in a time when science and technology let us see what's actually down
there under the waves. This dinner is designed to spawn discussions
both fanciful and factual about what lies under the sea.

Menu

Puffy Sea Stars

Shipwreck Fruit Salad in Cantaloupe Boats

Shipwreck Seafood Salad in Cucumber Boats

Shells in Tomato "Seaweed" Sauce

Coral Reef Cake

Game Plan

YOU CAN MAKE ONE OR BOTH OF THE SALADS FOR THIS DINNER. For example, if someone at your table is not a veggie- or seafood-eater, make a small portion of the fruit salad and make the seafood salad for the rest of the gang.

★ Thaw the frozen puff pastry for the Puffy Sea Stars.

★ Prep and bake (and nibble) the Puffy Sea Stars. ✋

★ Get the kids started on the Undersea Shadow Box.

★ Bring a pot of water to a boil for skinning the tomatoes for the Tomato "Seaweed" Sauce and the Shipwreck Seafood Salad, if you are making it. Prep a large bowl of ice water. Cut an X into the bottom of each tomato.

★ Meanwhile, if you are making the Shipwreck Fruit Salad, scoop out the melon boats and cut up the fruit to fill them.

★ If you are making the Shipwreck Seafood Salad, scoop out the cucumber boats and if time allows, start prepping the vegetables that will go into them.

★ When the water boils, follow the directions in the recipe for peeling and seeding the tomatoes. Add the vine-ripened tomato to the food processor for the Dilled Tomato Mayonnaise. Set the others aside for the sauce.

★ Prepare the Shipwreck Seafood Salad. Refrigerate until ready to serve.

★ Bring a pot of water to a boil and cook the shells. Drain and keep warm.

★ Cook the Tomato "Seaweed" Sauce.

★ Assemble the Fruit Salad and Shipwreck Seafood Salad Boats.

★ Mix the shells into the Tomato "Seaweed" Sauce.

★ Surf's up! It's Dinnertime!

★ Prep and cook the Coral Reef Cake. ✋

★ Smooth sailing to dessert!

Crafty Friday:
UNDER THE SEA SHADOWBOXES

USE YOUR IMAGINATION TO DECORATE THESE UNDERSEA SHADOWBOXES. Gather the materials listed below and any others that come to mind, and inspiration will come as surely as the tide!

1 shoebox per person

Blue construction paper

Craft glue

Transparent tape

Safety scissors

Green crepe paper

Green yarn and/or small green pompoms

Colored pipe cleaners

A handful of sequins

A handful of seashells or rocks

A few plastic pearls

Line the inside bottom and sides of the shoebox with the construction paper with glue or tape, cutting the paper to fit. Leave one long side uncovered. (That will be the sandy bottom of the sea.) If you like, you can cover the outside of the shadow box as well.

Create an undersea scene. Use crepe paper, yarn, or pompoms as seaweed and underwater plants. Form fish or mermaids (and mermen) by bending and cutting pipe cleaners and taping them to the construction paper. Make bubbles by gluing sequins to the construction paper. Glue seashells onto the bottom of the sea and glue pearls inside them.

Make your shadow box three-dimensional by taping some of your decorations to the bottom of the sea. Use pipe cleaners to help them stand up if necessary.

PUFFY SEA STARS

THESE EDIBLE SEA STARS ARE FUN TO MAKE. Use any combination of toppings that you and your kids will like. Or let each person select his or her own combination of toppings. Flavored and colored salts make an appealing presentation.

MAKES 8 PIECES

Nonstick cooking spray

1 sheet frozen puff pastry, thawed

1 egg, lightly beaten with 2 tablespoons water, for egg wash

1 tablespoon coarse salt, such as sea salt or flavored salt

1 tablespoon golden or black sesame seeds (optional)

1 tablespoon poppy seeds (optional)

1 tablespoon caraway seeds (optional)

Preheat the oven to 400°F. Lightly spray a baking sheet with nonstick cooking spray.

Place the puff pastry sheet on a work surface and cut crosswise into 10 (1-inch) strips. Cut each strip in half crosswise. You will have 20 strips measuring 1 inch by 4 to 5 inches.

Place 2 strips together to form a wide X. Repeat with 14 more strips, to make a total of 8 pastry Xs.

Cut the remaining 4 strips in half. Place a half-strip on each X, positioning the end of the strip in the center of the X to make a five-armed sea star; be sure to place the fifth arm so that it only touches the other two arms in the center.

Take the ends of one of the bottom strips, cross them over the top as though you were going to tie a knot, and press to seal the top half-strip into the pile. Fan the pieces out slightly, spacing them evenly to suggest five equidistant arms.

Using a pastry brush, brush on the egg wash so that it covers the pastry. Sprinkle lightly with salt and the toppings of your choice. (Don't oversalt; coarse salt can be intensely flavored.)

Bake for 15 to 20 minutes or until the stars have risen and are golden in color. When they are cool enough to handle, dig in!

What's a sea star?

SEA STARS USED TO BE CALLED STARFISH, but since they're not really fish, scientists have changed their name. Most sea stars have five arms, which gives them their star shape. Their mouths are on their underside, at the star's center. To eat, they push their stomachs up and out of their mouths. When they're done, they pull their stomachs back inside. If a sea star has an accident and loses one of its arms, it can grow a new one. Not bad for a creature that has no brain!

SHIPWRECK FRUIT SALAD IN CANTALOUPE BOATS

CUSTOMIZE THESE MELON BOATS WITH YOUR FAMILY'S FAVORITE FRUITS; use the suggestions below or whatever your family likes. You know your crowd, so you pick the varieties and the quantities; if your kids only like apple and melon, then use several apples, but if they like grapes, berries, pineapple, and apples, then a single apple will probably be enough. You get the idea. If you do use apples in this salad, be sure rub the cut surfaces with an orange segment or dip into orange juice to keep them from turning brown.

MAKES 4 SERVINGS

1 cantaloupe melon, cut in quarters and seeded

½ cup bite-sized pieces of fruit per person, such as seedless grapes, strawberry halves, blueberries, pineapple chunks (fresh or canned in their own juice), apple chunks and orange segments

Orange juice (optional, if you use apples but not orange segments)

With a melon baller, scoop out the flesh of the melon quarters into small balls, leaving enough so that the "boats" have sides.

If you are using apples, core and cut them into bite-sized wedges, rubbing them with a cut orange segment or dipping them into a cup of orange juice as you go to keep them from turning brown.

In a bowl, mix the melon balls and apple wedges, if you are using them, with the other fruit and toss lightly.

Spoon a heaping portion of salad into each melon boat.

SHIPWRECK SEAFOOD SALAD IN CUCUMBER BOATS

FENNEL AND FRESH DILL GIVE THIS SEAFOOD SALAD A DELICATE AROMA AND FLAVOR.
The tomato enlivens the mayonnaise dressing, so use the best one you can find—either from your own garden or the farmers' market, or a vine-ripened one from the supermarket. Please don't use fat-free mayo here; the texture just isn't the same as the real thing. If you don't want to fill the cucumber boats too full, any leftover salad will keep for two to three days, covered, in the refrigerator, and could certainly also be served on a bed of leafy greens. For a fun garnish, reserve four sprigs of fresh dill and use them for the "masts" of the boats.

MAKES 4 SERVINGS

Dilled Tomato Mayonnaise

1 medium tomato, vine-ripened or from your garden or the farmers' market

¼ cup stemmed and coarsely chopped fresh dill, plus 4 whole sprigs, for garnish

½ cup good-quality mayonnaise

Shipwreck Seafood Salad

4 plump pickling cucumbers, chilled

½ bulb fennel (anise), fronds removed, trimmed, and cut into bite-sized pieces (see note, next page)

8 ounces lump crabmeat, drained, picked over to remove any shell or cartilage, and flaked, or 1 (8-ounce) package pollack (imitation crabmeat), cut into bite-sized pieces

Boil a pot of water for peeling and seeding the tomato.

Spoon the mayonnaise into a food processor fitted with a metal blade. Add the dill.

When the water boils, peel and seed the tomato (see note, page 52). Place the tomato pulp into the food processor and process until the mayonnaise is coral-colored and flecked with tiny bits of green dill.

To make the boats, first peel the cucumbers. Then, working lengthwise with the vegetable peeler, cut away just enough flesh from one side of the cucumber so that it can sit flat on a plate without rolling. With the cucumber set flat like this, cut a thin lengthwise strip from what is now the top. Scoop out the seeds with a melon baller and discard them. Then scoop out some of the cucumber flesh to make the cucumber "boat." Cut the cucumber you've scooped out into bite-sized pieces, and place them into a glass or ceramic mixing bowl. Repeat with the remaining cucumbers.

Add the fennel, crab, and the mayonnaise to the bowl and toss to coat. Divide the salad evenly among the cucumber boats, letting it spill out over the sides a bit, and serve. Garnish with a sprig of dill for a "mast."

NOTE: If you are cooking the Shells and Tomato "Seaweed" Sauce, you can peel and seed the tomato for this salad along with those you'll use for the sauce. Just boil a pot of water big enough to hold all the tomatoes for both recipes and peel and seed as directed.

Fennel, sometimes called anise, is a wonderfully fragrant, slightly sweet-tasting vegetable that is eaten raw or cooked. To use, cut out the core and remove any dried-out or shriveled outer leaves from the bulb. Some folks eat the stalky "fingers," while others discard them; it's up to you. Do cut off the feathery fronds and discard most of those, though you can save some to use as a garnish. If you have leftover fennel, slice it raw into a salad. It's also delicious sautéed in olive oil with finely chopped garlic.

SHELLS IN TOMATO "SEAWEED" SAUCE

LOTS OF PEOPLE IN VARIOUS PARTS OF THE WORLD ENJOY EATING REAL SEAWEED, but the green stuff floating in this sauce is actually a stand-in—spinach, rich in iron and so good for you!

MAKES 4 SERVINGS

24 plum (Roma) tomatoes

1 pound medium pasta shells

2 tablespoons olive oil, plus more as needed

2 cloves garlic, crushed and finely chopped (See note, page 29)

1½ cups fresh baby spinach, or ½ cup frozen spinach, thawed

¼ to ½ teaspoon salt, or more to taste

Freshly ground black pepper to taste

Grated Parmesan or Romano cheese, for serving

Boil a pot of water for peeling the tomatoes. When the water boils, peel and seed the tomatoes (see note).

Cook the shells according to the package directions. When they're done, drain and keep warm.

For the sauce, heat the oil in a large, heavy nonstick skillet. When it sizzles, add the garlic and cook, stirring, for about 30 seconds, or until softened and golden. Add the spinach, stir to coat with the oil, and cook for 1 to 2 minutes, or until it wilts. Add the tomatoes and cook, stirring often and breaking them up with the side of a wooden spoon, for 10 to 20 minutes, or until the tomatoes have become a chunky sauce. Taste and season with salt and freshly ground black pepper, if you like.

With a slotted spoon, transfer the cooked shells into the sauce and toss to coat. Spoon the shells into serving bowls and serve with grated cheese.

To peel tomatoes, bring to a boil a stockpot of water large enough to hold all of them. Prepare a large bowl of ice water. Cut an X into the bottom of each tomato. When the water boils, carefully place the tomatoes into it. Boil for 30 seconds to 1 minute, and using a slotted spoon, transfer each to the ice water for about 30 seconds, to stop the cooking. Starting at the cut X, pull off the peel; it should come off easily. Halve the tomato, remove and discard the core, dig the seeds out with your hands and discard them. Proceed with the peeled, seeded tomatoes.

CORAL REEF CAKE

IF YOU CAME UPON THIS FRIED CAKE AT A CARNIVAL or country fair you'd know it as a funnel cake. For our imaginary undersea excursion, it's a coral reef—with the help of a little food coloring! To make these treats, you'll need a funnel with an opening about half an inch wide. Be careful when you make these, as the oil is hot and can splatter and burn! Let very small children stand back and watch.

MAKES 4 TO 6 CAKES

$1\frac{1}{4}$ cups all-purpose flour

3 tablespoons granulated sugar

1 teaspoon baking powder

$\frac{1}{4}$ teaspoon salt

$\frac{3}{4}$ teaspoon pure vanilla extract

1 cup milk, plus more as needed

Few drops of food coloring, red, pink, or any color of your choice

3 cups vegetable oil

Confectioners' sugar

Prepare a plate with a few layers of paper towels for draining the cakes and place it near the stove.

Combine the flour, sugar, baking powder, and salt in a mixing bowl. Add the vanilla, 1 cup milk, and the food coloring and mix to combine thoroughly. The batter should have the consistency of pancake batter.

Heat the oil in a deep 10- to 12-inch skillet until it reaches a temperature of about 360°F. (See note, page 54.) Position the mixing bowl next to the stove. Hold the funnel in one hand and plug the hole at the bottom tightly with your hand or finger. Scoop about $\frac{3}{4}$ cup of batter into the funnel.

Hold the still-closed funnel over the oil. Release your finger and drop the batter into the oil, moving the funnel back and forth to create a wiggly pattern. Don't drop too much dough in any one spot. If the batter doesn't flow from the funnel easily, add a little more milk, stir to incorporate, and try again.

Fry the cake for about 1 minute, or until it puffs a bit. Turn with tongs and cook for another minute, or until golden in color. Drain on the paper towels. (The food coloring might obscure the light-golden color, so after the cake cools a bit, you can break off a corner to see if it is cooked through.)

(continued on next page)

Repeat with the remaining batter, letting the oil reheat in between cakes.

Drain all the cakes on paper towels, blot lightly if necessary and serve topped with confectioners' sugar sprinkled over the top.

Deep-frying requires that the oil reach the right temperature. An electric skillet with a temperature control makes the task easy. You can also use a candy thermometer. If you don't have either, let the oil heat for a few minutes, until it shimmers, and if you are using a batter with food coloring, like this one, carefully place a piece of bread about half an inch square into the oil. (If you do not use a colored batter, you can drip a little batter into the oil. The food coloring can mask the color change that takes place during frying.) If it sizzles immediately and begins to turn golden brown within 45 to 60 seconds, the oil is hot enough.

TABLE TALK

What's a coral reef?

CORALS ARE UNDERSEA CREATURES whose origins date back million of years. There are many kinds of coral; some, known as stony corals, secrete a bony skeleton made of limestone. When they get together in colonies, their skeletons merge to create a habitat called a reef. The reef is an important habitat for fish, undersea plants, and animals. Coral reefs vary in color, shape, and size. Some are tiny, while others can weigh several tons. Some are round and ball-shaped, while others have knobs and stalks. Some are brilliantly colored. Because they shelter so many plants and animals, coral reefs are vital to the undersea ecology. They help us on land, as well, by providing barriers during storms and recycling carbon dioxide, which slows down global warming. Unfortunately, pollution, climate change, too much development on nearby land, overfishing, and other environmental hazards have put coral reefs in danger. A number of groups are working to save the world's coral reefs.

After-Dinner Fun: Reef Comber

TO SEE HOW BEAUTIFUL CORAL REEFS ARE, and to learn what you can do to help preserve them, search the Internet for "coral reef."

Dinnertime on a Pirate Ship

AHOY, MATEYS! FROM LONG JOHN SILVER TO CAPTAIN FEATHERSWORD, the appeal of the pirate lives on and on. Could it be the exotic locales they visit? The romance of living on the sea? Or maybe it's the cool way they talk? Here's a dinner for pirate fans, complete with some buried treasure in the main course and the dessert! *Arrgghh!*

Menu

Captain Antipasto's Wheel

Parrot Feather Salad

Treasure Chest Meatloaf

White Cap Twice-Baked Potatoes

Yellow Squash Doubloons

Floating Treasure Island

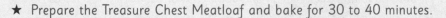

Game Plan

★ Soak the teabags for the Antique Treasure Map craft project in a cup of water.

★ Make (and nibble) Captain Antipasto's Wheel.

★ Prepare the Treasure Chest Meatloaf and bake for 30 to 40 minutes.

★ Drain the teabags and get the kids started on the Antique Treasure Maps.

★ Soak the hearts of palm for the Parrot Feather salad in passion fruit juice for 15 minutes.

★ Meanwhile, microwave the potatoes for the White Cap Twice-Baked Potatoes.

★ Prepare the vegetables for the Parrot Feather salad. Drain the hearts of palm, reserving the juice. Make the dressing using the reserved juice but do not toss with the salad.

★ When the potatoes are cool enough to handle, prepare them for their second baking.

★ Make the Yellow Squash Doubloons and keep warm.

★ Remove the meatloaves from the oven and let stand for 15 minutes. Increase the oven temperature and bake the potatoes for 15 minutes.

★ Add the hearts of palm to the salad and toss with the dressing.

★ Arrgghh! Dinner's Up!

★ Make the Floating Treasure Island.

★ Avast, ye swabbies! It's time for dessert!

DINNER PREP IN SMALL BITES:

Make the meatloaf the night before or earlier in the day. You can also bake your own meringues for the Floating Treasure Island (using the recipe from page 116), but you'll have lots left over.

FRIDAY NIGHT TIME-SAVER:

If time is short, bake the potatoes just once, but do mold them into white-cap wave shapes and add the "fish" below and on top. Use store-bought meringue cookies for dessert.

Crafty Friday:
ANTIQUE TREASURE MAPS

"X" MARKS THE SPOT ON THESE TREASURE MAPS, and dampened tea bags create the antique effect. Oak tag (thin, flexible poster board) is thick enough so that the tea won't soak through and cause it to tear. Cut the maps in any size you like. One 22 x 28-inch sheet will make a giant map, two medium-sized ones, or four small ones. Let your imagination sail away!

1 black tea bag per person

1 small glass of water

1 or 2 sheets of oak tag (thin, flexible poster board)

Markers or crayons

Calligraphy pens or markers (optional)

Stickers of fish, palm trees, pirates, or nautical themes

Soak the tea bags in the water for a few minutes until they are saturated, and squeeze them out over the sink well so that they don't drip. (If there are small children doing this project, it might be good for a grown-up to do this.) Discard the tea water, place the tea bags back into the empty cup, and set aside.

Cut the oak tag into map-sized pieces, sizing them so there are enough for everyone. Scallop the edges if you like to make them look like they've ripped over the years. Design a 1-inch border all around the edges of your map, decorating it with drawings, patterns, and stickers.

Draw the area inside the border. You can depict an island with water surrounding it or show a land route, but either way, it should have an "X" to mark the spot where the treasure is buried. Each map can also have a compass of arrows showing north, south, east, and west.

Along the route, label the landmarks (sand castles, fish, a pirate hat shop, or whatever you like) and pitfalls (palm trees with falling coconuts or a lagoon full of alligators). Younger children can draw these or use stickers, while older children can illustrate and spell out the names, as well. For those who can write, calligraphy pens are a fun way to make the maps look old.

To antique the maps, be sure the teabags have been wrung out very well so they aren't drippy. Blot and rub it over your map, just enough so that the map takes on an uneven golden-brown color, but not enough so that the liquid pools. (If there's too much liquid in one spot, wipe it up with the tea bag.) Let dry for 10 to 15 minutes and you've got an instant antique. Now, pretend it's a map of the room and try walking the route you've mapped out!

What's a pirate?

A PIRATE IS SOMEONE WHO ROBS SHIPS AT SEA. Piracy—the job of being a pirate—has been around for thousands of years—since people started sailing the seven seas. Some pirates were sailors who couldn't find other work; others were nasty people who liked stealing. Real pirates did not have an easy life; sailing a ship was hard work, and without refrigeration, their meals often consisted of crackers called hardtack, which they mixed with broth or coffee. Over the years, though, pirates have captured the imagination of writers, playwrights, and filmmakers, who have emphasized the exciting aspects of life at sea. Typically, pirates are depicted as spirited, rebellious souls who flew the Jolly Roger (a flag imprinted with a skull and crossed bones or swords), danced jigs, and wore their trademark two-corner or three-corner hats. These charming rogues showed great cunning in their raids on other ships, nimbly jumping from rigging to deck and back again, swords drawn. Pirate stories often feature buried treasure, although few pirates actually buried theirs.

Shiver me timbers! The pirate legend might not be true to historical fact, but it's a lot of fun to think about!

Can you name some famous fictional pirates?

Here are a few:

THE PIRATE KING, a character in *The Pirates of Penzance* by Gilbert and Sullivan (1879)

LONG JOHN SILVER, in the novel *Treasure Island* by Robert Louis Stevenson (1884)

CAPTAIN HOOK, in the play *Peter Pan* by James M. Barrie (1904)

JACK SPARROW, Pirate Lord of the Caribbean, in the Disney series *Pirates of the Caribbean*

CAPTAIN FEATHERSWORD, the gentle singing and dancing pirate who is a friend of the Wiggles, the Australian singing group for the preschool set.

What's a captain's wheel?

A CAPTAIN'S WHEEL, OR SHIP'S WHEEL, IS THE STEERING WHEEL OF THE BOAT.
It's connected to the rudder, which is a blade on the bottom of the boat that enables it change direction in the water. Before the ship's wheel was invented, sailors used a stick called a tiller to move the rudder.

CAPTAIN ANTIPASTO'S WHEEL

THE HUNGRY MATES AT YOUR TABLE WILL BE HAPPY TO navigate Captain Antipasto's wheel, with its pretzel "spokes" of salami, marinated mushrooms, tomatoes, and cucumbers. You can vary what's on the spokes any way you like, but make sure you use tidbits that are soft or you won't be able to skewer them. If you like, you can arrange harder antipasto tidbits that can't be skewered around the wheel on the plate. An easy option is a jar of marinated veggies, often called by the Italian name of *giardiniera* (gardener); just be careful when you shop, as some brands of giardiniera contain marinated hot peppers, which is fine if your crew likes them, but are likely to produce loud *Aargghhs* if they don't!

MAKES 4 ANTIPASTO WHEELS

24 (3- to 4-inch) thin pretzel sticks, plus more in case of breakage

3 ($\frac{1}{2}$-inch) cucumber rounds, each cut in quarters, to make 12 wedges

6 slices Genoa salami, each cut in half, then folded in half, to make 12 wedges

12 grape tomatoes

12 marinated mushrooms

4 (1$\frac{1}{2}$- to 2-inch) balls fresh mozzarella, plus a few more in case of breakage

Mixed marinated vegetables (giardiniera) or other antipasto tidbits, for serving (optional)

Spear a cucumber wedge with a pretzel stick, leaving about $\frac{1}{2}$ inch of pretzel at the end, so that you can spear a mushroom next to it. If you have trouble spearing the cucumbers with the pretzels, "drill" little holes in them with a sharp knife or metal skewer. Repeat with 11 more pretzels and the remaining cucumber wedges and mushrooms.

Spear a folded salami wedge with another pretzel stick, leaving about $\frac{1}{2}$ inch of pretzel at the end so that you can spear a tomato next to it. Repeat with the remaining 11 pretzels and the remaining salami wedges and tomatoes.

Place 1 mozzarella ball in the center of an appetizer plate. Insert 3 cucumber-mushroom pretzels and 3 salami-tomato pretzels into it, like spokes, alternating the two kinds, with the speared ingredients at the outside. If necessary, insert the pretzels into the cheese at different heights, so they'll fit securely. Repeat with the remaining cheese and skewered pretzel sticks.

If you are using giardiniera or other tidbits, scatter some pieces around the captain's wheel and serve. Let everyone pull out the spokes of the wheels and eat them.

PARROT FEATHER SALAD

PARROTS HAVE BEEN ASSOCIATED WITH PIRATES since Long John Silver made his debut in *Treasure Island*. This salad is inspired by the colors of the most common parrot species—green with brilliant bits of red and yellow—and by ingredients found in the tropics, where parrots live, and where many pirates traveled. Canned hearts of palm might have a residual "canned" flavor, but you can temper it if you soak them in the passion fruit juice that will later go into the salad dressing; the juice imparts a nice sweetness, as well. If someone at your table is allergic to nuts, just skip the macadamias.

MAKES 4 SERVINGS

½ cup canned hearts of palm (*palmito*), rinsed, drained, and cut into bite-sized pieces

½ cup passion fruit juice

¼ cup macadamia nuts

1 Romaine lettuce heart, trimmed, washed, dried, and torn

¼ cup red bell pepper cut into 1 x ¼-inch strips

¼ cup yellow bell pepper cut into 1 x ½-inch strips

1 tablespoon extra-virgin olive oil

1 tablespoon white balsamic vinegar

Salt and freshly ground black pepper to taste

In a medium bowl, soak the hearts of palm in the passion fruit juice for about 15 minutes.

Meanwhile, put the nuts into a plastic bag and smash to coarse pieces with a meat mallet or the bottom of a heavy pot. (This will take a bit of doing, but the bag will keep all the pieces contained.)

Combine the lettuce, bell peppers, and crushed nuts in a salad bowl. Remove the hearts of palm pieces from the juice, drain, and transfer to the salad, reserving the juice.

To make the vinaigrette, mix the oil, vinegar, and 2 to 3 tablespoons of the reserved passion fruit juice in a cup until thoroughly combined. Season with salt and pepper to taste and mix again. Just before you are ready to serve, toss the salad with the dressing.

Several species of tropical palm tree give us the vegetable known as hearts of palm, or palmito. The inner stem of the palm, it is beloved in Latin America, Asia, and other parts of the world, but it is still rather exotic in much of the United States. Once upon a time, the only way to harvest the heart of the palm was to cut down the tree, which killed the tree and made hearts of palm an expensive menu item indeed. In recent years, cultivated varieties with many stems have been developed, so the hearts can be harvested without killing the tree. You can find it fresh in areas where it is grown, but elsewhere it's largely canned.

TABLE TALK

Why are parrots associated with pirates?

PARROTS ARE PROBABLY ASSOCIATED with pirates because Long John Silver, of *Treasure Island* fame, kept one as a pet. In real life, most pirates probably didn't have the time or the space to have pets.

Can parrots really talk like people?

YES, PARROTS CAN TALK, but they don't always understand what they are saying. Their anatomy allows them to mimic human speech. Many parrot owners spend hours and hours teaching their pets to repeat words and phrases. Some species of parrot—typically, the bigger ones—can understand the words they learn to mimic and can apply them in context. The African Grey Parrot is one species that is known to communicate with humans using our language.

Can you talk like a parrot?

GIVE IT A TRY.

TREASURE CHEST MEATLOAF

THERE'S BURIED TREASURE IN THESE INDIVIDUAL MEATLOAVES—lovely, colorful nuggets of celery, carrot, onion, and red pepper. Because of their size, they cook more quickly than one big loaf.

MAKES 4 INDIVIDUAL LOAVES

1 tablespoon vegetable oil, plus more as needed

¼ cup sliced celery

¼ cup carrot cut in small dice

¼ cup yellow or white onion cut in small dice

¼ cup red bell pepper cut in small dice

1½ pounds ground beef

8 ounces marinara sauce

1 cup unseasoned breadcrumbs

1 large egg, lightly beaten

1 teaspoon salt

Preheat the oven to 375°F.

Heat the oil in a large nonstick skillet set over medium-high heat. Add the celery, carrot, and onion, and cook, stirring and shaking the pan frequently, for about 5 minutes, or until the vegetables are soft and the onions are translucent. Add the bell pepper and cook, stirring, for about 5 more minutes, or until softened and lighter in color. Remove from the heat and let cool.

Meanwhile, place the meat into a large mixing bowl. Add the marinara sauce, breadcrumbs, egg, and salt, and mix to combine thoroughly. Transfer about one-fourth of the meat mixture to a small bowl and set aside. Add the cooled vegetables to the large bowl and mix again to combine, so that there are vegetables of different colors throughout the meat.

Form the meat and vegetable mixture into 4 (5 x 3-inch) loaves, and place them into a roasting pan. If any vegetables are visible from the sides, poke them into the meat with a finger and cover the hole. Divide the reserved meat into 4 portions and pat 1 onto the top of each loaf, so the "treasure" vegetables won't be visible from the top as the loaves cook.

Bake the loaves for 30 to 40 minutes, or until they are nicely browned and an instant-read thermometer inserted into the center of each loaf reads 160°F. Let the loaves rest for 10 or 15 minutes before serving.

Can you talk like a pirate?

BOOKS AND MOVIES ABOUT PIRATES HAVE given us a concept of how pirates talked that probably bears little resemblance to real pirate lingo, but it's a lot of fun to imagine that they did talk this way—and even more fun to try it out yourself.

Here are some ideas to get you started.

AHOY! AHOY, THERE!—Hello!

ARRRR! OR ARRRGGGH!—An exclamation.

AVAST!—Pay attention!

BLOW ME DOWN!—A term of shock or displeasure. (If the sea winds are too strong, they can knock a sailor over.)

SHIVER ME TIMBERS!—Another term of shock or displeasure. (Timbers are heavy pieces of wood that support a ship; if they shiver, the sea is rough.)

MATEY—A way to address another person, as in "Ahoy, Matey." (A mate is an officer on a ship.)

YE—You, as in "Avast ye, Sailor!"

Is there really an International Talk Like Pirate Day?

IN 1995, TWO FRIENDS IN PORTLAND, OREGON, decided to establish International Talk Like a Pirate Day when, while playing racquetball, they started talking in stereotypical pirate fashion. They set the date as September 19. The new holiday caught the attention of newspaper humorist Dave Barry, who wrote about it in his syndicated column. The idea spread, and today, many people celebrate International Talk Like a Pirate Day. It's a great day to give talking like a pirate a try—or to cook up this dinner.

WHITE CAP TWICE-BAKED POTATOES

IT'S SMOOTH SAILING WITH THESE QUICK TWICE-BAKED POTATOES. The microwave speeds the first baking; then you mold them into "waves," add some goldfish-shaped crackers, and bake again in the oven for a few minutes. Think there's more than just fish floating in the sea? Add any other toppings you might like to make edible flotsam and jetsam.

MAKES 4 POTATOES

4 baking potatoes, washed, patted dry, and pierced with a fork

3 tablespoons butter or heart-healthy margarine

3 tablespoons milk

½ teaspoon salt, or to taste

24 goldfish-shaped crackers, plus more to taste

Freshly ground black pepper to taste (optional)

Chopped fresh chives, for garnish (optional)

Chopped cooked bacon, for garnish (optional)

Place the potatoes on a paper towel in the microwave oven and cook on high power for 11 to 12 minutes (or according to the "baked potato" setting on your microwave), until the potatoes are soft when pierced with a fork. Because microwaves can cook unevenly, test all 4 potatoes in several spots. If any are not baked through, return them to the microwave for another minute.

Allow to cool briefly, then cut the potatoes in half and scoop the cooked insides into a mixing bowl, keeping the jackets intact. Place the empty jackets on a baking sheet and set aside. (If they flop a bit, don't worry, you can remold them when you refill them.)

Preheat the oven to 400°F.

Add the butter to the potatoes in the mixing bowl, and mash with a potato masher a few times to melt it a bit. Add the milk and salt, and mash until creamy. Taste and season with more salt if necessary, and just combine—over-mashing will make the potatoes gummy.

Place 2 goldfish-shaped crackers into each baked potato jacket-half. Spoon the mashed potatoes into the jackets and mold the tops with your fingers, to look like waves.

Place the filled potatoes into the oven on the baking sheet and bake for about 15 minutes, or until the potatoes are slightly firm.

Remove from the oven, place 1 or 2 goldfish-shaped crackers on top of each potato half. If you wish, add some "flotsam and jetsam" by sprinkling with black pepper, chives, chopped bacon, or any other toppings of your choice.

TABLE TALK

What's a white cap?

IT'S A WAVE WITH A WHITE CREST.

What are flotsam and jetsam?

FLOTSAM IS THE FLOATING DEBRIS OF A SHIP WRECKED at sea or its cargo. Jetsam is cargo or equipment that is thrown overboard to lighten a ship's load in rough weather.

YELLOW SQUASH DOUBLOONS

THESE "GOLDEN COINS" ARE RENDERED MORE GOLDEN BY THE ADDITION OF butter and a little curry powder. The curry gives them a lovely flavor and fragrance, too. It burns easily, so add it just before you add the squash to the pot and keep an eye on the heat.

MAKES 4 TO 6 SERVINGS

1 tablespoon vegetable or olive oil

2 tablespoons unsalted butter

4 tablespoons chopped shallot (about 4 large shallots)

½ teaspoon curry powder

¼ teaspoon salt, plus more to taste

3 to 4 slender yellow (summer) squash, about 1½ pounds, sliced into ⅛-inch rounds

Heat the oil and butter in a nonstick skillet set over medium-high heat until the butter is nearly melted, but do not let it brown. Add the shallot and cook, stirring and shaking the pan, for about 30 seconds, or until slightly softened.

Reduce the heat to medium, add the curry powder and salt, and swirl to incorporate. Immediately add the squash and cook, stirring and flipping the slices frequently, for 6 to 8 minutes, or until they are golden-brown. If necessary, adjust the temperature and/or remove the skillet from the heat for a few seconds to keep the mixture from burning. Taste, season with salt if necessary, and stir to coat. Cook for a few more seconds, remove from the heat, and keep warm.

NOTE: The curry powder gives this dish an added dimension, but it can be omitted.

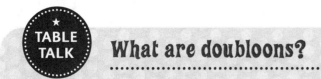
What are doubloons?

DOUBLOONS ARE GOLD COINS THAT SPAIN, its Spanish-speaking colonies, and other societies used as money for several hundred years, up until the nineteenth century. The name derives from the word for "double" because the doubloon was worth twice what Spain's standard gold coins were worth. They are associated with pirates because Spain was a leader in sea trade and the coins were often seized by pirates, who liked them because they could use them as money or melt them for their gold content.

FLOATING TREASURE ISLAND

FOR AN APPROPRIATE END TO A PIRATE DINNER, this recipe is a variation on the classic Floating Island. The original consists of meringues floating on a "sea" of custard. Here, the meringue remains, but the surrounding sea is a chilled mixed-berry soup that ups the nutritional content and is sure to tempt even the most berry-averse child. And kids will love hunting for the buried treasure at the bottom of the island! Note that the amount of sugar you add to the berry soup will depend on the sweetness of the berries. If you use fat-free half-and-half, look for a brand that does not contain corn syrup.

MAKES 4 SERVINGS

1 pound frozen mixed berries (any combination of strawberries, blueberries, raspberries, and blackberries)

2 cups light cream or fat-free half-and-half

¼ granulated or confectioners' sugar, plus more as needed

4 to 8 chocolate coins, unwrapped

4 to 8 meringue cookies

Combine the berries, cream, and about 1/4 cup of the sugar in a food processor fitted with a metal blade and process until smooth and creamy. Taste and, if necessary, add more sugar, pulsing the machine to combine.

Place 1 or 2 chocolate coins in each of 4 serving bowls. Pour about 1 cup fruit soup into each and top each with 1 or 2 floating island meringues.

Silly Hat Night

THE USUAL RULE OF REMOVING YOUR HAT FOR DINNER IS SUSPENDED TONIGHT!

Instead, everyone should wear a silly hat throughout the meal!

You can slap on your favorite silly hat or make one especially for the occasion.

And when you get to the table, there'll be hats galore!

Menu

Signora Caprese's Broad-Brimmed Hat

Curly Head Salad

Toque of the Town Soufflé

Mad Hatter Mushroom Caps

Fruity Hat Special

Game Plan

YOU CAN MAKE SOME OF THE COMPONENTS OF THIS DINNER AHEAD OF TIME, but others, like the pre-dinner munchies (Signora Caprese's Broad-Brimmed Hat), the Curly Head Salad, the dessert (the Fruity Hat Special), and most of the Toque of the Town Soufflé, are best made just before you eat them. Luckily, these dishes—even the soufflé—are fairly simple.

★ Make (and nibble) Signora Caprese's Broad-Brimmed Hat. ✋

★ Prepare the Mad Hatter Mushroom Caps, bake for 8 to 9 minutes, and keep warm. ✋

★ Prepare the Toque of the Town Soufflé, reduce the oven temperature, and bake for ✋ 30 to 40 minutes.

★ Get the kids started on Your Very Own Very Silly Hat.

★ Make the Curly Head Salad, but do not add the dressing.

★ Just before the soufflé is ready, toss the salad with the dressing and bring it and the mushroom caps to the table; then bring out the soufflé.

★ A tip o' the hat for dinner!

★ Make the Fruity Hat Special.

★ Hats off for dessert!

DINNER PREP IN SMALL BITES:

If you have time the night before or earlier in the day, stuff the Mad Hatter Mushroom Caps and bake just before serving. You can also measure out the cheese and ham filling for the soufflé.

FRIDAY NIGHT TIME-SAVER:

If time is short, use a bottled citrus-flavored dressing for the Curly Head Salad and, if you can find them, good-quality frozen stuffed mushrooms caps.

Crafty Friday:
YOUR VERY OWN VERY SILLY HAT

IF YOU DON'T HAVE A SILLY HAT LYING AROUND (OR EVEN IF YOU DO), you can make one right now. Everyone's hat will be an individual creation. Some ideas for decoration are listed below, but do pick and choose and add your own ideas as well.

1 plain baseball cap per person (preferably without much decoration) or $\frac{1}{2}$ sheet of white or colored poster board per person

Transparent tape

Craft glue

Any combination of the following:

Cloth patches with silly sayings

Self-sticking plastic jewels

Sticky foam letters

Wiggly plastic eyes

Pipe cleaners

Small fuzzy pipe cleaner insects on floral wire (often used to decorate summer tabletops, available in craft stores)

Safety scissors

1 (9 x 12-inch) sheet white or light-colored construction paper

Pens or markers

Trim the caps with your choice of decorations; use craft glue for items that aren't self-adhesive and let dry. Alternatively, make a top hat out of poster board: cut a long rectangle that will roll up to perch on top of the wearer's head. Cut a circular brim with an inside opening the same size as the stovepipe part, and use clear tape to fit the two parts together.

If you wish, make a face—or several faces—using the wiggly eyes and jewels. Or use pipe cleaners to make an angel's halo or devil horns at the top of the hat.

If you like, make a price tag à la Minnie Pearl: Cut a paper rectangle (about 2 inches x 1 inch), and punch a hole in it about $\frac{1}{2}$ inch from the edge. Write a silly price on it (such as $1.98—Minnie Pearl's price—or $1 million!) Loop the string through the hole and then through a safety pin, and pin it to the edge of the hat so that it hangs down and is visible to all. Be sure the pin is secure, and flatten it so that it won't scratch.

Or make a "For Sale" or "For Rent" or "Confused" sign—or any other sign you like, using the same procedure as the price tag. Write your silly saying on the sign, and pin it to the

Several (5-inch) lengths of string

4 to 8 small safety pins

1 hole puncher

edge of the hat. When everything is dry, put your silly hat on your head. Feel silly?

Who was Minnie Pearl?

MINNIE PEARL WAS THE STAGE NAME OF Sarah Ophelia Colley Cannon, a comedienne whose performances at the Grand Ole Opry in Nashville, Tennessee, were broadcast on radio and television for years. One of her trademarks was a silly straw hat that always had a price tag marked $1.98 dangling from the side. It looked as though she had left home in a hurry with her store-bought hat and had forgotten to take off the tag!

HOW MANY KINDS OF HATS CAN YOU NAME? What are the special features of each one? See the answers below for some suggestions.

Top hat; straw hat; derby hat; firefighter's hat; toque; witch's hat; cowboy hat; beret; baseball cap; hard hat; astronaut helmet; football helmet; police officer's hat; hairnet; pillbox hat; bonnet.

SIGNORA CAPRESE'S BROAD-BRIMMED HAT

THE ITALIAN ISLAND OF CAPRI HAS GIVEN THE WORLD A DELICIOUS GIFT: the Caprese salad. By tradition, this oh-so-simple salad consists of a platter of sliced vine-ripened tomatoes, sliced mozzarella, basil, olive oil, salt, and pepper—all fresh, and all utterly delicious. For Silly Hat Night, we've put the salad on slices of Italian or French bread and toasted it just a bit so that, if you use your imagination, it takes on the silhouette of a broad-brimmed, well-trimmed lady's hat. The name for the lady who might wear it? Signora Caprese, of course.

MAKES 8 "HATS"

8 bite-sized balls fresh mozzarella cheese

8 (1-inch) slices French or Italian bread, from a loaf about 3 inches wide

2 tablespoons olive oil

4 leaves fresh basil, cut in chiffonade (See note below)

8 grape or cherry tomatoes

Coarse salt to taste

Freshly ground black pepper (optional)

Preheat the oven to 300°F.

To assemble the bread hats, slice the mozzarella balls so that they sit on top of the bread without rolling off. Top with some of the basil strips, arranging them so they dangle over the cheese. Nestle cherry tomatoes among the cheese balls.

Drizzle each with a little olive oil. Sprinkle with salt and pepper if you like. Place on an ungreased baking sheet and bake for 10 to 12 minutes, or until the cheese is melted and the bread is toasted and golden but not browned.

To cut basil in chiffonade, trim away any thick stems and stack the leaves on top of one another. Roll into a cylinder, and using a sharp knife, cut the cylinder crosswise in $\frac{1}{8}$-inch rounds. Unroll them and you'll have nice thin strips of basil.

CURLY HEAD SALAD WITH ORANGE VINAIGRETTE

THIS SALAD GETS ITS "CURLY HEAD" FROM THE LETTUCE PATCH, in the form of curly endive, which has delicate, ever-so-thin, twisted leaves. (It's also known as frisée, which is French for "curly.") The mouth and eyes are made with orange segment "smiles" and grapes. And you make the nose with a home-made crouton. You can use a whole head of curly endive, or frisée, if you can find one and don't mind its slightly bitter flavor. The elegant salad is nice enough for company—whether you make individual "heads" or just toss it in a large bowl.

MAKES 4 SALADS

Orange Vinaigrette

Juice of 1 orange (about ⅓ cup)

1 teaspoon white wine vinegar or white balsamic vinegar

1 teaspoon Dijon mustard

1 teaspoon chopped fresh tarragon or ¼ teaspoon dried tarragon

3 tablespoons extra-virgin olive oil

Salt to taste

Freshly ground black pepper to taste

Salad

4 (4-inch) round rolls such as bulky, Kaiser, or brioche rolls

1 tablespoon olive oil

Salt to taste

1 (5- to 7-ounce) bag mixed salad greens that includes curly endive (frisée), washed and dried

To make the Orange Vinaigrette, whisk the orange juice, vinegar, mustard, and tarragon in a small bowl. Add the olive oil and whisk to combine thoroughly. Season to taste with salt and pepper if you like.

To make the salad, preheat the broiler. With a sharp knife, cut a circle in the top of each roll, leaving an edge of about ¼ inch, and make a bread "bowl" by pulling off the plug of bread in the center. Reserve the plugs for croutons. (You should get most of the bread out, leaving a deep bowl with only about half an inch of bread at the bottom.) Set the bread bowls aside.

To make croutons, brush the bread lightly with oil, sprinkle with the tarragon, and season with salt. Cut into ¼-inch pieces and place on a baking sheet. Set them under the hot broiler for 3 to 4 minutes, or until light-golden, being careful not to burn them. Remove from the oven and let cool. Set aside 4 croutons.

Meanwhile, set aside a small handful of curly endive, 4 orange segments, and 8 grape halves. Cut the remaining orange segments into chunks.

(continued on the next page)

1 orange, peeled, pith and seeds removed, and separated into segments

16 grapes, cut in half lengthwise

Toss the remaining greens with the cut orange pieces, remaining grapes, and cooled croutons.

When you are ready to serve, place the bread bowls into 4 salad bowls. Toss the salad with the Orange Vinaigrette and divide between the bowls. To make curly "hair," tuck a little of the reserved curly endive into one edge of each bowl, so that the leaves stick out over the bread a bit. In each bread bowl, position 2 reserved grape halves under the hair as eyes, a reserved crouton as a nose, and a reserved orange segment as a mouth. Place the salad bowls on the table so that each person can look down at a salad face. (If you have more salad than will fit into the rolls, you can serve it on the side.)

TABLE TALK

How many ways can you say "hat" in languages besides English?

Here are just a few:

SOMBRERO: Spanish

CHAPEAU: French

CAPELLO: Italian

HUT: German

CHAPÉU: Portuguese

HATT: Norwegian, Swedish

SHAAP KA: Russian

MÀO ZI: Chinese

MÙAK: Thai

MAD HATTER MUSHROOM CAPS

HERE'S THE VEGETABLE WORLD'S ANSWER TO THE FAMED HATMAKER'S TOPPER.

A handful of golden raisins offers a bright, tangy twist to this old favorite.

MAKES 12 MUSHROOM CAPS

12 large, white stuffing mushrooms, cleaned, with stems removed and reserved

1 tablespoon unsalted butter

1 teaspoon vegetable oil, plus more for drizzling

1 stalk celery, finely chopped

1 medium garlic clove, minced (See note, page 29)

1/4 cup chopped fresh parsley

1/8 teaspoon salt, plus more to taste

Freshly ground black pepper to taste

3/4 cup unseasoned breadcrumbs

1 large egg, lightly beaten

3 tablespoons golden raisins, coarsely chopped

Preheat the oven to 400°F.

Chop the mushroom stems coarsely and set aside.

Heat the butter and 1 teaspoon vegetable oil in a nonstick skillet set over medium-high heat until the butter melts. Add the celery and cook, stirring and shaking the pan occasionally, for 2 to 3 minutes, or until the celery is softened and translucent. Add the garlic and cook, stirring, for 30 seconds to 1 minute, or until softened, reducing the heat to medium if necessary. Add the chopped mushroom stems and parsley and cook for 4 to 5 minutes more, or until the mushrooms have released their liquid and the skillet is almost dry. Taste and season with salt and black pepper if necessary. Remove from the heat and transfer to a small mixing bowl. Let cool.

Arrange the mushroom caps on a baking sheet. Season lightly with salt and pepper.

Add the breadcrumbs, egg, and raisins to the cooked mushroom mixture, and mix well with a fork.

Spoon about 1 heaping tablespoon mushroom stuffing on each, packing it gently and using up all the stuffing. Drizzle the top of each with a little oil and bake for 8 to 9 minutes, or until the tops are just crisped and light golden-brown.

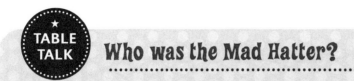

THE MAD HATTER, OR SIMPLY THE HATTER, was a character in Lewis Carroll's *Alice's Adventures in Wonderland*, published in 1865. Along with the March Hare and the Dormouse, the Hatter is one of the attendees at a never-ending Mad Tea Party that Alice wanders into. He wears a large hat with a price tag attached to it. In the nineteenth century, when Carroll lived and wrote, people who made hats were called hatters. At the time, mercury was used in hat making, and many hatters developed mercury poisoning, which interfered with their speech. Some people thought they were crazy. This could be why Carroll chose the hat-making trade for his very silly character. In any case, *Alice* is one of the silliest pieces of fiction ever, so after dinner, keep your silly hat on, open the book, and get ready for a silly treat.

TOQUE OF THE TOWN SOUFFLÉ

THE SOUFFLÉ, A FRENCH CLASSIC, IS REGARDED WITH SOME AWE by those who have never made one, but it's really just a fancy egg and cheese dish. The round dome reminds me of a chef's pouffy toque; hence, its place in this Silly Hat Night. A soufflé is fragile, yes, and must be brought to the table immediately on removal from the oven, while its dome is at its peak. Even if your soufflé falls, though, it's still a luscious treat. There are few things to know about soufflés, so do review the note on page 80 before you start to cook.

MAKES 1 (5½- TO 6-INCH)
SOUFFLÉ, 4 TO 6 SERVINGS

3 tablespoons unsalted butter, plus more for greasing

2 tablespoons grated Parmesan cheese, plus more as needed, for dusting

Preheat the oven to 375°F. Butter the bottom and sides of a 6-cup soufflé mold or round baking dish that is 5½ to 6 inches wide and 3 to 3½ inches deep. Sprinkle the mold with Parmesan cheese, rolling the pan gently on its side to ensure that the cheese is evenly distributed. Refrigerate until ready to use.

In a small saucepan set over medium-high heat, heat the

1 cup whole milk

3 tablespoons all-purpose flour

¼ teaspoon salt, plus more for whipping the egg whites and to taste

1 cup shredded Cheddar cheese

½ cup chopped ham

7 large egg yolks, lightly beaten

8 large egg whites

¼ teaspoon cream of tartar

milk for about 3 minutes to scald, or until just before it boils, being careful not to let it burn on the bottom.

Meanwhile, in a medium saucepan set over medium heat, make a Béchamel sauce: Melt 3 tablespoons butter, add the flour, and stir for about 30 seconds, or until a thick paste forms. Add the milk and stir for 30 seconds to 1 minute, or until the mixture thickens and coats the back of a spoon. Taste and season with salt. Remove from the heat, and stir in the cheese, ham, and egg yolks. Set aside.

With an electric mixer set at medium-low speed, beat the egg whites, a pinch of salt, and the cream of tartar in a clean, dry copper or stainless-steel bowl, increasing the speed to high after a minute. Beat for about 5 to 7 minutes, or until the whites form stiff peaks. When the beater is raised, the peaks should stand straight up. Don't overbeat or the whites will become too dry. (If you do, add another egg white and beat until stiff peaks form.)

Immediately fold the egg whites into the Béchamel mixture with a rubber spatula, a little at a time, using a gentle scooping, up-and-over motion to combine. Pour into prepared soufflé dish. Run your thumb around the inside edge of the soufflé mold to make a little "canal" around the edge of the batter; this will help it rise straight up. If your pan is less than 4 inches deep, make a collar of aluminum foil: Cut a strip of foil about 3 inches wide, and wrap it tightly around the pan so that it extends straight up.

Bake for 30 to 40 minutes, or until the soufflé has risen several inches above the rim of the mold and the center is firm and golden-brown. Do not open the oven door while the soufflé is baking. Remove the foil, if using, and bring to the table immediately.

Soufflés get their height from whipped egg whites; the air that you whip into them expands when exposed to the heat of the oven and makes the soufflé rise. When you separate the eggs, put the whites into a copper or stainless-steel bowl that you've washed and dried scrupulously. You don't want even a tiny bit of grease on the bowl; it will interfere with the rising. The same rule of impeccable cleanliness applies to the beaters. Also, don't let even a smidgeon of yolk into the bowl or it, too, will impede the rising. (If some falls in, scoop it out with a spoon right away.) Next, the height of the soufflé will depend in part on the dimensions of your baking dish—too wide or too deep and it won't rise enough; not deep enough and the batter will ooze out over the sides. If you don't have a soufflé dish, use a casserole as close in size to the specifications as possible. The collar of aluminum foil will help the soufflé to rise. You also want to treat beaten whites gently; use a folding motion to mix them into the batter and keep the oven door closed for at least the first 20 minutes of baking. A final note: Many French chefs suggest preheating the oven to 400°F or higher and then reducing the heat to 375°F when you put in the soufflé. That will fit right into your game plan if you make the other dishes for Silly Hat Night (Signora Caprese's Broad-Brimmed Hat and the Stuffed Mushroom Caps); your oven will have been set to 400°F already.

What's a toque?

A TOQUE IS A CHEF'S HAT. It's a French word that refers to a hat with no brim, which typically has a soft, pouffy top.

FRUITY HAT SPECIAL

HERE'S A DESSERT WORTHY OF THE BRAZILIAN SINGER, CARMEN MIRANDA, who was as famous for her fruit-topped hats as she was for her the energy and joy of her samba music and dancing. You'll need a waffle and an orange as the base for the "hat," but other than that, you can choose the fruits your crowd will like. The Orange-Scented Chocolate Sauce gives this dessert added character; you can use it for just about any dessert that calls for chocolate sauce. Grate the zest from the oranges you will use for the hat's base. To keep the ice cream from melting before you get your "hats" to the table, prepare all the fruit before you portion out the ice cream, but save the bananas for last, as they will turn brown when exposed to the air for long. If the folks at your table have small appetites, you might want to make fewer "hats" and share them.

MAKES 4 SERVINGS
Orange-Scented Chocolate Sauce

¼ cup chocolate syrup

Grated zest of 1 orange (See note, page 82)

Fruity Hat Special

4 frozen waffles, toasted and cooled

4 oranges

1 ripe mango (See note, page 82)

½ cup colorful fruit such as hulled strawberries, blueberries, green or red grapes, or pineapple chunks

4 ripe baby bananas, or 2 ripe bananas

4 large scoops vanilla ice cream

4 fresh mint sprigs (optional)

To make the Orange-Scented Chocolate Sauce, stir the zest into the chocolate syrup. Set aside.

To make the Fruity Hat Specials, place the cooled waffles on 4 flat dessert plates.

Peel the oranges, keeping the fruit inside intact. Trim off as much of the bitter white pith as possible. Then partially separate the orange segments, so that they remain attached at one end, like the petals of a flower. Carefully remove any pith from the center. Place a partially opened orange on each waffle.

With a sharp knife, cut into the mango lengthwise, making 8 wedges of equal size. Cut the wedges away from the pit and discard the pit. Peel the wedges and place 2 into each orange, so the tips emerge from the flower at an angle.

Cut the other fruit, except for the bananas, into bite-sized pieces if necessary.

If you are using baby bananas, peel them and cut them in half lengthwise. If you are using regular bananas, peel them *(continued on the next page)*

and cut them in half lengthwise and then crosswise. (Either way, you'll have 8 pieces.)

Place a generous scoop of ice cream on top of each orange "flower." Place 2 banana slices on each scoop of ice cream, positioning them so they stand vertically. Drizzle the Orange-Scented Chocolate Sauce over the ice cream. Top with remaining pieces of fruit, and garnish with a sprig of mint. Serve immediately.

The thin outer layer of the rind of an orange, lemon, or lime is known as the zest. This layer contains fragrant, flavorful volatile oils and is often used in baking. It is not to be confused with the inner peel and pith, which is very bitter. To get the zest, you can use the smallest holes of a grater. A very sharp paring knife will also work and will make zest strips, not grated zest. Be careful to get only the very outermost layer of the rind.

The tropical mango comes in hundreds of varieties, which range in color from green to green- yellow to red. Pick ripe mangoes that are slightly soft to the touch and have a sweet perfume. If your market only has hard mangoes, buy one a few days ahead, and let it ripen in a cool spot.

After-Dinner Fun: Sombrero Dancing

GET UP AND DANCE! The Mexican Hat Dance, called the *Jarabe Tapatío* in Mexico, was composed by Jesús González Rubio, a music professor from Guadalajara. Based on a variety of Mexican music and dance traditions, it tells the story of a man courting a woman. *Jarabe* can mean "sweet syrup" or "dance." *Tapatío* is someone or something from Guadalajara. English speakers who couldn't pronounce the real name called it the Hat Dance because at one point, the man drops his hat on the ground and the woman picks it up.

A version of the dance is often performed to the traditional melody, with everyone dancing around a hat. The steps are easy. Put your right heel out with your left foot flat on the ground; then jump and put your left heel out and your right foot flat. Alternate between the two moves three times, give two fast claps, and then repeat the pattern. If you know the tune, sing it.

AbbracaDinner!

MAGIC IS IN THE AIR! FAIRIES, WIZARDS, AND OTHER MAGICAL FOLK have never been more popular with the young set. Here's a dinner that makes a little magic and lots of yummy eating.

Menu

Carrot Stick Wands and Parmesan Poofs!

Wizard's Magic Pouch Salad

Pixie Salmon Patties

Golden Tresses Pasta with Olive Oil, Garlic, and Parsley

Fairy Dust Sugar Cookies

Game Plan

★ Make (and nibble) Carrot Stick Wands and Parmesan Poofs! ✋

★ Make the cookie dough and refrigerate for 1 hour. ✋

★ Get the kids started on their Wishing Pinwheel Wands.

★ Make the Wizard's Magic Pouch Salad filling and prep the peppers.

★ Make the Pixie Salmon Patties and keep warm.

★ Boil the water for the Golden Tresses Pasta with Olive Oil, Garlic, and Parsley.

★ Fill the peppers with Wizard's Magic Pouch Salad.

★ Make the pasta and drain.

★ Meanwhile, sauté the garlic and parsley for the pasta in the olive oil. Toss with the pasta.

★ Poof! Dinner!

★ Cut out, decorate, and bake the cookies.

★ Abbracadessert!

DINNER PREP IN SMALL BITES:

If you have time the night before or earlier in the day, bake the cookies or just make the dough and refrigerate it. Cook the fresh salmon and cut up the Wizard's Magic Pouch Salad filling, but don't toss it with the dressing or fill the pepper pouches.

FRIDAY NIGHT TIME-SAVER:

Use slice-and-bake cookie dough and sprinkle with colored sugar for the Fairy Dust Sugar Cookies. Canned salmon will work fine if you don't have time to cook fresh fillets.

Crafty Friday:
WISHING PINWHEEL WANDS

IN *SLEEPING BEAUTY*, A GROUP OF FAIRY GODMOTHERS USE THEIR MAGIC to endow a newborn princess with special gifts—the gift of beauty, the gift of song, and others. We can't give one another magical gifts, but it never hurts to send good wishes to those we love. And with these Wishing Pinwheel Wands, your beautiful wishes will look beautiful, too.

1 (9-inch) square construction paper per person, any color (each cut from a full sheet)

Safety scissors

Crayons or markers in rainbow colors

Glitter glue

1 unsharpened decorative pencil with an eraser per person

1 pushpin per person

Starting at one corner of the square of paper, cut inward on a diagonal about 5 inches. Repeat with the remaining 3 corners, so that the square has 4 triangular flaps. On each flap, use crayons or markers to write or draw a picture of your wish for the people at your table—happy times, jokes, laughter, music, good food, good health—whatever it is you wish. Trim with glitter glue, and let the glue dry for a few minutes.

Fold every other corner to the center of the square (there are now 8 corners and you will fold 4), overlapping them there, and use a push-pin to attach your pinwheel to the pencil's eraser. (A grown-up should do this unless older children are doing this project.) Position the pin so that the pinwheel is secure but the pointy end is contained within the eraser. Blow your wishes around the room!

CARROT STICK WANDS AND PARMESAN POOFS!

HERE'S A BIT OF KITCHEN MAGIC THAT WILL TAKE AWAY THE HUNGER PANGS that come while dinner's cooking. Every self-respecting fairy or wizard needs a wand, and a carrot stick makes an excellent one. (If it gets eaten, just grab another!) The number of carrots you use will depend on how many sticks—er, wands—your gang will eat. Figure about eight 4-inch sticks per carrot. As for the magic, the kids will get a kick out of watching the Parmesan transform from bits of shredded cheese into a cracker-like tidbit (known in Italian as *frico*); it happens in seconds, right before their eyes. You can make up a magic word to say as soon as you drop the cheese into the pan. Let them cool a bit; then watch them disappear—like magic!

MAKES 16 CARROT WANDS AND ABOUT 16 CHEESE "POOFS"

2 carrots, or more to taste

1 cup shredded Parmesan or Romano cheese

1 teaspoon cornstarch

Cut each carrot in half crosswise; then cut each half lengthwise in quarters to make 8 carrot sticks. Arrange on a larger serving platter in a starburst patter. (If the folks at your table will eat more carrots, by all means cut up more!)

Heat a nonstick 12-inch nonstick skillet over high heat. Combine the cheese and cornstarch in a small bowl and toss until the cheese is coated lightly.

Place heaping tablespoons in the pan, 4 to 5 at a time, keeping them at least 1 inch apart because they will expand slightly. (Don't forget to say your magic word.) Heat for 30 to 45 seconds, or until the cheese has melted into a pancake shape and the edges are just golden in color. Remove from the skillet with a spatula and cook the remaining cheese. Let the finished *Poofs!* cool for a minute or two before serving with the carrot stick wands.

NOTE: Reserve the carrot tops for some After-Dinner Fun (see page 93).

TABLE TALK

What's a fairy?

A FAIRY IS AN IMAGINARY CREATURE WITH MAGICAL POWERS. In folktales and stories, fairies are usually tiny people who use their magic to help humans—or make mischief for them. Many cultures have their own version of fairies: leprechauns, elves, pixies, brownies, gnomes, genies, trolls, and so on.

What's a wizard?

A WIZARD IS ANOTHER KIND OF IMAGINARY BEING who has studied and uses magic. If real-life studying involved magic, homework would always be fun! The word is related to the word "wise." Sometimes "wizard" is used to describe a very smart person or someone who knows a lot about a particular topic.

WIZARD'S MAGIC SALAD POUCH

THESE TASTY PEPPER POUCHES HOLD A MAGICAL MIXTURE OF FLAVORS. The finely chopped olives in the dressing add a perky "something extra" to the fresh chopped salad. (They also provide a nice tangy complement to the Pixie Salmon Patties in this dinner). The other key element in the salad dressing lies in the tomatoes; their juice serves as the acid in the vinaigrette, so reserve as much juice as you can when you cut them.

MAKES 4 SERVINGS

5 sweet Italian (Cubanelle) peppers

1 large vine-ripened tomato, cored and cut into $1/2$-inch cubes, with juice

$1/2$ cucumber, peeled and cut into $1/2$-inch cubes

1 tablespoon extra-virgin olive oil

$1/4$ cup green olives, with or without pimientos, finely chopped

$1/2$ teaspoon fresh oregano leaves, finely chopped, or $1/4$ teaspoon dried oregano (optional)

Salt and freshly ground black pepper to taste

Cut the stem ends off the peppers, and remove the seeds and membrane, keeping 4 of the peppers whole. Cut the remaining pepper into $1/2$-inch pieces.

Place the cut pepper, the tomatoes and juice, and the cucumber into a medium bowl. In a smaller bowl, mix the oil, olives, and oregano. Season with salt and pepper to taste. Pour over the salad and toss to mix thoroughly and coat the vegetables with the dressing.

Just before serving, stuff each pepper with salad.

IF YOU WERE A WIZARD, what magical tools would you keep in your pouch?

PIXIE SALMON PATTIES

PIXIES LIKE THESE PATTIES BECAUSE THEY'RE SO VERY TASTY. They're also kid-friendly, quick, and easy. And they're great for those nights when you're rooting around in the Pixie Pantry, wondering what to make for dinner.

MAKES ABOUT 16 PATTIES

1 pound fresh boneless salmon fillets with skin on or 1 (14.75-ounce) can salmon, black or gray skin and any bones removed

Vegetable oil for drizzling and frying

1 medium yellow or white onion, cut into 1-inch chunks

¼ cup chopped fresh parsley

¼ cup unseasoned breadcrumbs, plus more as needed

1 large egg

¼ teaspoon salt, plus more to taste

If you are using fresh salmon, preheat the oven to 475°F and oil a roasting pan lightly. Cut the salmon into pieces and place them into the pan. Drizzle a little oil on the top of each and bake for about 12 minutes, or until pink and opaque. Remove from the oven, and when cool enough to handle, peel off the skin.

Place the salmon, onion, parsley, breadcrumbs, egg, and salt into a food processor fitted with a metal blade and process until a chunky batter forms.

Pour ½-inch of oil into a 12-inch nonstick skillet set over medium-high heat. Position a plate lined with paper towels near the stove. Make a test patty: When the oil sizzles, carefully scoop about 1½ tablespoons of the batter and carefully drop it into the oil, but do not flatten it yet. Cook the patty for 1 to 1½ minutes, turn, and flatten gently with a spatula so that it is about ½ inch thick. Cook 1 to 1½ minutes longer, or until it is golden-brown and cooked through. Transfer to the paper towels and drain. Remove the skillet from the heat. (If the mixture does not hold together, add more bread crumbs to the food processor. Taste for seasoning, and add more salt to the batter if necessary. Pulse just to incorporate.)

Return the skillet to the heat, and when the oil sizzles, cook the remaining batter, spacing the patties around the skillet in a single layer, leaving about an inch between them. Work in *(continued on the next page)*

batches if necessary. Cook the patties for 1 to 1½ minutes, turn, and flatten gently with a spatula, so that the patty is about ½-inch thick. Cook 1 to 1½ minutes longer, or until it is golden brown and cooked through, adding more oil if necessary. Drain the patties on paper towels. Serve hot or cold.

How many famous fairies and wizards can you name?

Here are a few:

Tinkerbell from *Peter Pan*

Harry Potter and all his friends and teachers from the Harry Potter series

Cinderella's Fairy Godmother

The Wizard of Oz

Merlin the Magician, mentor of King Arthur and his Knights of the Round Table

Titania and Oberon and the rest of the fairies in Shakespeare's *A Midsummer Night's Dream*

The wizards of role-playing games and video games like *Dungeons and Dragons*

Flora, Fauna, Merryweather, and the evil Maleficent from the Disney version of *Sleeping Beauty*, along with other fairies from older versions of the tale.

Barbie's *Fairytopia* fairies

The wizards of J.R.R. Tolkien's Middle-earth

Abby Cadabby, the fairy from *Sesame Street*

The Disney Channel's *Wizards of Waverly Place*

WHAT WOULD YOU DO if you were just three inches tall?

GOLDEN TRESSES PASTA WITH OLIVE OIL, GARLIC, AND PARSLEY

THE REST OF THE WORLD MIGHT KNOW THIS EVER-SO-THIN PASTA AS ANGEL HAIR, but children can imagine whose delicate locks inspired this dish. In Italy, this olive oil and garlic sauce is called *aglio e olio* and is typically spiced up with hot pepper flakes, which you can add to the recipe below if you like, but for kids, parsley is a safer bet, and it's packed with Vitamin C and other nutrients. You can use this sauce as the basis for all sorts of additions, from cherry tomatoes to artichoke hearts to meatballs to sautéed shrimp, but it's luscious on its own as an accompaniment to the zesty Pixie Salmon Patties.

MAKES 4 SERVINGS

8 ounces angel hair (capellini) pasta

4 tablespoons olive oil, divided

1 medium garlic clove, finely chopped, plus more to taste (see note below)

1 teaspoon salt, plus more to taste

Freshly ground black pepper to taste (optional)

2 tablespoons finely chopped fresh parsley

Cook the pasta according to the package instructions. (Note that this thin pasta only takes a few minutes to cook once the water is boiled.) Drain.

Meanwhile, heat 2 tablespoons oil in a large nonstick skillet set over medium-high heat. When it sizzles, add the garlic and cook for 30 seconds to 1 minute, or just until softened and golden in color. (Do not let it brown; reduce the heat if necessary.) Remove from the heat. Transfer the pasta to the skillet and toss to coat. Then add the parsley and remaining olive oil to the skillet, and season with salt and pepper. Toss until the parsley is incorporated and heated through. Taste, season again if necessary, and stir once more. Serve hot.

The more finely you chop garlic, the more intense the flavor will be. If you like your garlic dishes very mild, then don't chop it at all. Instead, peel the clove, cook it in the hot oil for about 1 minute, and remove it. Proceed with the recipe.

FAIRY DUST SUGAR COOKIES

THESE DIMINUTIVE COOKIES ARE THE PERFECT SIZE FOR FAIRIES, PIXIES, and all kinds of magical sprites. Leftovers are also nice for packing into human lunchboxes. You'll need a shot glass or very small cookie cutter to make them. Kids will love sprinkling the shimmery "fairy dust" on these before they go into the oven. Use several colors to create a rainbow effect. (Colored sugar is available in the baking aisle of your supermarket. If you don't have it, you can use sprinkles, but it won't be quite the same.) Allow time to refrigerate the dough for at least 1 hour before forming and baking the cookies.

MAKES 3 DOZEN SMALL COOKIES

4 ounces (1 stick) unsalted butter, at room temperature

½ cup granulated sugar

¼ cup cream cheese, at room temperature

¼ teaspoon salt

½ teaspoon pure vanilla extract

1 large egg yolk, at room temperature

1¼ cups all-purpose flour, plus more for rolling out the dough

1 large egg white, lightly beaten with 1 teaspoon water, for egg wash

1 teaspoon water

¼ to ½ cup colored sugar

Place the oven rack in the middle position and preheat the oven to 370°F. Line 2 baking sheets with parchment paper. With an electric mixer set at medium speed, beat the butter in a mixing bowl for 20 to 30 seconds, or until very smooth. Add the sugar and beat at medium-high speed for 3 to 4 minutes, or until fluffy and very pale in color. Add the cream cheese and salt, and beat for 1 minute, or until smooth. Add the vanilla and egg yolk and beat at medium speed for about 30 seconds, or until incorporated well.

Turn off the mixer, scrape down the sides of the bowl, and mix in the flour by hand, just until combined. Gather the dough into a ball and flatten it gently into a disk about ½-inch thick. Wrap it in plastic wrap and refrigerate it for at least 1 hour. (Or see the note on the next page if you are making the dough in advance.)

When you are ready to bake, roll out the dough on a lightly floured work surface until it is about ⅛-inch thick. Cut out cookies with a shot glass or a 1¾-inch cookie cutter, rerolling the scraps and cutting them as you go. Place the cookies on the baking sheets, about 18 cookies per sheet, spacing them close together, as they don't spread when baked.

Gently brush a thin layer of the egg wash onto the top of the cookies. Sprinkle the cookies with colored sugar. Bake, 1 sheet at a time, for 6 to 9 minutes, or until the edges just begin to brown. Cool the cookies for 1 minute on the sheet; then, with a thin metal spatula, carefully move them to a cooling rack to cool completely.

This wonderfully versatile dough can easily be doubled and the cookies can be made smaller or larger and any shape you like. You can make this dough ahead of time. It will keep for up to 2 days, wrapped in plastic, in the refrigerator. For longer storage, the dough can be wrapped in plastic and then foil and frozen for up to a month. Thaw frozen dough, still wrapped, in the refrigerator overnight.

After-Dinner Fun: Fairy Tops

MY GRANDMOTHER FANNIE ALWAYS HAD A FEW feathery carrot tops growing in her kitchen; she taught my mother Janice to make them, and they taught me. Now I've passed on the tradition to my daughter. I've rechristened them as Fairy Tops for this dinner (they're the perfect size for a couple of wee folk to romp in), but whatever you call them, they're lots of fun, and so simple! Reserve a few of the cut carrot tops from the Carrot Stick Wands and Parmesan *Poofs*! and place them in a saucer or small dish with about ¼ inch of water. Leave them for a few days, replenishing the water as needed. You'll see them sprout tiny shoots that grow into feathery greens. When they get mushy, start again with new carrot tops.

Into the Forest

THE FOREST HAS BEEN PART OF ALL OUR LIVES SINCE, WELL . . . FOREVER.
Think about how many fairy tale characters find themselves in the woods, where they have adventures, confront fearsome obstacles, and head for home stronger and better than before. In the real world, the forest was once a supermarket of sorts, where people hunted or gathered nuts, berries, and wild mushrooms to eat, and got wood and other materials for building and fuel. While we might not rely on forests in our daily lives anymore, in recent times, scientists have taught us that forests are vital to the health of the planet. This dinner will get you thinking about forests real and imaginary, with dishes that are just the thing for a cozy supper, safe at home.

Menu

Rain Forest Smoothie

Broccoli Forest Primeval

Forest Floor Mushroom Soup

Toad-in-the-Hole, British-Style

Toad-in-the-Hole, American-Style

Little Hansel and Gretel Houses

Game Plan

THIS COMFORT-FOOD DINNER CAN BE MADE IN MANY WAYS. There are two pre-dinner snacks here, a smoothie and veggie nibble; you can make one or the other—or both. There are also two main courses, a British and an American version of Toad in the Hole. (I couldn't offer one without the other!) Again, you can make one or both. If you've still got room, there's soup and dessert. (Of course, there's always room for dessert!)

★ If you are serving the Rain Forest Smoothie, make (and drink) it.

★ If you are serving the Broccoli Forest Primeval, make (and nibble) it.

★ Get the kids started on the Save the Rain Forest Poster.

★ If you are making the British-Toad-in-the-Hole, mix it up and bake for 25 to 29 minutes.

★ Make the Forest Floor Mushroom Soup and keep warm.

★ If you are making the American Toad-in-a-Hole, cook it now.

★ Ring the dinner bell!

★ Assemble the Little Hansel and Gretel Houses.

★ Time for after-dinner sweets!

DINNER PREP IN SMALL BITES:

If you have time the night before or earlier in the day, make the Forest Floor Mushroom Soup. You can also prep the Broccoli Forest Primeval and the British Toad-in-the-Hole, but wait until just before dinnertime to cook them. The kids can also do the Little Hansel and Gretel Houses, but you might have to make extra, as they're likely to want to eat them on the spot!

FRIDAY NIGHT TIME-SAVER:

If time is short, opt for the smoothie and the American Toad in the Hole, and serve a high-quality prepared soup.

Crafty Friday:
SAVE THE RAIN FOREST POSTER

WHY DO WE NEED RAIN FORESTS? COUNT THE WAYS ON A DECORATIVE POSTER that will get you thinking about an important environmental issue. If you need some ideas, read Table Talk "What's a rain forest?" on page 98.

1 sheet oak tag or poster board per person

Crayons or markers

Computer and printer (optional)

Magazines to cut up

Safety scissors

Glue sticks

Think of a slogan or title for your poster. It can be as simple as "Save the Rain Forest" or "We Love Rain Forests," or something more complicated and clever. Figure out where you'll place your title on your poster—at the bottom, at the top, or somewhere in the middle—and carefully write it out. The letters should be big enough to see if you were to hang the poster on the wall and look at it from across the room. Or, if you prefer, you can type out your title on your computer and print it out.

Then think of ways in which the rain forest is important. You can draw pictures to illustrate each idea, or look through magazines and cut out pictures to paste on to the poster. Before you put anything on paper, though, plan your poster so you'll be able to fit everything in. Leave room under or above the pictures to label them if you like. You're now a rain forest advocate!

RAIN FOREST SMOOTHIE

THIS SATISFYING SMOOTHIE WILL MAKE YOU APPRECIATE THE RAIN FOREST in a way that's up close and personal, because it's made with delicious rain forest products—mango and passion fruit juice. There are two versions here, one rich and one light. If your foresters are ravenous, go with the richer version, but if they eat like little birds, choose the light one.

MAKES 3½ TO 4 CUPS
Rich Rain Forest Smoothie

1½ cups frozen mango chunks
   (from the frozen food aisle)

2 cups frozen vanilla yogurt

¼ cup granulated sugar

1½ cups passion fruit juice

Place the mango, frozen yogurt, sugar, and juice into a blender and blend until smooth and creamy. If necessary, stop the blender and mix to be sure it's thoroughly blended and all the mango chunks are being chopped. Frozen mango can take a while to blend, but keep going until you have a nice, thick, creamy drink. Pour into glasses and serve.

Light Rain Forest Smoothie

2½ cups frozen mango chunks
   (from the frozen food aisle)

¼ cup granulated sugar

1½ cups passion fruit juice

1 cup milk

Place the mango, sugar, juice, and milk into a blender and follow the blending instructions above.

What's a forest?

A FOREST, ALSO CALLED A WOODLAND OR WOODS, is a place where trees and other smaller plants grow densely together.

What's a rain forest?

A RAIN FOREST IS A TALL, VERY DENSE FOREST THAT GETS LOTS OF RAIN. There are two kinds: tropical and temperate. The tropical rain forest gets at least 100 inches each year and is quite humid and hot. The temperate rain forest also gets lots of rain but isn't as hot.

Rain forests are located in Central and South America, Africa, Asia, Australia, and even North America, in Alaska. They only cover about 6 percent of the Earth's surface, but they are home to millions of kinds of plants and animals, and they provide us with food, medicine, and materials we use every day. For example, rubber is made from trees that grow in some rain forests. Foods from the rain forest include sugar; cacao beans (used to make cocoa and chocolate); and tropical fruits such as pineapples, mangoes, passion fruit, papaya, guava, and many others. Plants in the rain forest have been made into medicines to treat diseases like cancer and arthritis. Rain forests also help clean our air; as their plants "exhale," they produce oxygen that people and animals need to breathe. They "inhale" carbon dioxide, which gives them the carbon they need.

Sadly, much rain forest has been destroyed by people who have not been careful about how many trees they cut down. Cutting too many trees without planting new ones and not being careful about the resources we use not only destroys the homes of the rain forest's people and animals but deprives us of all the things that the rain forests do for us. There are lots of groups working to save the rain forests, and most have Web sites that are packed with information. Check them out after dinner!

BROCCOLI FOREST PRIMEVAL

WHEN I WAS A LITTLE GIRL, MY MOTHER WOULD SOMETIMES recite lines of poetry she had learned in school. I couldn't resist naming this appetizer after one of her favorites. The original poem (see Table Talk on page 100, if you don't recognize it) refers to pine and hemlock trees, but this forest is made of broccoli. If you thought only the giants in folktales and legends could uproot trees and eat them, you haven't visited the Broccoli Forest! Raw broccoli can be tough to digest and unpleasant to chew, so even when it's finger food, as it is here, I like to cook it a bit. Here it's flavored with a classic Italian-style combination of olive oil, lemon juice, garlic, and salt. Be sure to have napkins at the ready, as this lip-smacking preparation can make for greasy fingers.

MAKES 1 TO 2 "FORESTS"

12 ounces fresh broccoli crowns
  (or about 1 pound broccoli, stems
  trimmed)

⅓ cup olive oil

1 medium garlic clove, finely chopped
  (See note, page 29)

½ teaspoon salt

1½ teaspoons fresh lemon juice

2 to 4 large (6 to 7 inches long) sturdy
  pieces rye or Italian or Tuscan-style
  sandwich bread

Cut the broccoli crowns into individual "trees," making sure that each has a "trunk" that is 1 to 1½ inches long, and place into a large microwavable container with a lid.

In a small bowl, mix the oil, garlic, salt, and lemon juice. Pour over the broccoli, seal tightly, and shake to coat. Remove the lid and place it loosely over the container, so that it is open just slightly. Microwave on high power for 2 to 3 minutes, or until the broccoli has softened slightly but is still crisp. Let cool.

When the broccoli is cool enough to touch, place 2 slices of bread, one on top of the other, on a plate. Stand the broccoli trees in it, poking the stem end through the holes in the bread, until the slice is completely covered. If you can't fit all the broccoli into this "forest," repeat with the remaining 2 slices of bread. Serve, letting everyone pull up the "trees" and eat them—and then pick at the bread, which will have absorbed some of the flavored oil, if you like. (Leftover broccoli will keep, covered, in the refrigerator, for 2 to 3 days. Toss it into some pasta or a salad.)

What is the "forest primeval"?

PRIMEVAL MEANS VERY, VERY OLD. This phrase is from a poem by Henry Wadsworth Longfellow called "Evangeline," and it tells the story of a woman of that name who lived in Arcadia. The first line is: "This is the forest primeval. The murmuring pines and the hemlocks . . . " If you've ever stood in a forest and heard the wind rustling through the tree branches so it almost sounded like they were murmuring, you know what he was writing about!

FOREST FLOOR MUSHROOM SOUP

THE FOREST FLOOR DOESN'T GET MUCH LIGHT, which makes it a good place for mushrooms to grow. Long ago, people often went into the forest to pick mushrooms to eat, but they knew what to look for. (In some parts of the world, certain groups still pick mushrooms in the forest together as part of their cultural heritage!) Today we buy mushrooms from the supermarket. (See Table Talk, page 102.) You can use any combination of store-bought mushrooms you like. Sautéing them first makes their earthy flavor even stronger.

MAKES 4 CUPS

1 tablespoon vegetable oil

1 tablespoon unsalted butter

2 to 3 tablespoons chopped shallot (2 to 3 large)

1 pound white mushrooms and 8 ounces other fresh mushrooms such as cremini or porcini, or 1½ pounds white mushrooms, sliced

½ teaspoon salt, plus more to taste

3½ cups beef stock

Heat the oil in a large stockpot set over medium-high heat. Add the butter and when it has melted, add the shallot, and cook, stirring and shaking the pan for 30 seconds to 1 minute, or until soft and translucent.

Add the mushrooms, stir to coat them with the butter mixture, sprinkle with ½ teaspoon salt, and cook, stirring occasionally, for 10 to 15 minutes, or until they have released their liquid and most of it has evaporated.

Add the beef stock and cook for 1 or 2 minutes, or until heated through. Using an immersion blender, purée the mushrooms until thick and creamy. Or cool the soup briefly;

1 teaspoon arrowroot, or as needed

Freshly ground black pepper to taste

Low-fat sour cream, for garnish (optional)

Fresh parsley, chopped, for garnish (optional)

then transfer in batches to a food processor or blender and blend until smooth. (Do not overfill a processor or blender or it will leak.) Be very careful while blending, and crack the lid when you are finished to allow steam to escape. Return the smooth soup to the pot and reheat as needed. If it seems too thin, add the arrowroot and cook for 1 more minute. Taste and season with salt and pepper. Stir well. To serve, spoon the soup into 4 serving bowls and top each with a dollop of sour cream and a sprinkling of parsley.

Many cooks will tell you never to wash mushrooms with water but to use a special mushroom brush to clean them instead. Sometimes bits of soil can be hard to brush away; if so, it's fine to wash them quickly or wipe them with a damp paper towel. Know, however, that they absorb water like sponges, so don't immerse them for any length of time, as the water will dilute their flavor and soften them. Cultivated "wild" mushrooms, called exotics by their growers, will have more intense, mushroomy flavors. Dried wild mushrooms are a tasty alternative to expensive or hard-to-find fresh exotics; reconstitute them in warm water for about twenty minutes to soften and clean them of any residual soil. You can also strain the soaking liquid and use some of it in the soup or freeze it and save it for another time. It has a very earthy flavor, though, that kids might not appreciate.

TABLE TALK

What's a mushroom?

A MUSHROOM BELONGS TO THE FAMILY of living things known as fungus. It's not a plant, although some folks mistakenly think so, because it can grow out of the ground. Unlike plants, mushrooms don't have green leaves that produce their food but get their nourishment from the soil. They reproduce with tiny spores. There are thousands of different kinds of mushrooms, some wild and some produced by farmers as food.

Why shouldn't we pick wild mushrooms?

SOME MUSHROOMS CAN MAKE PEOPLE VERY, VERY SICK. In the olden days, many people knew the difference between edible mushrooms and harmful ones just by looking at them. Today we don't get our food from the wild, so we've forgotten a lot about what to look for. The thing to remember is this: Never pick or eat a mushroom that you find growing outside. We only eat mushrooms from stores or markets, or from a mycologist (someone who has studied mushrooms extensively).

Another reason not to pick wild mushrooms is that some are endangered species.

Precooked sausages, also labeled as "fully cooked," can speed your cooking time and ensure that sausages are cooked thoroughly when they are an ingredient in a more complex dish like this. If you can't find any that are already cooked—or if you're a sausage connoisseur who prefers uncooked sausage—follow the package instructions for cooking your links before adding them to this recipe.

TOAD-IN-THE-HOLE, BRITISH-STYLE

IF YOU WERE WALKING IN THE WOODS, YOU MIGHT JUST LOOK DOWN and see a toad in a hole, and that's why this dish appears here. Personally, I don't think it looks much like a real toad in a hole, but someone long ago must have, because Toad in the Hole has been traditional British comfort food for ages. It's made with a savory batter similar to the one used for Yorkshire pudding, but where Yorkshire pudding requires drippings from a roast, Toad-in-the- Hole is made with sausage. (I guess the sausages looked like toads peeking out of a hole to whoever named the dish.) I like lighter chicken sausages, but you can use pork if you prefer.

MAKES 4 SERVINGS

2 tablespoons olive oil

10 to 12 small (about ¾ to 1 ounce each) precooked chicken, turkey, or pork breakfast sausage links (see note, page 102)

1 small yellow onion

3 large eggs

1 cup whole milk

¾ cup plus 2 tablespoons all-purpose flour

½ teaspoon salt

Position the oven rack in the lower-middle position and preheat the oven to 450°F. Heat the oil in a 9-inch nonstick ovenproof skillet set over medium-high heat. Add the sausages and cook, stirring and shaking the pan, for 5 to 7 minutes, or until they are golden brown on all sides. If the sausages are browning too much, reduce the heat to medium.

Meanwhile, grate the onion into a large bowl, using the small holes of the grater, so the onion is reduced almost to a paste.

Combine the eggs, milk, flour, onion, and salt in a mixing bowl, and whisk for 1 to 2 minutes, or until the mixture has the consistency of a very smooth, thin batter.

If the sausages have released too much fat, spoon some off until you have only 1½ tablespoons of fat still in the pan. Pour the pudding mixture into the skillet, being careful not to splatter any of the hot fat. Immediately place the skillet into the oven. Bake for 10 to12 minutes, or until the top of the pudding is just golden-brown. Reduce the heat to 350°F and bake for another 15 to 17 minutes, or until deep golden-brown and very puffed up. Carefully remove the hot skillet from the oven. Slice and serve immediately.

TABLE TALK

IS A TOAD THE SAME AS A FROG? Scientists maintain that toads and frogs belong to the same animal family, but some nonscientific folks make the distinction that toads spend most of their time on land, while frogs spend their time in or near the water. Both frogs and toads are amphibious, which means they hatch from eggs laid in the water. They hatch as tadpoles—creatures similar to fish—but soon grow legs that allow them to walk—and jump—on land.

TABLE TALK

LOTS OF STORIES AND FAIRY TALES TAKE PLACE IN THE FOREST. Can you think of any? Can you make up one of your own?

TOAD-IN-THE-HOLE, AMERICAN-STYLE

SOMETIMES CALLED EGG-IN-A-HOLE OR EGGIE-IN-A-BASKET, this is the American version of the "Toad," and it's a super-quick comfort food dinner that kids will love. Hearty appetites will want two slices of bread, while delicate eaters might want just one. Then again, you never know when a delicate eater will turn into a human vacuum cleaner. Never fear; the recipe expands and contracts with ease.

MAKES 4 SERVINGS

1 teaspoon butter per slice of bread, softened, or heart-healthy margarine, for spreading

4 to 8 slices sandwich bread such as rye, Italian, challah, or any other favorite

Nonstick cooking spray

4 to 8 large eggs

Salt and freshly ground black pepper to taste

Butter the bread on both sides, covering each side completely, including the crusts, so that it does not burn. With a round or square cookie cutter, cut a 2-inch hole in each, reserving the cut pieces. (You can fry them along with the large slices unless there are little mouths that want to eat them immediately.)

Spray a large nonstick skillet or frying pan with nonstick cooking spray, covering it generously, and set over medium heat. Place the bread into the skillet in a single layer, working in batches if necessary, and fry for 1 to 2 minutes, or until golden in color.

Turn with tongs. Crack the eggs into a cup, one at a time, pouring each egg into one of the holes of the bread as you go. Fry for 3 to 4 minutes longer, or until the eggs are firm and cooked through. If the pan gets too dry before the eggs are cooked, add more butter. (If a yolk breaks and the egg becomes runny, let it cook for a minute and then, with a fork, try to lift it and tuck it back into the hole. It won't affect the flavor, but the presentation will be nicer.) Work in batches if necessary, keeping the first batch warm while you work on the second. When all are done, transfer 1 or 2 cooked "toads" to each plate and serve immediately.

LITTLE HANSEL AND GRETEL HOUSES

A BIG, ELABORATE GINGERBREAD HOUSE, MADE ESPECIALLY FOR the holiday season, is a thing of beauty that can be savored, piece by piece, for weeks. These small, portion-controlled houses are quick to assemble and can offer a night or two of fun and treats at any time of the year. Graham crackers afford an easy building material; just buy a high-quality brand cracker that won't crumble to bits before you're done. Or use square or rectangular gingerbread or other cookies. Note that you'll need 3 squares for each house to create an edible lean-to that's perfect for the good witches of your local forest.

MAKES 4 TO 8 "HOUSES"

6 to 12 best-quality graham crackers, broken in half to make squares, or
12 to 24 square or rectangular gingerbread or other cookies, plus more in case they crumble

Prepared frosting for "gluing"

Assorted small candies (or large ones, such as gum drops, that can be cut) in a variety of colors

Make an A-frame gingerbread house by placing 1 graham cracker square on a plate or work surface. With a small spreader or a finger, spread some of the frosting on 2 opposite edges, making sure that the frosting covers each edge completely. Alternatively, you can pipe the frosting from a piping bag or a zip-top plastic bag with a small hole cut in a corner. This will be the house's floor.

Use 2 more graham cracker squares to make the sides. Spread or pipe some frosting along 2 opposite edges of each square. Hold the squares so that the frosted edges are at the top and bottom, attach the bottom edges to the frosted edges of the floor, and press lightly; then tilt the sides together until the frosted edges touch and press lightly again to make a triangular structure.

Let your house sit for a few minutes to allow the graham crackers to adhere to the frosting and plan your decoration. Use the frosting to attach the candies to the house to make colorful trimmings. Admire your work . . . and then gobble it up!

You're a Grand Old Flag

THIS DINNER MAKES AN IDEAL SUMMER HOLIDAY MEAL FOR A SMALL GROUP; its red, white, and blue theme will take you from Memorial Day right through Flag Day, July 4, and Labor Day—and it's good anytime in between. For larger parties, just increase the quantities.

Menu

Stars and Stripes Dips and Chips

(Red Tomato Salsa, White Bean Dip, and Blue Corn Chips)

Patriotic Potato Salad

Red, White, Blue, and Green Salad

Yankee Doodle Chicken Skewers

Red, White, and Blue Mess

Game Plan

KIDS WILL BE INTRIGUED BY A DESSERT CALLED RED, WHITE, AND BLUE MESS—and they'll love the sweet meringues and fresh berries in it. Take note, though; if you make them from scratch, the meringues need to dry in the oven at very low heat for an hour or more. That will tie up the oven, and you still need something to cook the chicken in—for a shorter time at a much higher temperature. A backyard grill is the perfect solution, especially since this is a summer dinner. Or, if you want to do all the cooking indoors and are lucky enough to have two ovens, no problem. If not, allow enough time to bake the meringues well before you prep the rest of the dinner. That way your chicken will come to the table piping hot and moist.

★ Make (and nibble) the Stars and Stripes Dips and Chips. ✋

★ Make the meringues for the Red, White, and Blue Mess and bake them for 65 to 75 minutes. ✋

★ Get the kids started on the Brushwork Fireworks project.

★ Prep potatoes for the Patriotic Potato Salad and microwave them for 15 to 20 minutes.

★ Make the marinade and marinate the chicken for the Yankee Doodle Chicken Skewers for at least 15 minutes. Prep the other ingredients for the skewers and set aside.

★ Make the vinaigrette for the potato salad. Remove the potatoes from the microwave, drain, and let cool. Dress the potato salad.

★ Prep the Red, White, Blue, and Green Salad and the dressing, but do not dress the salad yet.

★ Grill or broil the chicken for 10 to 12 minutes.

★ Dress the salad.

★ It's dinnertime in the U.S. of A.!

★ Remove the meringues from the oven and let cool. Prep the whipped cream and berries for the Red, White, and Blue Mess and assemble the dessert.

★ Dessert for all!

Crafty Friday:
BRUSHWORK FIREWORKS

WHO DOESN'T LOVE THE FIREWORKS THAT ACCOMPANY SUMMER HOLIDAYS? Kids will love creating their own sparkly fireworks silhouettes on paper. You don't use a regular paintbrush for this project; instead, you'll need some old scrub brushes—or stock up on some inexpensive new ones. If you have them on hand, some baby bottle brushes will make a smaller fireworks orb and give your work of art perspective.

Acrylic paint in red, white, blue, and any other colors of your choice

Paper plates

1 black (9 x 12-inch) sheet construction paper per person

1 round scrub brush for each color of paint (the kind used for scrubbing dishes)

Bottle brushes (optional)

Glitter glue in various colors

Pour the paint, a little of each color, on paper plates, keeping the colors separate and leaving room to dip a scrub brush into each. (A dinner-sized plate will have room for 2 or 3 colors.)

Dip the round end of a brush into one of the colors, making sure there is a light coat of paint all the way around the brush. If the paint covers the brush in a giant gob, remove some paint by wiping it back onto the plate. The paint should just cover the bristles lightly.

Press the bristles on the paper to make a circular fireworks pattern.

(continued on next page)

Swap brushes and repeat, making as many fireworks explosions as you like. Overlap some of them. Use a bottle brush to make a smaller fireworks silhouette if you like.

Let the paint dry a bit, and then use the glitter glue to make sparkly arcs around and within the fireworks circles. Don't forget to say "ka-boom!"

What's a flag?
What's the meaning of the United States flag?

A FLAG IS DESIGNED TO REPRESENT A COUNTRY, state, city, or group of people. The design of the United States flag has thirteen red and white stripes and fifty white stars on a blue background. These decorations have a special meaning: More than two hundred years ago, the people in what is now the United States decided they did not want to be ruled by the king of England and they fought a war for freedom. At the time, they were grouped into thirteen territories called colonies. People from all the colonies got together and decided what their flag would look like. The thirteen stripes represent the thirteen original colonies. The stars represent the fifty states that now make up the United States. But the flag didn't always look like this. The first flag had thirteen stars in a circle on the blue background. Over the years, as more states became part of the country, stars were added to the flag. Some people think the red, white, and blue used in the flag had a special meaning, but if they did, the people who designed the flag never explained it.

WHAT DOES FREEDOM MEAN TO YOU?

STARS AND STRIPES DIPS AND CHIPS

KETCHUP WAS ONCE THE MOST POPULAR CONDIMENT IN THE U.S. OF A., but salsa, an import from our neighbors south of the border, overtook it years ago and now it's an American staple. Here, it's paired with a white bean dip and blue corn chips, for a true red, white, and blue treat. Use a food processor for the bean dip, but cut the salsa ingredients by hand so the tomato doesn't become too liquidy.

MAKES 1¾ TO 2 CUPS SALSA AND 1 CUP BEAN DIP

Red Tomato Salsa

3 medium tomatoes, vine-ripened or from your garden or the farmers' market, cored and chopped (about 2 cups)

1 tablespoon finely chopped red onion, plus more to taste

¼ to ½ jalapeño pepper, seeds and membranes removed, and finely diced (½ to 1 tablespoon), or to taste (see note below)

Juice of ½ lime (1½ to 2 tablespoons)

3 to 4 sprigs fresh cilantro, chopped,

⅛ teaspoon salt, plus more to taste

White Bean Dip

1 (14-or 15-ounce) can white kidney (cannellini) beans, rinsed and drained

Juice of 1 lime (about 3 to 4 tablespoons)

2 tablespoons extra-virgin olive oil

1½ teaspoons cumin, or to taste

¼ teaspoon salt, plus more to taste

Blue corn chips, for serving

To make the salsa, mix the tomatoes, onion, jalapeño, lime juice, and cilantro leaves, if using, and mix to combine. Season with salt to taste and set aside to let the flavors meld.

To make the white bean dip, combine the beans, lime juice, olive oil, cumin, and 1 teaspoon salt in a food processor fitted with a metal blend, and process until creamy. Taste and add more salt if necessary and process just to mix.

To serve, spoon the salsa and bean dip into small serving bowls, and set out a bowl of blue corn chips.

Like other hot chile peppers, jalapeños' stinging heat comes from a substance in them called capsaicin, and you'll feel it not just in your mouth but on your hands—and on your face and in your eyes if you happen to touch them after cutting them. Some cooks wear rubber gloves for cutting chiles; you might not go to that extreme, but do be careful when handling them. You can put plastic sandwich bags on your hands while chopping. To lessen the heat in a recipe, remove and discard the membranes and seeds and just use the pepper flesh.

YANKEE DOODLE CHICKEN SKEWERS

WHY YANKEE DOODLE? BECAUSE THESE EASY GRILLED CHICKEN KABOBS ARE just dandy! For this dish, you'll need eight (12-inch) skewers. You can use either metal or wooden skewers, but if you use wood, soak them in water for at least 20 minute before putting the food on them so they don't burn on the grill. Starting with partially frozen chicken makes it easier to cut.

MAKES 4 SERVINGS

(8 SKEWERS)

2 tablespoons ketchup

1 tablespoon soy sauce

1 tablespoon olive oil, plus more
   for drizzling

2 boneless, skinless chicken breast
   halves, partially frozen

Nonstick cooking spray

4 precooked garlic or plain chicken
   sausages, each sliced diagonally into 6
   pieces

2 small to medium yellow or white
   onions, each cut into 8 wedges

16 grape or cherry tomatoes

Mix the ketchup, soy sauce, and 1 tablespoon oil in a shallow, nonreactive glass, ceramic, or plastic container. Cut the partially frozen chicken breasts into $\frac{1}{2}$-inch chunks and place them into the marinade, turning to coat. Marinate for at least 15 minutes, or until you've prepped the rest of the dinner. (If you find that you are delayed for much longer, cover and refrigerate.)

When you are ready to cook, spray the grill rack or broiler pan with nonstick cooking spray and preheat the grill to medium-high heat or preheat the broiler.

Assemble the skewers, threading each with a piece of sausage, a wedge of onion, a chunk of chicken, and a tomato, repeating the pattern once, and ending with a piece of sausage. Brush the tomato and onion with a little oil. Discard the chicken marinade. Place the skewers on the grill or broiler pan, and grill or broil for 10 to 12 minutes, or until the chicken is cooked through and no longer pink inside.

The marinade might look like a yummy basting sauce, but once it is used to marinate chicken or any other animal protein, you never know if it is contaminated with salmonella or other foodborne bacteria, because they are colorless and odorless. If you are tempted to use the marinade for basting, be sure that you stop basting at 3 to 5 minutes before you finish cooking; this will allow the heat to kill any bacteria that might be lurking in it. Better yet, make up a fresh batch of marinade and use it for basting.

TABLE TALK
Who is Yankee Doodle?

A YANKEE IS ANOTHER WORD FOR AN AMERICAN. When the people of the thirteen colonies decided they didn't want to be ruled by the king of England, they had to fight a war before they were free to set up their own country. The English soldiers who fought against them made fun of them with a song that called them "Yankee Doodles." The colonists proudly wrote their own version of the song and it became a popular marching song. If you know "Yankee Doodle," try singing it now. If not, check it out on the Internet after dinner.

PATRIOTIC POTATO SALAD

IF YOU'VE NEVER CUT INTO A PURPLE POTATO BEFORE, you're in for a colorful surprise. Not only does the skin have a purplish cast but the innards show off lovely shades of purple and blue. Alongside the blushing red skins and white flesh of the red potatoes, you've got a very patriotic potato salad. The purple potato, which originated in South American but is now grown in the United States, has thick skin that must be removed for potato salad. The red skin, however, is thin and delicate and perfectly edible—not to mention, it's the vital third color for a red, white, and blue dinner.

MAKES 4 TO 6 SERVINGS

12 ounces baby red-skinned potatoes, washed and cut into quarters

12 ounces baby purple potatoes, washed, peeled, and cut into quarters

½ teaspoon salt, plus more for boiling the potatoes

1½ tablespoon red wine vinegar

2 teaspoons Dijon mustard

4 tablespoons olive oil

3 tablespoons minced shallots (about 3 large shallots)

4 to 6 kalamata olives, pitted and chopped (about 1½ tablespoons)

Place the quartered potatoes into a microwave-safe container and fill with water to cover. Add a dash of salt and microwave on high power for 15 to 20 minutes, or until the potatoes are easy to pierce with the tines of a fork. Drain and let cool.

Meanwhile, make the vinaigrette: In a small mixing bowl, mix the vinegar, Dijon mustard, oil, and ½ teaspoon salt, and mix until combined and golden in color. Stir in the shallots and olives.

Pour the vinaigrette over the cooled potatoes and toss lightly. Let stand for at least 15 minutes before serving.

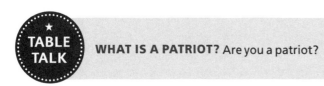

★ TABLE TALK

WHAT IS A PATRIOT? Are you a patriot?

RED, WHITE, BLUE, AND GREEN SALAD

EVEN YOUR SALAD BOWL CAN GO RED, WHITE, AND BLUE! Mild white balsamic vinegar makes for a delicate dressing that won't overpower the blueberries.

MAKES 4 SERVINGS

3 tablespoons olive oil

1 tablespoon white balsamic vinegar

1 heart Romaine lettuce, trimmed, washed, dried, and torn

½ red bell pepper, cut into 1 x ¼-inch strips (about ¾ cup)

½ cup fresh blueberries

½ cup crumbled feta cheese

To make the vinaigrette, mix the oil and vinegar in a small bowl until thoroughly combined.

Combine the lettuce, bell pepper, blueberries, and cheese in a large salad bowl.

When you are ready to serve, pour the vinaigrette over the salad, toss gently to coat, and serve.

RED, WHITE, AND BLUE MESS

THIS DESSERT WAS INSPIRED BY A TREAT ENJOYED AT ETON, the famed British school. There it's called Eton Mess, and it consists of crushed meringues topped with strawberries or raspberries and whipped cream. On this side of the pond, I've added blueberries to make it a real Red, White, and Blue Mess! The meringue recipe here makes more than you'll need to serve four to six people, but it's difficult to do meringue cookies with fewer than the three egg whites called for. If kids are around, though, leftovers shouldn't be a problem. You can enjoy them, with or without berries, another night.

MAKES ABOUT 40 MERINGUES
Meringues

3 large egg whites

$\frac{1}{16}$ teaspoon salt

$\frac{1}{8}$ teaspoon cream of tartar

$\frac{3}{4}$ cup granulated sugar

MAKES 4 TO 6 SERVINGS
Fruit Topping

1$\frac{1}{2}$ pints strawberries

1 to 2 tablespoons granulated sugar, or to taste

$\frac{1}{2}$ pint blueberries

Whipped cream

1 cup heavy cream

1 tablespoon confectioners' sugar

Position the oven racks in the middle and lower-middle positions, and preheat the oven to 225°F. Line 2 baking sheets with parchment paper.

With an electric mixer set at medium-low speed, beat the egg whites and salt in a mixing bowl for about 30 seconds, or until foamy. Add the cream of tartar and beat for 1 to 2 minutes, or until the whites begin to hold soft peaks. (The peaks will rise when you lift the beaters from the mixture but will fall immediately.) Gradually add the sugar, pouring it in slowly while still beating. This should take about 30 to 45 seconds. Scrape down the bowl.

Increase the mixer speed to medium-high and continue beating for 5 to 6 minutes, or until the meringue becomes glossy and stiff. When the beater is raised, the peaks of meringue should stand straight up. Rub a bit of the meringue between two fingers. It should feel smooth. If any gritty sugar remains, continue beating for another 1 to 2 minutes, or until it is dissolved.

With a clean spatula, transfer the meringue to a pastry bag fitted with a plain ⅛-inch tip or a 1-gallon resealable plastic bag. If you are using a plastic bag, seal it tightly and then snip one of the bottom corners to create a ⅛-inch opening.

Pipe small, flat disks, 1½ inches in diameter and ⅛ inch high, onto the parchment, spacing them close together, as they don't spread when baked. Pipe about 20 disks onto each sheet.

Bake the meringues for 65 to 75 minutes, or until they are completely dried out. They should not take on any color. To test if they are done, remove 1 cookie and let it cool at room temperature for 3 or 4 minutes. When fully baked, it should snap in half with perhaps some crumbs, but no stickiness. If they are not yet crisp, continue baking the meringues for another 5 to10 minutes.

Remove the pans from the oven and cool the meringues on the sheets. They will dry a little more from the heat of the pans. Once completely cooled, they can be removed easily by peeling them off the parchment.

While the meringues are baking, rinse the strawberries, pat them dry, remove the hulls, and cut them into ¼-inch slices. Add the granulated sugar; starting with just a little, then tasting and adding more if the berries need a little more sweetness. Reserve half the sliced, sweetened strawberries. Transfer the remaining strawberries to a small bowl and mash with a fork.

Rinse the blueberries and pat them dry. Mix with the reserved sliced strawberries.

To make the whipped cream, pour the cream into a mixing bowl, add the confectioners' sugar, and whip with a whisk or an electric mixer set at low to medium speed until soft peaks form. (The peaks will rise when you lift the beaters from the mixture but will fall immediately.)

Assemble the "mess" just before serving so the meringues retain their crunch. Crumble about 20 meringue disks into the whipped cream. Scoop a large dollop of this mixture into each of 4 to 6 small bowls. Top each with 1 to 2 tablespoons of the mashed strawberries and swirl into the whipped cream. Top each mess with a large spoonful of the reserved strawberries and blueberries. Serve immediately with more meringue disks for crumbling on top as desired.

TABLE TALK

IF YOU MADE A FLAG FOR YOUR FAMILY, what would it look like?

TABLE TALK

DO YOU KNOW some other names for the United States flag?

After-Dinner Fun

CHECK OUT THE FLAGS OF OTHER COUNTRIES in an encyclopedia or on the Internet.

Two of the flag's nicknames are Old Glory and the Stars and Stripes.

An Evening at the North Pole

THE NAME MIGHT SOUND WINTRY, BUT THIS EVERYTHING-COLD DINNER IS designed for a hot summer night, when you can't imagine eating hot food and you need to think cool thoughts. It's mind—and meal—over matter, with a cold feast and some cold facts about the coldest places on Earth.

Menu

Cool as a Cucumber Watermelon Salsa with Pita Crisps

Snowy Cold Cauliflower Soup

Cold Roast Beef Sandwiches with Ho-Ho-Ho Spread

Vegsicle Salad

High-Speed Baked Alaska

Game Plan

★ Make (and nibble) the Cool as a Cucumber Watermelon Salsa with Pita Crisps.

★ Cook the cauliflower for the Snowy Cold Cauliflower Soup.

★ Get the kids started on the "Poughlar" Bear.

★ Make the Cold Roast Beef Sandwiches with Ho-Ho-Ho Spread.

★ Finish the cauliflower soup and chill.

★ Make the Vegsicle Salad and dressing. Just before you are going to serve, dress the salad.

★ Brrr! Time to eat!

★ Make the meringue topping for the High-Speed Baked Alaska, assemble it, and bake for about 4 minutes.

★ Warm up with a cool dessert!

DINNER PREP IN SMALL BITES:

If you have time the night before or earlier in the day, make the Snowy Cold Cauliflower Soup and the Ho-Ho-Ho Spread for the Cold Roast Beef Sandwiches.

FRIDAY NIGHT TIME-SAVER:

If time is short, use a good-quality bottled fruit salsa and a prepared flavored cream cheese instead of the Watermelon Salsa and Ho-Ho-Ho Spread.

Crafty Friday:
"POUGHLAR" BEAR

HERE'S A POLAR BEAR SCULPTURE WHOSE NAME COMES FROM the fact that it's made from a simple dough—a "poughlar" bear, if you will. Don't try eating this dough; it's nontoxic, but not very tasty. If you make a standing bear, be sure to make the legs thick enough so that your sculpture won't fall over.

½ cup all-purpose flour per person, plus more as needed

½ cup table salt per person, plus more as needed

¼ cup water per person

Permanent markers

Mix the ingredients together in a bowl until you have a moldable dough. If the mixture is too soupy or squishy, add a little more flour and salt.

Divide the mixture equally among all the sculptors and have each person form a polar bear. You can make it reclining on the ice, curled up asleep, or standing on all four legs or on two. Or, if you like, make a baby polar bear and its mother.

Place the bears on a microwavable plate and microwave on high power for 1 to 3 minutes, or until hardened. Remove from the microwave and let cool.

When the bears are cool enough to touch, draw the bear's eyes, nose, and mouth with markers. Say hello to your bear!

★ TABLE TALK

What's a polar bear?

A POLAR BEAR IS THE WORLD'S LARGEST BEAR. It can grow up to 10 feet tall. Its white or yellowish fur is thick and it has a thick layer of fat under its skin, all to help it live in the cold Arctic. Sadly, in recent times, pollution and climate change have caused much of the Arctic ice to melt, which has made it harder for the polar bears to hunt for food, and scientists have listed them among animals that are in danger of dying out. Several groups are working to save the polar bear. To find out more about the polar bear and what you can do can do to help, check it out on the Internet after dinner.

COOL AS A CUCUMBER
WATERMELON SALSA WITH PITA CRISPS

THE INGREDIENTS IN THIS REFRESHING SALSA MIGHT SEEM an unlikely combination, but they include two of the coolest foods you can find without raiding the freezer. Spoon a little on a toasted pita wedge and you'll see.

MAKES ABOUT 3½ CUPS

2½ cups (1/4-inch) chunks watermelon, black seeds removed

½ cucumber, cut into ¼-inch chunks (about 1 cup)

1 teaspoon honey mustard

2 tablespoons chopped fresh dill

1 or 2 pita breads, plus more to taste, for serving

Combine the watermelon, cucumber, honey mustard, and dill in a medium serving bowl, and toss until the melon and cucumber have released some of their liquid and the mustard and dill are distributed throughout the salsa.

Toast the pita bread and cut it into 1½-inch wedges. Place the dip in its bowl on a serving platter. Surround with pita wedges and let everyone spoon some of the salsa onto the pitas.

What's the North Pole?

THE NORTH POLE IS THE NORTHERNMOST POINT on the planet Earth, in the middle of the Arctic Ocean. It's very cold there—so cold that the ocean is covered with floating ice that can be as much as ten feet thick. Because of the way the Earth is tilted in relation to the sun, the light from the sun hits the North Pole and the area surrounding it very differently from the rest of the planet. As a result, it doesn't have day and night as we know them, but six months of constant light and six months of darkness.

What's the South Pole?

THE SOUTH POLE IS THE SOUTHERNMOST POINT on the planet. Unlike the North Pole, it's on land, near the middle of the continent of Antarctica. The area around the North Pole is cold, but at the South Pole, it's even colder; it's the coldest, driest place on Earth. In fact, the temperature there has plunged to more than 100 degrees below zero. Think about that on a hot summer day and you'll feel cooler in no time!

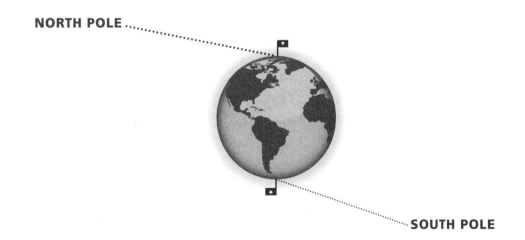

NORTH POLE

SOUTH POLE

SNOWY COLD CAULIFLOWER SOUP

CAULIFLOWER IS ONE OF THOSE FOODS THAT DIVIDES PEOPLE INTO TWO CAMPS— those who like it and those who don't. I happen to love it, and I'm not above trying to convert the Cauliflower Don'ts of the world into Cauliflower Dos. This soup will be delicious warm from the pot (see note on next page), but for this dinner, cold is the way to go, and for that, frozen cauliflower is key. Not only does it speed the prep time, but a few frozen florets help chill the cooked soup without diluting the flavor.

MAKES ABOUT 4 CUPS

1 (14.5-ounce) can chicken stock

1 (20-ounce) bag frozen cauliflower

¾ cup light cream or fat-free half-and-half, plus more to taste

Salt to taste (optional)

Bring the chicken stock to a boil in a medium saucepan. Meanwhile, set aside 4 large cauliflower florets. (If the bag you are using has only small florets, grab a small handful.) When the stock begins to boil, add the remaining cauliflower and cook, occasionally pushing down any florets that rise above the liquid, for about 15 minutes, or until very soft.

Prepare 2 bowls for an ice bath, one slightly larger than the other. Fill the larger one halfway up with ice water, and nestle the smaller into it, making sure that the water level is not so high that that it will spill into the smaller bowl.

Remove the pot from the heat and process with an immersion blender until you have a creamy soup, or carefully transfer the hot cauliflower to a food processor fitted with a metal blade and process until creamy. There will be some tiny chunks of cauliflower in the soup.

Transfer the soup to the small bowl in the ice water bath and stir in the cream. Place the reserved frozen cauliflower into it and let stand for 10 to 15 minutes, or until chilled. Taste and season with salt if necessary. Divide the soup among 4 soup bowls. You can discard the frozen cauliflower or attempt to eat it!

This soup can be eaten warm or cold. Note that cold tends to minimize strong flavors, so you might need to add salt once it is chilled. If you reheat any leftovers and find that the soup is too salty, add a bit more cream and heat very gently. If you plan to serve it warm from the pot, you can use fresh or frozen cauliflower; both will be delicious.

★ TABLE TALK

WHEN IT'S HOT OUT, how do you keep cool?

WHEN IT'S COLD OUT, how do you stay warm?

COLD ROAST BEEF SANDWICHES WITH HO-HO-HO SPREAD

COLD ROAST BEEF DRESSES FOR DINNER WITH THIS HO-HO-HO SPREAD, so named because its red, green, and white hues might remind you of a plump someone who is said to live at the North Pole. You can easily customize the spread to suit everyone at your table. If someone objects to scallions, leave them off his or her sandwich. Same goes for the cranberries. But as I always say, "First taste one bite. You just might like it."

MAKES 4 SANDWICHES

Ho-Ho-Ho Spread

3 to 4 tablespoons sweetened dried cranberries

1/2 cup cream cheese or light cream cheese

2 scallions, sliced

Sandwiches

8 slices pumpernickel or other hearty, flavorful bread

3/4 pound thinly sliced cold roast beef

4 leaves romaine lettuce

To make the spread, chop the dried cranberries coarsely and pour them into a small mixing bowl. Add the cream cheese and scallion and mash until thoroughly incorporated.

Spread 4 slices of bread with 1 1/2 to 2 tablespoons Ho-Ho-Ho Spread each. Top each with 1 leaf of lettuce, folding it to fit. Divide the roast beef among the sandwiches and top each with a slice of bread. Cut each in half and serve.

TABLE TALK

Does anybody live at the North and South Poles?

WHILE THE NORTH POLE ITSELF IS IN THE MIDDLE OF THE ICY ARCTIC OCEAN, the area surrounding it (extending more than 1,000 miles beyond the pole) touches land in Canada, Denmark (Greenland), Finland, Lapland, Norway, Sweden, the Russian Federation, and the United States (Alaska). Known as the Arctic, this area is very cold, but people have learned to adapt, and have lived there for hundreds of years. There's lots of wildlife in the Arctic, including polar bears, reindeer, caribou, lemmings, whales, seals, walruses, snow geese, snowy owls, and others. They have special qualities that enable them to live in the cold, such as thick fur coats and extra layers of fat under their skin.

The South Pole is in the middle of the large land mass called Antarctica. It's colder than the Arctic and has never been home to many people—except for scientists who have traveled there to study it. But penguins, whales, and other creatures live along the edge of Antarctica and in its surrounding waters.

Does anybody else live at the North Pole?

OH, YES . . . It's said that Santa Claus and his elves live there, too!

VEGSICLE SALAD

WHEN MY DAUGHTER WAS TINY, SHE DEVELOPED A FONDNESS FOR EATING *frozen peas. Was I ever relieved when the pediatrician told me that lots of kids do—and that it's perfectly okay! This salad makes use of kids' affinity for cold, frozen things and hits the spot on a hot night. The dressing gives it a grown-up kick, which kids can opt to try—or not.*

MAKES 4 SERVINGS

Caper Vinaigrette

1½ tablespoons red wine vinegar

3½ tablespoons olive oil

2 tablespoons capers, rinsed and drained

Vegsicle Salad

4 cups torn iceberg lettuce or a mixture of iceberg and Romaine lettuces

1 cup frozen mixed vegetables or ⅓ cup frozen peas, ⅓ cup frozen carrots, and ⅓ cup frozen corn, rinsed in a colander but still frozen

Grated Parmesan cheese, for sprinkling

Combine the vinegar and oil and mix thoroughly. Add the capers and mix again. Set aside.

Combine the lettuce and frozen vegetables in a salad bowl and toss lightly.

Just before serving, add the dressing to the salad, sprinkle with Parmesan cheese, and toss to coat. Top with a light sprinkle of cheese and serve.

HIGH-SPEED BAKED ALASKA

IF YOU AND I WERE PASTRY CHEFS AT A FANCY RESTAURANT, we'd spend hours making and then molding the ice cream and baking the cake for this dessert, all from scratch. But we're not—so we can substitute store-bought cake and ice cream and come up with an impressive, delicious confection in less than half an hour! Cold at the core and warm on the outside, covered with light, delectable meringue, it might (or might not) remind you of an igloo. You'll need to work quickly, or the meringue will fall and the ice cream will melt before you get it into the oven, but if you set up your work space efficiently, you'll be able to assemble your Baked Alaska before you can say, "It's cold inside!" Serve as soon as it comes out of the oven. Store leftovers in the freezer.

MAKES 6 TO 10 SERVINGS

1½ cups vanilla ice cream–orange sherbet combo or other ice cream of your choice

1 (1 pound) plain loaf pound cake

4 large egg whites

⅛ teaspoon salt

⅛ teaspoon cream of tartar

½ cup granulated sugar

On a piece of parchment paper, use a spoon to form the ice cream into a 1 to 1½-inch-high log that's just slightly smaller and narrower than your pound cake, allowing for a cake border around the ice cream when you assemble the Baked Alaska. Cover and return it to the freezer.

Adjust the oven rack to the middle position and preheat the oven to 475°F. Slice the pound cake in half lengthwise to make two layers, making the bottom one a little thicker than the top. With a sharp knife, scoop out a ½-inch deep oval or rectangle from the bottom layer, leaving an edge of about ½ inch, to make a "cake bowl." Set the cake scraps aside with the top cake layer. Place the bottom cake layer in a baking dish pretty enough to go from oven to table, and set aside.

Set up your work space so that all your components will be close at hand and you'll have room to pack the ice cream into the bottom cake layer, quickly seal it with the top layer and the cake scraps, and then cover it all with meringue.

With an electric mixer set at medium-low speed, beat the

Little Hansel and Gretel Houses, page 106

Broccoli Forest Primeval, page 99

Fairy Dust Sugar Cookies, pages 92-93

Sunnyside-Up Pineapple-Apricot Upside-Down Cake, pages 140–41

Antique Treasure Maps, pages 58-59

Inside-Out Turkey, Cheese, and Cranberry Relish Wraps, pages 137–38

Bat 'n' Ball Banana Split, page 142

Popperjack, page 27, and Chili Dawgs, pages 28-29

Curly Head Salad with Orange Vinaigrette, pages 75–

Your Very Own Silly Hat, pages 72-73

Chicken à la King in a Pastry Crown, pages 149–50

Castle Cupcakes, pages 152–54

Tuna Po'Boy with Olivey Aioli, pages 209–10

Signora Caprese's Broad-Rimmed Hat, page 74

X-Ray Vision Summer Rolls, pages 196–97

End of the Rainbow Lentil Salad, page 211

Paparazzi Pepperoni Pop Star Pita Pizzas, pages 174–75

Wooden Spoon Prince
and Princess Puppets, page 145

egg whites and salt in a mixing bowl for about 30 seconds, or until foamy. Add the cream of tartar and beat for 1 to 2 minutes, or until the whites begin to hold soft peaks. (The peaks will rise when you lift the beaters from the mixture but will fall immediately.) Gradually add the sugar, pouring it in slowly while still beating. This should take about 30 to 45 seconds. Scrape down the bowl.

Increase the mixer speed to medium-high and continue beating for 5 to 6 minutes, or until the meringue becomes glossy and stiff. When the beater is raised, the peaks of meringue should stand straight up. Rub a bit of the meringue between two fingers. It should feel smooth. If any gritty sugar remains, continue beating for another 1 to 2 minutes, or until it is dissolved.

Now is the time to work quickly. Take the molded ice cream out of the freezer and place it into the depression of the bottom cake layer. Place the top cake layer over it and use the scraps to seal any spots on the side where the ice cream is visible.

Spoon the meringue over the entire cake, smoothing it where necessary to create a mound of white swirls. Bake for 3½ to 5 minutes, or until the meringue is just lightly browned and firm to the touch. Serve immediately.

TABLE TALK — Where is Alaska, and why is this dish named for it?

ALASKA IS THE NORTHERNMOST OF THE UNITED STATES. It is not attached to the rest of the states but instead borders our neighbor, Canada. Part of Alaska is within the Arctic Circle, and it is quite cold. The United States purchased Alaska from Russia in 1867, but it didn't become a state until 1959. Baked Alaska was invented more than 100 years ago, although its exact origin isn't agreed upon. French chefs made a similar dessert and called it a Norwegian omelet. (Norway is also in the Arctic.) In the nineteenth century, an American chef renamed it Alaska Florida, because it was both hot like Florida and cold like Alaska. In the early twentieth century, it was rechristened "Baked Alaska," and the name stuck.

After-Dinner Fun: Globe Trotters

ON A GLOBE, FIND THE NORTH AND SOUTH POLES, the Arctic and Antarctic Circles, and Alaska. Find where you live and see how far away you are from the poles.

Then go to your computer and check out the National Oceanic and Atmospheric Administration's North and South Pole webcams to see live photos of the beautiful, if frigid, top and bottom of the Earth!

Backwards Night

TONIGHT'S THE NIGHT TO LET YOUR INNER SILLY PERSON STEP OUT!

For starters, have everyone come to dinner dressed in something backwards or inside out. Put your shirt on backwards, put your pants on inside out, and pick socks or shoes that don't match. But that's only the beginning. The menu consists of slightly off-kilter items like a Bumpy Smoothie and an Inside-Out Wrap, and, of course, a twist on a classic, the Sunnyside-Up Pineapple-Apricot Upside-Down Cake. Let the silliness begin!

Menu

Bumpy Smoothie

Inside-Out Turkey, Cheese, and Cranberry Relish Wraps

Nutty Pepper Slaw

Sunnyside-Up Pineapple-Apricot Upside-Down Cake

Game Plan

★ Make (and drink) the Bumpy Smoothie. ✋

★ Glaze the pecans for the Nutty Pepper Slaw and bake for 10 minutes. ✋

★ Make the Sunnyside-Up Upside-Down Cake and bake for 42 to 49 minutes. ✋

★ Get the kids started on the Picasso Project.

★ Make the Inside-Out Turkey, Cheese, and Cranberry Relish Wraps.

★ Make the Nutty Pepper Slaw.

★ emitrenniD!

★ Remove the Sunnyside-Up Pineapple-Apricot Upside-Down Cake from the oven and let cool.

★ tresseD!

DINNER PREP IN SMALL BITES:

If you have time the night before or earlier in the day, glaze and bake the pecans for the Nutty Pepper Slaw, make the Inside-Out Turkey, Cheese, and Cranberry Relish Wraps, and bake the Sunnyside-Up Pineapple-Apricot Upside-Down Cake.

FRIDAY NIGHT TIME-SAVER:

If time is short, use coleslaw or other premade slaw instead of the Nutty Pepper Slaw. It's hard to find a prepared upside-down cake, but if you're pressed, substitute another cake or dessert that you can turn upside down.

Crafty Friday:
PICASSO PROJECT

AT THE BEGINNING OF THE TWENTIETH CENTURY, many artists began to change the way they made art—and some people thought the results looked upside down and backwards! But over time, people got used to art that didn't look exactly like the real world, and realized that it could be quite interesting. In this project, the kids get to pick up where Pablo Picasso left off. It's the perfect project for Backwards Night. If you like, for inspiration, read the Table Talk: Who was Pablo Picasso? (page 134) and check out some of Picasso's artwork in a book, if you have one, or on the Internet.

Construction paper in various colors, cut in circles, triangles, and rectangles of different sizes

1 (9 x 12-inch) sheet construction paper per person

Old newspapers and magazines

Sheet music that can be cut up (optional)

Wallpaper scraps (optional)

Safety scissors

Glue sticks

You can start the kids out with precut shapes or ask them to cut their own.

Make a picture by gluing shapes to your full sheet of construction paper. Cut the construction paper into smaller shapes and also cut embellishments out of newspaper, sheet music, or wallpaper and glue them on to their artwork. Voilà! A masterpiece!

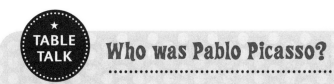

PICASSO WAS ONE OF THE MOST INFLUENTIAL ARTISTS of the twentieth century. Along with other artists of the same time, he did not try to make pictures and sculpture that re-created the world with photographic realism. Instead, he made art in ways that represented how he felt or what he thought about his subject—or how he felt and thought about their shapes and colors. Picasso made art in many styles and forms; one of his best-known styles is Cubism, in which he and other artists looked at their subjects, figured out what shapes they contained, and reassembled the flat shapes to make unrealistic images that depicted the subjects in new and sometimes jarring ways. (For example, a person's head might look like a circle or an upside-down triangle; legs might be thin rectangles or thin upside-down triangles.) The Cubists, as they were called, used paint and made collages of wallpaper, sheet music, newspaper, and other materials.

When Picasso and the other Cubists first showed their work, many people thought they were crazy. Some still do. But if you get used to looking at it, Cubism can be exciting and even beautiful! It's fun to look at the world from a different perspective.

BUMPY SMOOTHIE

HERE'S A SMOOTHIE WITH BUMPS, courtesy of your favorite breakfast cereal. I think the fruit provides enough sweetness, but taste it for yourself; you might like it a little sweeter or you might have picked up an exceptionally tart bag of berries. If so, add a little sugar or honey.

MAKES 3½ TO 4 CUPS

3 ripe bananas, peeled

2 cups frozen strawberries or other frozen berries

1 cup milk

Granulated sugar or honey to taste (optional)

1 cup dry cereal such as flakes, granola, or O-shaped oat cereal

In a blender, combine the bananas, frozen berries, and milk. Blend until smooth and creamy. Taste and, if necessary, add the sugar, starting with 1 teaspoon. Add the cereal and pulse a few times, or until the cereal is broken up slightly but still distinguishable. Serve immediately.

You can't go wrong making a smoothie; it's the ultimate in flexibility. You will need at least two elements: one frozen and one liquid. You can blend any combination of frozen berries, frozen bananas (sliced before you freeze them), frozen yogurt, ice, fresh berries, peeled apple chunks, fresh bananas, fresh berries, milk, juice, sugar, honey, chocolate syrup, piña colada mix—or whatever strikes your fancy.

Have you ever heard of a palindrome?

A PALINDROME IS A WORD OR PHRASE that's the same whether you read it from beginning to end or end to beginning. Some examples:

Anna	Eye	Madam, I'm Adam.
Hannah	Race car	Able was I, ere I saw
Noon	SOS	Elba.

INSIDE-OUT TURKEY, CHEESE, AND CRANBERRY RELISH WRAPS

THE TORTILLA'S ON THE INSIDE OF THESE YUMMY WRAPS, so they need special handling, but if you follow the directions, they're quick and easy. The cheese serves as the wrapper here, so rectangular slices work best; squares tend to crumble. Look for the rectangle-shaped cheese at the deli counter or packaged in the dairy aisle. Likewise, Swiss or Muenster cheese are the best choices; other sliced cheeses will fall to pieces. You'll need 16 toothpicks to hold these together. They'll keep, refrigerated, for a day or two and are an ideal do-ahead for dinner at the beach or a picnic in the park. Salty sweet-potato chips make a nice accompaniment, and they carry on the night's backwards theme.

MAKES 8 WRAPS

Cranberry Relish

½ cup sweetened dried cranberries

¼ cup grated Parmesan cheese

2 teaspoons hot dog relish

2 teaspoons olive oil

Put the cranberries, Parmesan cheese, relish, and oil into a food processor fitted with a metal blade, and process until the cranberries are chopped into crumbs and the mixture is slightly sticky and holds together when you press it. Trim the round edges from 8 tortillas to make 8 rectangles in the same dimensions as the cheese.

Place a slice of cheese on a work surface. Top with a slice of turkey breast, and fold in the edges to conform to the shape

Wraps

4 to 8 flour tortillas

8 rectangular (about 6 x 3 inches) slices Swiss or Muenster cheese or some of each (packaged slices from the deli)

8 slices deli or packaged turkey breast

1 medium cucumber, sliced in half crosswise and then in eighths lengthwise to make 16 (3-inch) strips

Packaged salty sweet-potato chips, for serving (optional)

of the cheese if you need to. Top with a trimmed tortilla. Place 2 cucumber sticks just inside one of the short edges of the wrap. Spoon about 1½ teaspoons of the cranberry relish next to the cucumber, forming a thin strip of relish and leaving about ¼ inch on the edges of the wrap so the relish won't fall out when you roll it. Press the relish lightly and roll the cheese, turkey, and tortilla over the cucumber and relish. Secure with 2 toothpicks. Cut in half on a diagonal, and if necessary trim the other side of the wrap so that it's flat and can stand upright. Serve with sweet-potato chips if you like.

What is it about finger food that kids love? You can turn these wraps into a finger food dinner or even a cocktail party nibble by using 3 toothpicks per wrap and cutting each into 3 smaller pieces.

NUTTY PEPPER SLAW

THAT'S RIGHT—NUTTY! LITERALLY! This crisp, colorful salad is loaded with luscious maple-glazed pecans and goes nicely with casual fare like the Inside-Out Wraps in this dinner. It will travel well, too.

MAKES 4 TO 6 SERVINGS

Nonstick cooking spray

1 tablespoon unsalted butter, melted

3 tablespoons pure maple syrup, divided

1 cup pecan pieces

1 medium green bell pepper, stemmed and seeded,

1 medium red bell pepper, stemmed and seeded

1 medium carrot

2 to 3 tablespoons seasoned rice vinegar

Preheat the oven to 375°F. Spray a baking sheet with nonstick cooking spray.

Mix the melted butter and 2 tablespoons maple syrup in a container with a lid; add the pecans, seal, and shake to coat all the nooks and crannies thoroughly. Arrange the pecans on the baking sheet in a single layer and bake, watching carefully to keep them from burning, for about 8 minutes, or until they are crisp. Set aside.

Meanwhile, shred the peppers in a food processor fitted with a shredding attachment, or cut into thin matchsticks that are about 1 inch long. Shred the carrot in the food processor or with a vegetable peeler. (Make crosswise cuts with a knife in 5 or 6 spots on the peeled carrot and shred lengthwise with the peeler. Make more cuts as you peel if needed.)

Place the pepper, carrot, and pecans into a salad bowl. Mix the remaining maple syrup and 2 tablespoons rice vinegar in a cup until incorporated. Pour the dressing over the salad and toss to coat. Taste and add another tablespoon vinegar if necessary. Toss again and serve. Any leftovers can be kept, covered, in the refrigerator for 2 to 3 days. The vegetables will exude their liquid with time, so you might want to drain the salad a bit in a fine-mesh sieve before serving.

Just like it sounds, seasoned rice vinegar is a mild vinegar distilled from rice and seasoned with salt and sugar or other sweetener. (I like the brands sweetened with plain old sugar.) It is used as a salad dressing or dipping sauce, alone or in combination with other ingredients. You'll find it in Asian grocery stores and, increasingly, in the vinegar section at mainstream supermarkets.

TABLE TALK

Can you speak Pig Latin?

Pig Latin isn't Latin; it's an all-mixed-up English-language game in which speakers drop the initial consonant of every word and add it to the end, followed by an "ay." For example, in Pig Latin, "backwards" translates as *ackwords-bay*. If the word begins with a vowel, just add an "ay" to the end. "Upside down" would be *upside-ay own-day*.

Try saying the names of everyone at the table in Pig Latin. Then try having a conversation in Pig Latin. How fast can you go?

SUNNYSIDE-UP PINEAPPLE-APRICOT UPSIDE-DOWN CAKE

THIS CAKE GOT ITS NAME BECAUSE THE APRICOTS inside the pineapple rings reminded me a little of sunny-side-up eggs. For this recipe you will need an ovenproof skillet or saucepan that that is relatively deep—at least 2 inches for a 9-inch skillet or 1¾ inches for a 10-inch skillet—so there's room for the batter to rise. Use canned pineapple packed in juice, not syrup, and reserve the juice for both the topping and the batter. Canned apricot halves usually come in syrup; choose a can with light syrup or juice if you can find one.

MAKES 1 (9- TO 10-INCH) CAKE

Syrup

3 tablespoons unsalted butter

5 to 7 canned pineapple rings packed in juice, drained, juice reserved

¾ cup light brown sugar

5 to 7 canned apricot halves in light syrup, drained

Cake

1¾ cup all-purpose flour

2 teaspoons baking powder

¼ teaspoon salt

8 ounces (2 sticks) unsalted butter, at room temperature

¾ cup plus 2 tablespoons granulated sugar

1½ teaspoons pure vanilla extract

Move the oven rack to the middle position and preheat the oven to 350°F.

In a deep, 9- or 10-inch ovenproof skillet, melt 3 tablespoons butter, 2 tablespoons of reserved pineapple juice, and the light brown sugar. Adjust the heat to medium-low and cook, stirring occasionally, for about 3 minutes, or until syrupy. The sugar will not have completely dissolved.

Turn off the heat under the skillet and arrange the drained pineapple rings in it, with 1 ring in the center and the others in a circle around the edge. Use as many as will fit without overlapping. Place an apricot half, round-side down, in the center of each pineapple ring.

Sift the flour, baking powder, and salt into a medium bowl. In a separate bowl, using an electric mixture set at medium speed, beat the remaining butter for about 2 minutes, or until very smooth. Add the granulated sugar, increase the mixer speed to medium-high, and beat, for about 5 minutes, scraping down the bowl 2 or 3 times, or until fluffy and very light in

2 large eggs

1 large egg white

3 tablespoons whole milk

color. Reduce the speed to medium, add the vanilla, and beat for 10 seconds. Add the eggs and egg white, one at a time, beating for about 20 seconds to incorporate after each addition.

In a small bowl or measuring cup, mix 4 tablespoons of the reserved pineapple juice with the milk.

Add one-third of the flour to the batter, beat at low speed for about 20 seconds, scrape down the bowl, and add half the juice-milk mixture. Beat well for 20 seconds and continue adding a third of the dry ingredients and the second half of the wet ingredients, beating well after each addition. The batter will be thick enough to scoop.

Drop large scoops of batter evenly over the pineapple and apricots in the skillet. Spread the batter smoothly to the edges of the skillet. Bake immediately in the preheated oven for 42 to 49 minutes, or until the cake is golden on top and a toothpick inserted into the center comes out clean. Let the skillet cool for 7 to 8 minutes on the counter; then place a rack over the cake and, with oven mitts on your hands, carefully invert the skillet to release the cake. Cool the cake on a rack, over a piece of foil or parchment to catch any drips. Cool the cake completely and serve.

After-Dinner Fun: Wordsmith

GATHER SOME WORD FINDER OR SCRAMBLED-WORD PUZZLES. You can find them in books, in some newspapers, or on the Internet. Or make them up! Of course, make sure they are the right age-and skill-levels for your kids. Here's a scrambler to get you started:

emit ylimaf si emit rennid

(Answer can be found below)

TABLE TALK

The Chair That Was Not There

Bend your knees and see how long you can stay in a sitting position while "sitting" on air. Sit down all the way or it will be too easy.

Answer: Dinner time is family time.

Ye Royal Dinner

IN THE PAST FEW YEARS, PRINCESSES AND ROYALTY IN GENERAL
have become the hottest thing for kids (or, at least, for little girls).
But stories of glamorous royal figures who have fantastical adventures and
solve difficult problems have been around for ages; they figure prominently in
the folktales passed from parents to children around the world. These tales are not
static, however. In her most recent appearances, the princess doesn't need to wait
for the prince to save the day; she works with him to overcome the obstacles they
face. And then, of course, they all live happily ever after. This dinner brings some
of the magic of "Once upon a time" to your dinner table, with, among other
things, an edible crown and an honest-to-goodness Castle Cupcake for kids
to decorate. And then, of course, you'll all eat happily ever after.

Menu

The Princess and the Sugar Snap Peas

Queen of Hearts Salad

Chicken à la King with a Pastry Crown

Castle Cupcakes

Game Plan

★ Thaw the frozen puff pastry for the Chicken à la King Pastry Crown.

★ Make (and nibble) the Princess and the Sugar Snap Peas. ✋

★ Prep the Castle Cupcakes and bake for about 30 minutes. ✋

★ While the cupcakes are baking, prep the Puff Pastry Crowns for the Chicken à la King. ✋

★ Get the kids started on the Wooden Spoon Prince and Princess Puppets.

★ Start the Chicken à la King.

★ When the cupcakes are done, remove them from the oven and let cool. Bake the pastry crowns for about 20 minutes.

★ Finish the Chicken à la King and keep it warm.

★ Prep the salad and the dressing, but don't cut the pears or dress the salad until just before serving.

★ Finish the salad and dress it. Place the pastry crowns on dinner plates, and spoon the Chicken à la King into them.

★ Hear ye, hear ye: Time to eat!

★ Make the frosting and assemble and frost the Castle Cupcakes. ✋

★ By royal proclamation, it's time for dessert!

DINNER PREP IN SMALL BITES:

If you have time the night before or earlier in the day, make the minted vanilla yogurt for the Princess and the Sugar Snap Peas (the minty quality will become a little more intense with time), and bake the Castle Cupcakes.

FRIDAY NIGHT TIME-SAVER:

If time is short, use store-bought cupcakes and mini-cupcakes and assemble and frost them to make Castle Cupcakes. (You might have to scrape off whatever frosting came on them.)

A WOODEN SPOON CAN MAKE AN ADORABLE PUPPET that is easy to manipulate. Each person can make one—or for a more complicated story line—two or more. If you have enough spoons, you can make a whole cast of characters: a prince, a princess, a queen, a king, and their royal subjects. When it's time for the puppet show, the puppeteers can crouch behind the couch or the table and hold the puppets up over their heads so that only the puppets can be seen. Practice your royal voices!

1 wooden spoon per puppet

1 (6-inch x 8-inch or larger) piece of felt or other fabric per puppet

Safety scissors

1 (4-inch x 6-inch) piece tulle, netting, or shiny fabric per puppet, or several short lengths of shiny ribbon

1 colored pipe cleaner per puppet

2 small plastic self-adhesive eyeballs per puppet or a blue, green, brown, black, or purple marker

1 small self-adhesive pink or red heart or crescent moon, or a red or pink marker

Ribbon or yarn for hair

Craft glue

Silver or gold pipe cleaner or aluminum foil

Dress your puppet in royal robes: Wrap a large piece of felt around the handle of the spoon, cutting it to fit if necessary. Wrap a piece of tulle, netting, shiny fabric, or ribbon—or a combination of these if you have extra—around the felt, cutting it to the size you like. Tie securely with a pipe cleaner where the puppet's waist would be. If the handle of the spoon is completely covered with fabric, arrange it so that your own hand can fit underneath. If there's some spoon handle sticking out, this will be your handle.

Make your puppet's face in the concave bowl of the spoon. Stick on the eyes or draw them on with marker. Use a stick-on heart or moon for a mouth or draw on the mouth with marker. Cut yarn or ribbon to make hair, and carefully glue it to the top edge of the spoon's bowl.

Make a crown with the silver or gold pipe cleaner, fit it to your puppet's head, and trim any excess with scissors. Alternatively, form a crown with small lengths of aluminum foil; roll them into a ring, then add a scalloped or pointed top.

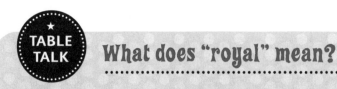

TABLE TALK — **What does "royal" mean?**

"Royal" is a word used to describe kings, queens, princesses, princes, their families, and their households. At one time, most countries were ruled by a royal family. The job was typically passed within the family from the king or queen to the eldest son or daughter, who would pass the job to his or her eldest son or daughter, and so on. As time passed, some countries gave up this system, which is called a monarchy, in favor of rulers elected by the people every few years. Some countries combine the two systems and have a monarchy and an elected government. Because of its association with kings and queens, the word "royal" is used to describe all sorts of things—usually of the best quality.

THE PRINCESS AND THE SUGAR SNAP PEAS

IN THE TALE OF THE PRINCESS AND THE PEA, the test of a true princess was her extreme sensitivity. So delicate was her constitution that she was bothered by a tiny pea placed under the pile of mattresses she slept on. With all respect, I think the fairy tale got it wrong; my test of a true princess is whether she eats her green veggies. In fact, I'm sure that even the princess who felt the pea under the mattresses would have liked sugar snap peas; their sweet, crunchy character makes them a fine snack just plain. Because this is a royal dinner, they've got an escort: a minted yogurt dip that's cool and refreshing and just right.

MAKES 4 SERVINGS

1 (6 to 8-ounce) container low-fat or nonfat vanilla yogurt

2 tablespoons chopped fresh mint

8 ounces sugar snap peas

In a small serving bowl, mix the yogurt and mint until thoroughly combined. Let stand for at least 5 minutes or refrigerate until ready to serve.

If necessary, trim the peas by breaking off the tiny tough tips and pulling off the "strings" all the way down the seams of the pods.

To serve, place the yogurt dip in its bowl on a large serving platter. Surround with the sugar snap peas and serve.

QUEEN OF HEARTS SALAD

THE QUEEN OF HEARTS MIGHT BE BEST KNOWN FOR HER TARTS, but she was also a champion salad-maker. This one has two kinds of hearts: marinated artichoke hearts and red bell pepper hearts. The kids will enjoy snapping the pepper to make the hearts, and if it takes a few tries to master the technique, that's okay—in this salad, even broken hearts make for a happy ending!

MAKES 4 SERVINGS

Dressing

1 tablespoon white balsamic vinegar

2 tablespoons extra-virgin olive oil

Salt and freshly ground black pepper to taste (optional)

Salad

1 large red pepper with deep ridges

4 cups washed, dried, and torn Romaine or other lettuce

1 (6.5-ounce) jar marinated artichoke hearts, drained and cut into bite-sized pieces

1 ripe Bosch or Anjou pear

To make the dressing, mix the vinegar and oil in a small bowl until thoroughly combined. Season with salt and pepper to taste, if you like, and set aside.

To make your red pepper into hearts, slice it crosswise into rings about ¼-inch thick. Carefully remove the seeds and membrane, keeping the rings whole. Place 1 ring on a work surface and pick the side with the 2 best "scallops" as the top of your heart. Directly across from the center of the scallop, cut the pepper ring. Position the loose ends so that they form the bottom of the heart shape; if necessary, snap the curves just next to where you've cut to straighten out the sides of the heart, but don't let the pepper break anywhere else. (You might have to snap a few curves to make a proper heart, but be careful not to break the pepper. If it does, set your "broken heart" aside and try again with another pepper ring.) Repeat with 3 more pepper rings for a total of 4 hearts. Set these aside.

Slice all the remaining pepper, including any broken hearts, into ½-inch pieces. Place the lettuce into a salad bowl and toss lightly with the cut pepper and artichoke.

Just before you are ready to serve, core the pear and cut the flesh into bite-sized pieces. Add them to the salad bowl and toss the salad with the dressing. Divide the salad among 4 bowls, top each with a red pepper heart, and serve.

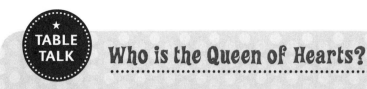

Who is the Queen of Hearts?

THE QUEEN OF HEARTS CAME TO LIFE AS ONE OF THE 52 IMAGES in a deck of playing cards. Playing cards have been around all over the world for many centuries; they are thought to have originated in China or India. Card games came to Europe sometime in the Middle Ages. At first they were decorated with all sorts of pictures, but by the sixteenth century, card makers had figured out a standard system: Each deck of cards was imprinted with four kinds of symbols, or suits—hearts, spades, diamonds, and clubs. Within each suit, the cards were assigned numbers or one of three royal characters—the king, the queen, and the jack. The Queen of Hearts is the queen card in the heart suit.

The Queen of Hearts is also the main character of the famous English nursery rhyme that begins, "The Queen of Hearts, she baked some tarts, all on a summer's day. . . . " It was published in the late 1700s but might have been composed earlier than that. The short rhyme tells how the queen's tarts are stolen by the Knave of Hearts but recovered by the King of Hearts, who punishes the knave, who, in turn, promises not to steal again:

The Queen of Hearts, she made some tarts, all on a summer's day;
The Knave of Hearts, he stole the tarts and took them clean away.
The King of Hearts called for the tarts and beat the Knave full sore
The Knave of Hearts brought back the tarts and
Vowed he'd steal no more.

In 1805, Lewis Carroll cast the Queen of Hearts as a character in *Alice's Adventures in Wonderland*. Alice meets the Queen of Hearts, a rather grouchy monarch who, when displeased with someone, shouts, "Off with his head!" Luckily for most of these poor souls, her husband, the king, pardons them, and their heads remain where they belong. As in the nursery rhyme, the Knave of Hearts makes off with her tarts and is put on trial. And you know what the Queen shouts as a verdict! Just in the nick of time, Alice wakes up from her fantastical dream, so the Knave, too, gets to keep his head.

CHICKEN À LA KING IN A PASTRY CROWN

THIS CLASSIC DISH IS SO REGAL IT COMES WITH ITS OWN "CROWN" of puff pastry balls. The crown is based on the Saint Honoré, a French dessert confection named in honor of the patron saint of bakers. In this version, instead of a sweet cream filling, this crown is filled with Chicken à la King. By cooking the components one after the other in a single skillet, you are layering and intensifying the flavor of the dish. Some bits of caramelized chicken and garlic remain to flavor the mushrooms, and in turn, bits of caramelized mushroom, chicken, and garlic are left to flavor the savory sauce. If at any point the pan seems too dry, add a bit more oil or butter.

MAKES 4 SERVINGS
Pastry Crowns

Nonstick cooking spray

2 sheets frozen puff pastry, thawed

1 large egg, lightly beaten with 2 tablespoons water, for egg wash

About 2 tablespoons frozen green peas, plus more as needed

1½ to 2 teaspoons sesame seeds

Chicken à la King

3 tablespoons unsalted butter, divided

2 tablespoons olive oil, divided

2 cloves garlic, finely chopped, divided

1½ pounds skinless, boneless chicken breasts or chicken breast tenders, trimmed (white tendon removed), pounded to a thickness of ¼-inch and cut into bite-sized pieces

Place the oven rack in the middle position and preheat the oven to 400°F. Spray a baking sheet with nonstick cooking spray.

Spread 1 sheet of puff pastry on a work surface. Make 2 lengthwise cuts in each to make 3 strips. Make 9 crosswise cuts in each, so that you have a total of 30 squares. Roll each square into a small ball. Repeat with the remaining sheet of puff pastry.

Arrange the balls on the prepared baking sheet end-to-end in 4 rings of 15 balls each, dipping each ball into in the egg wash as you press it into the ring. The rings should each be about 4 to 5 inches wide and should be spaced on the baking sheet so that they don't touch. Use a pastry brush to coat any uncoated spots on the rings with egg wash. Press 1 green pea into the top of each ball and sprinkle each ring with sesame seeds. Press the seeds gently so that they adhere. Bake for about 20 minutes, or until golden-brown and nicely puffed. Remove from the oven and let cool for a few minutes. Then, with a spatula, carefully detach the pastry crowns from the baking sheet. If any break, just put them back together.

(continued on the next page)

1 teaspoon salt, plus more to taste, divided

8 ounces white mushrooms, sliced

3 tablespoons all-purpose flour

½ cup whole milk

1 (14.5-ounce) can chicken stock

Freshly ground black pepper to taste

2 tablespoons fresh chopped parsley, for garnish (optional)

Meanwhile, make the Chicken à la King. Heat 1½ teaspoons butter and 1 tablespoon oil in a large nonstick skillet set over medium-high heat until the oil shimmers and the butter is melted. Add 1 teaspoon garlic, and cook, stirring, for 20 to 30 seconds, or until softened and translucent. Add the chicken, season with about ¼ teaspoon salt, and cook, stirring and shaking the pan for 6 to 7 minutes, or until cooked through and just golden in color. Transfer the chicken to a large, clean platter.

Return the skillet to the heat, add 1½ teaspoons butter and 1 tablespoon oil, and heat until the butter is melted. Add the remaining garlic and cook, stirring, for 20 to 30 seconds, or until softened and translucent, but not browned. Add the mushrooms, season with ¼ teaspoon salt, and cook, stirring and shaking the pan, for 5 to 6 minutes, or until they have released their liquid, it has evaporated, and the mushrooms are just golden in color. Transfer the mushrooms to the platter with the chicken.

Return the skillet to the heat and make a Béchamel sauce: Reduce the heat to medium-low, add 2 tablespoons butter and the flour, and stir for about 30 seconds, or until a thick paste forms. Add the milk and stir for 30 seconds to 1 minute, or until the mixture thickens and coats the back of a spoon. Add the chicken stock and stir for 4 to 6 minutes, or until the sauce is creamy and again coats the back of a spoon. Taste and season with salt and black pepper, if necessary. Return the chicken, mushrooms, and any juices from the platter to the skillet. Stir and heat through for about 1 minute longer.

To serve, place 1 cooled pastry crown on each of 4 dinner plates. Spoon about a quarter of the chicken, mushrooms, and sauce into the center of each crown. Sprinkle with parsley if you like, and serve.

You can also use boneless chicken thighs for this dish. But because they are dark meat, they must cook longer. Cook until the chicken is no longer pink, its juices run clear, and a meat thermometer inserted into a thick piece reads 165°F.

TABLE TALK

Where did all the stories about princesses and princes come from?

PRINCESSES AND PRINCES WERE CONSIDERED VERY IMPORTANT PEOPLE back in the days when royal families ruled most everywhere, so people made up lots of tales about them. Before printed books were widespread, people told their favorite stories out loud, passing them from parent to child or from friend to friend. Many of the tales we know best were collected by the Brothers Grimm. Jacob and Wilhelm Grimm were born in Germany in 1785 and 1786, respectively. They started collecting and writing down folktales as young men, and in time, the brothers published several volumes that made their name as famous as the tales they collected. Their stories came not just from Germany but all over Europe. There have been other collectors of tales, too, notably Andrew Lang, a Scottish writer born in the nineteenth century, who collected and published a series of folktales titled with colors (*The Blue Fairy Book, The Red Fairy Book,* and others). In the twentieth century, these tales were retold on film and in cartoons by the Walt Disney Company.

Can you think of any favorite stories of princesses and princes?

CASTLE CUPCAKES

NOTHING BUT A CASTLE CUPCAKE WOULD DO for this dinner, so I asked my friend Cindi Kruth, a master baker, for help. Not only did she come up with something charming and fun for kids to put together, her carrot cake is simply the best I've ever tasted. The frosting is a simple but delicious cream cheese and confectioners' sugar mixture that can be used for these carrot cupcakes or for spice cake. Cindi's ingenious castle decorations are described below, but you can decorate these with pretty much any combination of small candies, dried fruits, or nuts that you like.

MAKES 12 CASTLES (12 REGULAR AND 12 MINI-CUPCAKES)

Cupcakes

Nonstick cooking spray (optional)

2 cups all-purpose flour, plus more for dusting

1 teaspoon baking powder

¾ teaspoon baking soda

½ teaspoon salt

1 teaspoon ground cinnamon

¼ teaspoon grated nutmeg

Pinch of ground cloves

3 large eggs at room temperature

¾ cup lightly packed light-brown sugar

¾ cup granulated sugar

1 cup vegetable oil

½ teaspoon pure vanilla extract

Line a 12-cup cupcake tin and a 12-cup mini-cupcake tin with paper wrappers, or spray the insides of the cups with nonstick cooking spray and dust lightly with flour. Place the oven rack in the middle position, and preheat the oven to 375°F.

Sift the flour, baking powder, baking soda, salt, cinnamon, nutmeg, and cloves into a large mixing bowl. In another large bowl, whisk the eggs and sugar for about 2 minutes, or until the sugar is thoroughly dissolved and the mixture is light in color. Whisk in the oil and vanilla extract until just combined.

Add the flour mixture to the egg mixture, and stir until they are just blended. Add the carrot and nuts, if you like, and stir just to blend all the ingredients.

Scoop or spoon the batter into the prepared cups, filling each about two-thirds full. Bake the mini-cupcakes for 18 to 22 minutes and the regular-sized cupcakes for 26 to 31 minutes, or until the tops appear dry, the cupcake springs back when gently pressed, and a toothpick inserted into the center comes out clean.

Meanwhile, to make the frosting, beat the cream cheese with an electric mixer set at medium speed until very smooth.

2 cups lightly packed grated carrot

¾ cup toasted pecans, chopped (optional)

Cream Cheese Frosting

8 ounces cream cheese

4 ounces (1 stick) unsalted butter, at room temperature

4 cups confectioners' sugar

1 teaspoon pure vanilla extract

1 to 2 tablespoons heavy cream, as needed

Few drops pink or other food coloring (optional)

Decorations

12 chocolate or white chocolate kisses, unwrapped

24 vanilla or chocolate mini Tootsie Rolls, unwrapped

24 Tootsie Rolls or 36 to 48 caramels, unwrapped

Several thin strands of licorice (pulled off a rope)

24 to 36 yellow, white, or clear gumdrops or other "gummy" candies

24 or 36 red gumdrops or other "gummy" candies

Add the butter and beat again until very smooth. Sift the confectioners' sugar into the bowl, reduce the speed to low, and beat until combined. Add the vanilla and beat until the mixture is smooth and fluffy. If it is too thick for spreading, drizzle in 1 or 2 tablespoons heavy cream. Beat at medium speed until smooth. If you like, tint with a drop of food coloring.

To decorate the cupcakes, when they have cooled a bit, remove the paper wrappers from 1 regular-sized carrot cupcake and 1 mini-cupcake. Cut a thin horizontal slice off of the top of the larger cupcake to make it flat, and turn it upside down on a flat dish. Do the same to the mini-cupcakes if necessary. (You can eat the trimmings!) Place a small spoonful of icing on top of the larger cupcake and place the mini-cupcake upside down on top of it to make a castle.

Frost the entire castle. If the frosting is difficult to spread evenly without getting crumbs on the outside, do the best you can with a thin coating of frosting and chill the cupcakes in the freezer for 10 minutes or so to firm them up. They will be easier to finish frosting neatly if they are cold.

Place the chocolate or white kiss on top to complete the castle silhouette.

To make towers, place the Tootsie Rolls on a work surface and roll out with your hands until they are wide and very flat. Wind up the flattened Tootsie Roll to make a cylindrical shape. Place one tower on either side of the front of the castle.

To make doors and drawbridges, roll 2 Tootsie Rolls or 3 or 4 caramels in your hands to soften, then flatten them out, cutting them into rectangles with rounded tops. Attach to the

(continued on the next page)

frosting on the side of the larger cupcake, standing it up straight, like a door. Roll what's left of the Tootsie Roll into a flat rectangle and mark it with a toothpick or butter knife to look like a wooden bridge. Place it on the plate in front of the castle doors. Cut the licorice strand in 1-inch pieces and arrange like drawbridge chains.

To make windows, flatten the yellow gumdrops or gummy candies and cut them to make tiny rectangles or squares. (Yellow or other light colors look best as windows.)

To make a flag, flatten a red gumdrop or gummy candy and shape it into a thin triangle. Pierce 1 side with a toothpick and insert the toothpick into the mini-cupcake next to the chocolate kiss.

NOTE: If you prefer to make these with white cake, use the batter for Microphone Cupcakes (You Might Even Be a Pop Star!, page 176). The proportions that are there will make 8 castle cupcakes; for 12 castle cupcakes, multiply the batter 1½ times. Bake for 18 to 24 minutes.

TODAY, CASTLES ARE THE VERY LARGE AND VERY FANCY HOMES OF royal families. Hundreds of years ago, the first castles were also large, and they were often occupied by royalty, but they were designed as fortresses, to keep enemies out. Castles were very strong buildings and typically had high, thick walls and bars on the very small windows.

Once a castle was built, another protection was added: A big hole was dug all the way around it and filled with water. This moat, as it was called, made it even more difficult for the king's or queen's enemies to get in. But the people who lived and worked in the castle needed a way to get in and out. The solution was a drawbridge, which was attached to the castle in place of a door. When someone wanted to cross the moat to get in or out of the castle, the drawbridge could be lowered by chains to make a bridge. Once the person had crossed it, the drawbridge was pulled, or drawn, up again, leaving the castle safe and secure.

Home on the Range

THE OLD WEST IS ANOTHER LOCALE THAT FIGURES IN THE AMERICAN IMAGINATION.
The full story of the West is a lot more complicated than the legend depicted by Hollywood, but oh, what a legend! Cowboys doing daredevil stunts astride majestic horses. Good guys and bad guys clearly defined by the color of their hats. Native Americans in colorful feathers and paint. (Never mind that not every tribe wore them; the legend was one size fits all.) This dinner invokes the legend of the Old West and offers up some authentic Western flavors, both old and new.

Menu

Howdy Pardner Guacamole

Old West Salad with Pinto Beans, Cactus Bits, and Ranch Dressing

Native American Fry Bread

Chuck Wagon Chicken-Fried Steak with Onion Cream Gravy

Cookie's Apple-Apricot Cobbler

Game Plan

★ Make (and nibble) the Howdy Pardner Guacamole. ✋

★ Mix up the batter for the Native American Fry Bread and let it rest for 30 minutes. ✋

★ Get the kids started on the Dream Catcher craft.

★ Prep the beans for the Old West Salad and roast for 5 minutes. Remove from the oven and let cool. Prep the other salad components, but don't toss them together yet. Prep the Ranch Dressing and set aside to pass at the table.

★ Fry the Native American Fry Bread.

★ Prep and cook the Chuck Wagon Chicken-Fried Steak, and let it rest for 10 minutes. Cook the Onion Cream Gravy and assemble the salad.

★ Ring the cowbell! It's eatin' time!

★ Prep Cookie's Apple-Apricot Cobbler and bake for about 20 minutes. ✋

★ Time for dessert!

DINNER PREP IN SMALL BITES:

If you have time the night before or earlier in the day, roast the beans for the Old West Salad. You can make the Ranch Dressing, but know that its buttermilky bite becomes a bit more intense with time. You can also prep the components for Cookie's Apple-Apricot Cobbler, but don't cook or bake them; the cobbler is best hot out of the oven.

FRIDAY NIGHT TIME-SAVER:

If time is short, buy good prepared guacamole. For a quicker and lighter main course than the Chuck Wagon Chicken-Fried Steak, you can grill or broil plain steaks and serve them with the Onion Cream Gravy. You can also use a good-quality flour tortilla, warmed lightly in the oven, to approximate the Native American Fry Bread.

A DREAM CATCHER IS AN AUTHENTIC NATIVE AMERICAN CRAFT, but, to be historically accurate, it was not a craft of the Old West, though you'll find it in the West today. It originated with the Ojibwa tribe, who lived in what is now known as the Great Lakes region. In the twentieth century, the dream catcher tradition spread to other tribes, and today you can find dream catchers made by Native American artisans all around the country—North, South, East, and West. It's easy to understand why the dream catcher is so popular: It's a craft that comes with a lovely tale. According to Ojibwa (also spelled as "Chippewa") tradition, if you hang a dream catcher on your door, the patterned web inside will catch the bad dreams and keep them from entering, while good dreams will pass through. You can make your dream catcher with any kind of ring or round tubing that is 4 to 6 inches wide. I've used an inexpensive option—the inside ring of a wooden embroidery hoop—but I've seen them made from metal rings, bent willow, and other materials. You can use any kind of twine, waxed thread, or yarn to make the web and wrap and decorate the ring, but I like multicolored yarn, as it makes a visually interesting craft. Your web can be as complex as a spider's or as simple as a square, a star, or an X.

1 ball of multicolored yarn

Safety scissors

1 (4- to 6-inch) wooden ring from the inside of an embroidery hoop, per person

Small plastic beads

Small bells with loops that can be threaded with yarn (optional)

Small plastic shells that can be threaded with yarn (optional)

1 bag colorful feathers

Craft glue

To make your dream-catcher's web, think about the pattern you'd like to make. Cut a piece of yarn that is 4 to 6 times the diameter of your hoop (depending on the complexity of your pattern). Tie one end to the hoop with a double knot. Stretch the yarn across the hoop in various directions to make your pattern, tying it at each point where it crosses the hoop to keep it in place. If you wish, you can add a bead to the interior of the web; tradition has it that this bead lets us keep the wisdom of our good dreams. Tie the end of the yarn and cut off any leftover yarn.

Cut a long (4 to 6 yards) piece of yarn. Tie one end to the hoop with a double knot and wrap the yarn tightly around the

(continued on the next page)

whole circumference of the hoop, so that all the wood is covered; weave it between the strands of the web wherever necessary. The length of this piece of yarn will depend on the size of your hoop. If you cut a piece that is too short, just tie it when you get near the end, cut another piece, and keep wrapping. If it's too long, tie it when you finish wrapping the hoop and cut off the leftover.

Cut a 12-inch piece of yarn to make a hanger for your dream catcher. Loop it through the hoop, wrapping it once or twice in the center of the top end (as if it were the 12 o'clock position), so that it will stay in place. Then tie the ends securely to make a loop from which to hang the dream catcher.

To decorate your dream catcher, cut 4 (8-inch) pieces of yarn per hoop. Tie 1 to each side of the hoop at the 3 o'clock and 9 o'clock positions, using double knots and letting most of the yarn dangle. Tie the 2 remaining pieces to the bottom, at the 5 o'clock and 7 o'clock positions, again using double knots and letting most of the yarn dangle. (If you wish, you can use more than 4 pieces of yarn.)

Add some simple beadwork to your dream catcher: Thread 1 to 4 beads halfway up one of the decorative pieces of yarn on the side of the hoop. If you wish, add a small bell or shell. Tie a double or triple knot in the yarn at the halfway mark to keep the beads and bell from sliding down. Repeat with the remaining 3 pieces of yarn.

Trim your dream catcher with feathers: Put a dab of glue at the sharp end of 1 or 2 feathers, stick them together if you're using 2, and wrap the glued end tightly with the end of the yarn, leaving enough yarn at the end to tie a knot. Let dry.

Who are Native Americans and how did they end up in the Old West?

THE NATIVE AMERICANS (NOW CALLED AMERINDIANS in some circles) were the first people to live in the lands known as the Americas. At the height of their civilization, between 1000 B.C. and 1000 A.D. (which began 3,000 years ago), there were some 600 different groups, or tribes, in North America alone, speaking almost as many languages and living according to a variety of religions and community traditions. After Christopher Columbus arrived in 1492, large numbers of Europeans began to sail across the Atlantic. They began to take land occupied by the Native American tribes, pushing them farther and farther west, at first informally, and later in forced government-sponsored resettlement programs that restricted the Native Americans to areas known as reservations. Many Native Americans died along the way, both in battles against the European settlers and from diseases and harsh conditions that they introduced. This was a sad chapter in United States history. In more recent years, Native Americans have begun to rebuild their communities and proudly return to their traditions.

HOWDY PARDNER GUACAMOLE

AVOCADOS ORIGINATED IN CENTRAL MEXICO SEVERAL THOUSAND YEARS AGO and were a favorite of the Aztec peoples who lived there. They called them *ahuacatl*. When the Spanish conquistadores came to the Americas, they were treated to a mashed-avocado preparation called *ahuacamulli*, which was virtually the same as modern guacamole. Large-scale avocado cultivation was introduced to California in the late 1800s. Guacamole might not have been typical cowboy food, but about 100 years later, it had found its way onto every Southwestern menu from the streets of Laredo to the avenues of Hoboken—and with good reason; it's mighty tasty, pardner. If there's any guacamole left over, it will keep, covered in the refrigerator, for about 1 day. Squeeze a good amount of lime juice over the top before pressing plastic wrap down onto the guacamole to keep it from oxidizing and turning brown.

MAKES ABOUT 2 CUPS

½ cup finely chopped sweet onion, such as Vidalia

12 grape tomatoes, finely chopped

3 tablespoons fresh lime juice

½ teaspoon salt, plus more to taste

3 small ripe avocados

Tortilla chips, for serving

Combine the onion, tomatoes, lime juice, and salt in a mixing bowl.

Cut the avocado lengthwise, twist to remove the pit, spoon the flesh into the bowl, and mash until the avocado is smooth and creamy and all the vegetables are thoroughly incorporated. Taste, season with salt if necessary, and mix to combine. (If you are in a rush, you can do the chopping and mixing in a food processor fitted with a metal blade, but you'll get a very creamy guacamole; pulse slowly if you want to retain a bit of texture from the onions.) Serve with chips.

Look for ripe avocados that are just slightly soft to the touch but not mushy. If only hard ones are available, let them ripen at room temperature for a few days. To remove the pit, make a lengthwise cut around the whole avocado and twist the 2 sides until they separate. The pit will be attached to one side; use a spoon to remove it. Immediately sprinkle all surfaces or mash the whole thing with an acid such as lime juice to prevent it from turning brown.

Git Along Little Doggies

A COWBOY IS, IN THE SIMPLEST DEFINITION OF THE WORD, somebody who takes care of cows. In the mid-1800s, there was a great effort by the emerging cattle industry to move large herds across vast expanses of the West. This was done by cowboys who rode horses alongside the herds as they went. It was hard work to keep all the cattle going in the proper direction, and cowboys were expert horsemen who used complicated roping techniques to control the cows. They had plenty of help from their dogs, who often became their best friends on the trail. The broad-brimmed hats that kept the sun out of their eyes became their trademark. Few—if any—women joined in on these cattle drives, but in the late 1800s, the industry changed; instead of moving cattle over wide-open spaces, the land was divided into ranches separated by barbed wire fences. Many cowboys married, and in some cases, their wives and daughters took on ranching duties, effectively becoming cowgirls. Some expert cowboys and cowgirls became performers; they demonstrated their riding and roping skills at shows called rodeos, and later in movies and on TV.

OLD WEST SALAD WITH PINTO BEANS, CACTUS BITS, AND RANCH DRESSING

THIS SALAD IS FULL OF WESTERN TIDBITS. First, ranch dressing is a tangy buttermilk dressing that actually was invented on a dude ranch called the Hidden Valley Ranch in the 1960s; this is a do-it-yourself version. Second, *pinto* means "painted" in Spanish; the word was applied to both the speckled beige beans and multicolored ponies of the West. Finally, the desert is home to many varieties of needle-studded cactus plants, and some cactus bits have made their way into this salad—but don't worry, the needles are removed before you ever buy them! In Mexico and some areas in the Southwestern United States, a variety of cactus known as *nopale* is considered a delicacy. You can buy nopales (or, in tidbit form, *nopalitos*) ready to eat in a light brine solution in Mexican markets and some grocery stores. They're really quite tasty! If you can't find them, the salad will be just as good without.

MAKES 4 SERVINGS AND ABOUT 1 CUP DRESSING

Ranch Dressing

½ cup mayonnaise

½ cup low-fat buttermilk

1 clove garlic, finely chopped (about 1 teaspoon)

½ tablespoon chopped fresh chives, or to taste

¼ teaspoon salt, plus more to taste

Salad

Nonstick cooking spray

1 (15.5-ounce) can pinto beans, rinsed and drained well

To make the dressing, combine the mayonnaise, buttermilk, garlic, chives, and salt in a bowl and mix until thoroughly incorporated. (If you wish, you can do this in a blender or mini-chopper, in which case, you can cut the garlic roughly and let the machine do the fine chopping.) Let stand for at least 10 minutes.

Preheat the oven to 350°F. Spray a baking sheet with nonstick cooking spray. Pour the drained beans onto the sheet, toss with the salt and cumin, and then spread them in a single layer. Bake for 5 minutes, or until dry. Remove from the oven and let cool.

In a salad bowl, combine the lettuce, tomato, cactus bits, if you are using them, and cooled beans, and toss lightly. Divide among 4 salad bowls, and pass the dressing at the table.

½ teaspoon salt

¼ teaspoon cumin

4 cups washed, dried, and torn
  Romaine lettuce

12 cherry or grape tomatoes, halved

¼ cup jarred cactus paddles
  (*nopalitos)*, or to taste, drained and
  cut into bite-sized pieces (optional)

"Home on the Range"

THE RANGE WAS THE VAST, OPEN LAND WHERE COWBOYS herded cattle, moving them from feeding grounds to the railroads, where they would be transported to places all over the country. "Home on the Range" is a song about the beauty of the range. The words were written by Brewster Higley in the 1870s, and it became the state song of Kansas. Do you know this song? Try singing it now. Or after dinner, check it out on the Internet.

What did Native Americans eat?

BEFORE THEY WERE PUSHED ONTO RESERVATIONS, NATIVE AMERICANS got food from many sources, depending on where they lived. They were hunters, gatherers, or farmers, or all three; the local climate and geography determined the mix. They hunted, fished, and foraged for nuts, seeds, roots, berries, and other wild plants. In the Southwest and several other regions, farming was an important source of food. The chief crops of the Native Americans of North America were corn, beans, and squash, which were known in some tribes as the Three Sisters. The tribes of the Southwest, where rain was sporadic, learned to build complex irrigation systems to water their crops.

NATIVE AMERICAN FRY BREAD

THIS TASTY BREAD WAS BORNE OF HARDSHIP. When the Native Americans were forced onto reservations, they couldn't rely on the land for their traditional sources of food; instead, much of their diet came from the supplies provided by the federal government. Fry bread was developed by ingenious Native American cooks and has become a staple of Native American cuisine.

MAKES 4 FLATBREADS

2 cups all-purpose flour, plus more for dusting

2 tablespoon nonfat powdered milk

2 teaspoon baking powder

$\frac{1}{2}$ teaspoon salt

$\frac{3}{4}$ to 1 cup warm water or milk

1 teaspoon plus about 1$\frac{1}{2}$ cups vegetable oil, or more as needed, divided

Combine the flour, powdered milk, baking powder, and salt in a medium bowl and stir to combine. Add $\frac{3}{4}$ cup water and mix well to form a ball of dough. If the batter seems too dry, add a little more water. Turn the dough onto a lightly floured board and knead until it is soft and smooth, but not sticky. Form the dough into a ball. Brush a medium bowl with 1 teaspoon oil. Turn the dough into the bowl to coat it with oil. Cover and set aside to rest for 30 minutes.

When you are ready to fry the dough, heat about 1$\frac{1}{2}$ cups (about 2 inches) of oil in a deep, heavy pot or skillet to about 360°F. (See note, page 54, for a tip on how to determine the temperature if you do not have a thermometer for deep-frying.) Line a plate with paper towels and set aside.

Dust a work surface with flour and turn dough out onto it. Divide it into 4 pieces of equal size, and cover the remaining dough while you work with 1 piece, dusting with flour as necessary. Pat 1 ball of dough into a 5- to 6-inch circle, about $\frac{1}{4}$-inch thick around the edges and thinner in the center. With your finger, poke a small hole in the center to keep the fry bread from puffing too much.

When the oil is hot enough, carefully slide the flattened dough into the hot oil and cook for 1 to 2 minutes, or until bottom is golden-brown. Turn with tongs and cook for 1 to 2 minutes, or until golden on the other side. Transfer to the paper towels to drain and cool a bit. Repeat with the remaining batter to make 3 more breads.

CHUCK WAGON CHICKEN-FRIED STEAK

WHEN THEY WERE OUT ON THE RANGE, cowboys didn't have a very interesting diet, but they looked forward to nights when the cook fixed chicken-fried steak. It is still a local treasure in the Southern and Western United States. Traditionally, it is served with fried onions and a "cream" gravy made from the steak drippings, flour, and milk. In this version, the onions and sauce are rolled into one Onion Cream Gravy.

MAKES 4 SERVINGS

$\frac{1}{3}$ cup all-purpose flour

1 egg

1 cup unseasoned breadcrumbs

2 teaspoons cumin

$1\frac{1}{2}$ teaspoon salt, divided

4 round or rump steaks, about 6 ounces each

Freshly ground black pepper to taste (optional)

$\frac{1}{2}$ cup vegetable oil, plus more as needed

2 large onions, sliced in rounds and then into half-moons

1 (14.5-ounce) can beef stock

Pour the flour into a shallow bowl. Beat the egg lightly in another shallow bowl. Pour the breadcrumbs into a third shallow bowl, add the cumin and $\frac{1}{2}$ teaspoon salt, and stir to incorporate. Season each steak with about $\frac{1}{4}$ teaspoon salt and pepper to taste, place them between 2 sheets of waxed paper, set on a work surface, and pound lightly with a meat mallet to a thickness of about $\frac{1}{4}$ inch.

Dip 1 steak into the flour, tapping lightly to remove any excess, then into the egg, and finally into the crumbs, turning to coat and tapping lightly to remove excess. Set on a plate and repeat with the remaining steaks. Reserve the excess flour.

When you are ready to cook the steaks, heat about $\frac{1}{2}$ cup oil in a large nonstick skillet to about 360°F. (See note, page 54, for a tip on how to determine the temperature if you do not have a thermometer for deep-frying.) Prepare a clean platter lined with paper towel. When the oil is hot enough, carefully place the steaks into it, in a single layer, working in batches if necessary. Cook for 2 to 3 minutes, or until deep

(continued on next page)

golden in color, and turn with tongs. Cook for 2 to 3 minutes more for medium, or until to the desired degree of doneness. Transfer the steaks to the paper towels and let rest for 10 minutes.

Drain out all but 3 or 4 tablespoons oil from the skillet. Return the skillet to the heat. Toss the onion slices in the reserved flour and tap to remove any excess. Carefully place the onion into the oil and stir to coat. Cook, stirring occasionally, for about 10 minutes, or until softened and translucent. Add the stock and cook for 5 to 7 minutes, or until a thick sauce that can coat the back of a spoon forms. Remove from the heat.

Place a steak on each of 4 plates and divide the Onion Cream Gravy between them. Serve immediately.

Mighty Tasty Vittles

A CHUCK WAGON WAS THE HORSE-DRAWN WAGON that traveled with the cowboys when they herded cattle from place to place on the range. It carried bedding, supplies, and most importantly, food, cooking equipment, and a cook who prepared the cowboys' meals. A cowboy's work was exhausting, and the food served at the chuck wagon had to be filling, but the ingredients had to travel well without refrigeration. Cowboys usually ate seated around the campfire. A typical meal would consist of dried beans cooked with bacon; beef from the herd, either boiled, stewed, fried, or barbecued; and sourdough biscuits baked over the campfire. Desserts were sweetened with molasses or corn syrup. Occasionally, the cowboys would enjoy dried fruit. Vinegar pie, with a sweet jelled filling, was a treat.

COOKIE'S APPLE-APRICOT COBBLER

NO, THERE ARE NO COOKIES IN THIS COBBLER; it's named for the cooks who traveled with the cowboys. Invariably, they were called "Cookie." On the trail, they didn't have a lot of fancy supplies to work with. Dried fruit was probably as close as you could get to produce. But when you rehydrate and sweeten it, as we do here, it makes a nice treat, whether you've spent a day roping steer or book-l'arnin' in school.

MAKES 4 SERVINGS

Fruit Filling

½ cup packed light-brown sugar

3 cups dried apples, any bits of core removed, roughly cut into ½-inch pieces

¼ cup dried apricots, cut into ¼-inch pieces

Sweet Biscuit Topping

1 cup all-purpose flour

¼ cup plus 1 teaspoon granulated sugar, divided

½ teaspoon baking powder

¼ teaspoon baking soda

⅛ teaspoon salt

1 teaspoon cinnamon

6 tablespoons (¾ stick) unsalted butter, cut into pieces

½ cup low-fat buttermilk

1 teaspoon pure vanilla extract

Vanilla ice cream for serving (optional)

Place an oven rack in the middle position and preheat the oven to 400°F.

Combine 2 cups of water and the brown sugar in a 9- or 10-inch ovenproof nonstick skillet or greased cast-iron skillet set over medium heat and cook for 2 to 3 minutes, or until the sugar is dissolved. Add the apples and apricots and simmer for about 5 minutes, or until the fruit is soft and moist and the liquid has the consistency of a thin syrup. Remove from the heat.

Meanwhile, in a large mixing bowl, combine the flour, ¼ cup sugar, baking powder, baking soda, salt, and cinnamon. Add the butter and work it into the flour until the mixture has the consistency of coarse meal.

Combine the buttermilk and vanilla in a cup and add to the flour mixture, stirring to incorporate thoroughly and form a sticky dough.

Spoon the dough over the cooked fruit, distributing it as evenly as possible. (It won't be perfect.) Sprinkle the remaining 1 teaspoon sugar evenly over the dough and bake for about 20 minutes, or until a toothpick inserted into the center of the biscuit topping comes out clean and the biscuit is golden. Serve warm, with ice cream if you like.

Frontier Talk

COWBOYS DEVELOPED THEIR OWN VOCABULARY, much of which sounds quaint to our modern ears. Why not try talking like a cowboy tonight? Here are some cowboy expressions:

AW, SHUCKS: An expression of disappointment or embarrassment

AIMIN': Intending

CITY SLICKER: Someone from the city, with fancy manners and dress

DOWNRIGHT: Thoroughly

DUDE: A fancy guy, probably a city slicker

GRUB: Food

HANKER: Want

HOWDY: Hello

MUCH OBLIGED: Thank you

PARTNER OR PARDNER: Buddy

PLUMB: Thoroughly

RECKON: Believe

TENDERFOOT: A newcomer inexperienced in cowboy life

TUCKERED OUT: Tired

YAHOO!: Hooray!

YEEHAW!: Hooray, also an expression to make the cows move

YIPPEE!: Hooray!

You Might Even Be a Pop Star!

FROM THE BOBBIE-SOXERS WHO SWOONED OVER FRANK SINATRA TO THE mini-skirted fans who screamed for the Beatles to the kids of today who sell out entire Hannah Montana concert tours in minutes, kids have always had a special relationship to the performers who make "their" music—whatever that music might be. This dinner is designed to celebrate our favorite star performers—whether we see them on stage, on TV, or sitting across from us in the living room! So everyone put on your shades for dinner tonight, strike a pose for the photogs, and prepare to rock the house!

Menu

Bling Cherry Bites

Ham It Up Salad

Paparazzi Pepperoni Pita Pizzas

Microphone Cupcakes

Game Plan

★ Make (and nibble) the Bling Cherry Bites. ✋

★ Prep the Microphone Cupcakes and bake for about 20 minutes. ✋

★ Get the kids started on the Autographs Please! picture frame craft.

★ Prep the components of the Ham It Up Salad and dressing, but do not combine them or dress the salad yet.

★ Prep and cook the pizza sauce and assemble the Paparazzi Pepperoni Pita Pizzas. ✋ Bake for 5 to 6 minutes.

★ Assemble the salad and toss with the dressing.

★ When the pizzas are done, cool a bit, cut, and arrange the pieces to make stars.

★ Grab a bite!

★ Make the frosting and frost the Microphone Cupcakes. ✋

★ Have a posh dessert!

DINNER PREP IN SMALL BITES:

If you have time the night before or earlier in the day, bake the Microphone Cupcakes. Prep and cook the pizza sauce.

FRIDAY NIGHT TIME-SAVER:

If time is short, use good-quality jarred pizza sauce. Use cake mix instead of baking the cupcakes from scratch.

CREATE PROPERLY SPARKLY FRAMES FOR PHOTOS OF THE POP STARS who live in your house—complete with their autographs! Have your pop stars sign their photos with pen or marker, or have them sign the mat underneath it if that's easier. (If you choose to sign the mat instead of the photo, you can also use glitter glue.) Foam picture frames are available in craft party stores. You can substitute small, precut artist mats.

MAKES ONE FRAME PER PERSON

1 rubber foam picture frame per pop star

Safety scissors

1 photo or printout of a photo of each pop star

White or light-colored paper for matting (optional)

Colored pens, markers, or glitter glue

4 strips of self-adhesive plastic jewels per pop star or strips of sequins that can be cut

Craft glue (if you use sequin strips)

Sparkly self-adhesive letters or small individual self-adhesive jewels (optional)

Sparkly self-adhesive stars, hearts, or other decorations (optional)

Open your picture frame and see how your photo will fit into it. If necessary, cut the photo to fit. Or make a mat for the photo by measuring and cutting the white paper to fit into the frame and mounting the photo on it. If you make a mat, you can position the photo so that the border is the same size all the way around, or you can leave extra space at the bottom for the autograph, as it will probably be easier for kids to write on the paper than directly on the photo. Have each pop star autograph his or her photo or mat and let dry.

To decorate the frame, first plan your design. Stick on the jewel strips or cut and glue the sequin strips to make a border.

If you like, spell out the words "Pop Star!," "Bling!," or "Music!" on the frame with self-adhesive letters or create the letters with small, self-adhesive jewels.

If you like, decorate any remaining space with stars, hearts, or other decorations. Put the photo into the frame and seal it up, or if you have used glue, wait for everything to dry before you put the photo into the frame.

BLING CHERRY BITES

POP STARS DON'T GO ANYWHERE WITHOUT THEIR BLING-BLING, but in this case, the bling is in the Bing—Bing cherries, that is.

MAKES 16 BITES

1 (8-ounce) package regular or reduced-fat crescent roll dough

½ cup shredded extra-sharp Cheddar cheese

48 dried cherries, preferably Bing

Place an oven rack in the middle position and preheat the oven to 375°F.

Separate the dough along the perforated lines and place the 8 resulting triangles on a work surface. Cut each triangle crosswise to make 16 pieces; these need not be the same shape and size.

Place a pinch of cheese in the center of each triangle and top with 3 cherries. Fold the 3 corners of each triangle in and over the cheese and cherries to make a pouch. Pull the dough gently to seal, but don't worry if any holes remain.

Place the pouches on an ungreased baking sheet, spacing them evenly, and bake for about 10 minutes, or until the cheese inside is melted and the dough is golden in color. Let cool a bit, as the cheese can get quite hot, and serve.

The Bing cherry, the most popular variety of cherry on the market, is a sweet and juicy treat. It was named for Ah Bing, who helped develop it. Bing was born in China and, like many of his countrymen, came to the United States in the 1800s. Bing found work assisting a horticulturalist named Seth Lewelling. It was in the Lewelling nurseries that he cared for the cherry graft that would be named for him.

HAM IT UP SALAD

BECAUSE "HAM" CAN REFER TO SOMEONE WHOSE PERFORMANCE IS over the top, I just had to get some ham into this Pop Star dinner. Here, it's combined with two classic L.A.-style ingredients: avocado and alfalfa sprouts, for a salad that is over the top in flavor.

MAKES 4 SERVINGS

1 clove garlic, finely chopped

½ teaspoon salt, plus more to taste

1 small avocado

2 tablespoons fresh lemon juice, divided

2 tablespoons olive oil

4 rectangular slices deli or packaged ham

½ cup alfalfa sprouts

Freshly ground black pepper to taste (optional)

4 cups washed, dried, and torn Romaine lettuce leaves

Place the finely chopped garlic into a cup with the salt and let stand for 5 minutes.

Cut the avocado lengthwise, twist to remove the pit, and spoon the flesh into a small bowl. Immediately mash the avocado with 1 teaspoon lemon juice so that it does not turn brown, mashing until creamy.

Pour the remaining lemon juice into the cup with the garlic, mix, and let stand for 1 or 2 minutes. Strain out the garlic and discard, reserving the lemon juice.

Place the sprouts into a small bowl and toss with ½ tablespoon of the seasoned lemon juice. Place the ham slices on a work surface. Spread each with one quarter of the avocado, and top each with one quarter of the sprouts. Roll each ham slice up and cut crosswise into 4 small rolls.

Mix the remaining seasoned lemon juice with the olive oil. Taste and season with salt if necessary. Place the lettuce into a bowl. When you are ready to serve, toss with the dressing to coat. Arrange the ham rolls on top, and serve. Or if you wish, divide the dressed lettuce between 4 salad bowls, top each with 4 ham rolls, and serve.

PAPARAZZI PEPPERONI POP STAR PITA PIZZAS

HERE'S PAPARAZZI THAT ANY POP STAR WOULD BE GLAD TO MEET: individual pizzas with homemade sauce, cut before they come to the table to form stars. I tried using a serrated knife for the cutting, but Maria Soriano-Person, the wonderful food stylist for this book, had a better idea: Sharp kitchen shears will give you a nice clean cut. This recipe makes six to eight pita pizzas; small appetites will want just one, while larger appetites might want two or more. Between bites, see if you can say the name of this dish three times in a row.

MAKES 6 TO 8 PIZZAS

1 tablespoon olive oil

1 garlic clove, finely chopped

¼ cup grated onion (about 1 small onion)

1 tablespoon tomato paste

2½ cups canned tomato sauce

½ teaspoon dried oregano

1 tablespoon grated Parmesan cheese

1 teaspoon salt

½ to 1 teaspoon sugar (optional)

6 to 8 (5½ -inch) pita breads

1½ to 2 cups shredded mozzarella cheese (about ¼ cup per pizza)

Sliced pepperoni to taste

Other toppings of your choice, such as sliced fresh or sautéed mushrooms, olives, sliced meatballs (optional)

Place an oven rack to the middle position and preheat the oven to 400°F.

Heat the oil in a large nonstick skillet over medium-high heat until it sizzles. Add the garlic and cook, stirring for about 30 seconds, or until soft and golden. Add the onion and cook, stirring and shaking the pan, for 1 to 2 minutes, or until softened. Add the tomato paste and sauce, oregano, grated cheese, and salt. Cook, stirring, for 7 to 8 minutes, or until slightly thickened and any acidity has cooked out of the sauce. Taste and season with salt if necessary. If the sauce is too acidic, add a little sugar, if you like.

Place the pitas on a baking sheet. Spoon 2 to 3 tablespoons of sauce on each, leaving a ½ -inch border all the way around the pita. Sprinkle each with ¼ cup cheese. Top with pepperoni or any other toppings of your choice. Bake for about 5 to 6 minutes, or until the cheese is melted and bubbly and the crust is lightly browned. Remove from the oven and let cool for a few minutes.

Place a pita pizza on the work surface. With kitchen shears, cut it in half and then cut each half in thirds. Take 1 of the wedges and cut it to make a diamond (you can eat the scraps!). Arrange the 5 remaining wedges on a dinner plate, points out, to form a star. Place the diamond in the center. Repeat with the remaining pizzas. For those at your table who are having more than one pizza, use the wedges to make a bigger (11-point) star, place a diamond in the center, and serve.

Who are the paparazzi?

PAPARAZZI ARE PHOTOGRAPHERS WHO LIKE TO follow famous people like pop stars around and try to take their picture. That's why pop stars sometimes wear sunglasses and hats; when they aren't in the mood to be photographed, they hope the paparazzi won't recognize them.

MICROPHONE CUPCAKES

THESE YUMMY CUPCAKES GIVE NEW MEANING TO THE PHRASE "Sing for your supper!"
You can sing into them—the batter is baked into flat-bottomed ice cream cones so, when they're all frosted and
decorated, they resemble microphones—but you'll probably want to gobble them up. My friend Cindi Kruth
developed the recipe for this book, and the batter is designed to bake inside ice cream cones without drying
out or overflowing the cones. Cindi warns not to overfill the cones here, but if you follow the instructions below,
you'll get only good feedback. For the chocolate buttercream frosting, she offers this advice: Cocoa varies in
intensity and thickening power, so start out with the quantities of cream and cocoa suggested and add more
as needed. You can add up to $\frac{1}{4}$ cup more cocoa for more intense chocolate flavor. If you do, add more cream
to get the desired consistency.

MAKES 12 CUPCAKES AND 2½ CUPS FROSTING

Cupcakes

4 ounces (1 stick) unsalted butter, at room temperature

$\frac{3}{4}$ cup granulated sugar

2 large eggs

1$\frac{1}{4}$ cup all-purpose flour

$\frac{1}{4}$ teaspoon baking powder

$\frac{1}{2}$ teaspoon baking soda

$\frac{1}{8}$ teaspoon salt

$\frac{1}{3}$ cup sour cream, at room temperature

1$\frac{1}{2}$ teaspoons pure vanilla extract

12 flat-bottomed ice cream cones

Place the oven rack in the middle position and preheat oven to 350°F.

Beat the butter with an electric mixer set at medium speed, preferably with a whisk attachment, for 1 minute to 90 seconds, until very smooth. Gradually pour in the sugar. Beat at medium-high speed for 5 to 6 minutes, or until the mixture is fluffy and very light in color, scraping down the side and the bottom of the bowl every minute or two. Add the eggs, one at a time, and beat for 10 to 15 seconds after each addition.

In a separate bowl, sift together the flour, baking powder, baking soda, and salt.

In a measuring cup or small bowl, mix the sour cream, and vanilla until incorporated.

With the mixer set at low speed, add about $\frac{1}{2}$ cup of the flour mixture to the butter mixture. Beat for 10 to 15 seconds and scrape down the bowl. Add half the sour cream mixture and beat for 10 to 15 seconds to combine. Scrape the bowl

Chocolate Buttercream Frosting

4 ounces (1 stick) unsalted butter, at room temperature

½ cup unsweetened cocoa powder (naturalized or alkalized), plus more to taste

3 cups confectioners' sugar

Pinch salt

1 teaspoon pure vanilla extract

5 to 8 tablespoons heavy cream

Decoration

½ cup black sparkly sugar (available in kitchen or craft shops) or chocolate sprinkles

again. Continue alternating between the flour mixture and the sour cream, beating after each addition. During these additions, the mixture might appear slightly curdled, but it will come together smoothly by the time you are finished with all the additions.

Divide the batter evenly among the cones, and place them in a 12-cup muffin tin. If the cones tip over in the muffin cups, scrunch up some aluminum foil and tuck it around them to hold them upright. The batter should be ¼ to ½ inch below the top of the cone. Do not overfill the cones. Bake for 20 to 26 minutes, or until a toothpick inserted into the middle of a cupcake comes out clean and the tops are lightly golden.

Meanwhile, make the frosting. With an electric mixer set at medium speed, beat the butter in a mixing bowl. Sift in the unsweetened cocoa powder, confectioners' sugar, and salt. Beat at low speed to combine. Drizzle in the vanilla and 5 to 6 tablespoons heavy cream. Beat until the mixture is very smooth and fluffy. If it is too thick for spreading, drizzle in another 1 or 2 tablespoons heavy cream. Beat on medium until smooth. (Taste, and if you'd like a more intense chocolate flavor, add a little more cocoa powder and beat in enough cream to get a spreadable consistency.)

To decorate, frost the cupcakes with chocolate frosting, mounding it to a rounded shape on top of each to resemble the top of a microphone. Spread some of the frosting down over the top 1½ inches of the cone. Dip the frosted part of the cupcake into black sparkly sugar or chocolate sprinkles.

After-Dinner Fun: Have a Pop Star Concert

AFTER DINNER, EVERYONE CAN PERFORM A FAVORITE POP STAR SONG. This activity is not just for kids; grown-ups have to perform songs that were popular when they were young! If you like, put on your bling or special pop star costume, dim the lights, and shine a spotlight (a flashlight or a lamp) at the performer. If anyone plays an instrument, now's the time to get it out. After each person performs, a round of applause is in order. When everyone has performed, you can trade autographs!

Gracious Night

THIS MEAL IS INSPIRED BY MY MEMORIES OF LONG-AGO GRACIOUS LIVING
college dinners: we'd dress up, serve hors d'oeuvres, and use our nicest manners. The food here is on the fancier side, and if you'd like, you can dress for dinner and get out the linen and good china, too. The activities are designed to help everybody learn some basic etiquette. I hasten to add that this dinner need not be stuffy or rigid. I was lucky enough to interview the etiquette expert Peggy Post some years ago. Etiquette, she said, is a set of guidelines that is based on being considerate of one another; its purpose is to make our lives function more easily. Making the people around you feel comfortable (whether with "please" and "thank you" or not chewing with your mouth open) is always right, whether you're all dressed up for Gracious Night or having a movie night in your pajamas.

Menu

Monogram Canapés

Fancy-Schmancy Salad with Caviar Dressing

Finger-Lickin' Chicken Cordon Bleu

Gussied-Up Asparagus

Curry Curry Couscous

Cherrymisu

Game Plan

★ Make (and nibble) the Monogram Canapés. ✋

★ Get the kids started on setting the table and making the Pretty Place Cards craft.

★ Prep the Fancy-Schmancy Salad and the Caviar Dressing and pour it into a serving bowl or pitcher to pass at the table. Cover both and chill until you are ready to serve.

★ Prep the components of the Curry Curry Couscous and the Gussied-Up Asparagus, but don't cook them yet.

★ Prep the Finger-Lickin' Chicken Cordon Bleu bundles, brown them on the stove, bake for about 15 minutes, and let rest for 5 to 10 minutes.

★ Meanwhile, cook the Curry Curry Couscous and keep warm, and assemble the salads. Cook the Gussied-Up Asparagus and toss the asparagus with the Orange Soy Sauce.

★ Dinner is served!

★ Prep the Cherrymisu. ✋

★ Care for a dessert?

DINNER PREP IN SMALL BITES:

If you have time the night before or earlier in the day, make the caviar dressing for the Fancy-Schmancy Salad and keep it refrigerated. Prep the chicken bundles for the Finger-Lickin' Chicken Cordon Bleu and keep refrigerated. Make the chocolate-cherry sauce and prep the mascarpone cheese for the Cherrymisu.

FRIDAY NIGHT TIME-SAVER:

If time is short, buy some fancy frozen hors d'oeuvres. If you're really pressed, you can also buy a good precooked chicken from your local market or a frozen chicken cordon bleu.

Crafty Friday:
PRETTY PLACE CARDS

PLACE CARDS ARE INVALUABLE FOR LARGE FORMAL AFFAIRS when lots of people are all trying to figure out where to sit at once, but they're also fun for intimate dinners, especially when they are personalized by the dinner guests.

1 (3- x 5-inch) index card for each person at the table

Pencils

Colored pens or markers

Wrapping paper or wrapping paper scraps

Glue sticks

Fold the index card in half crosswise so that it stands up on the table. Place the folded card flat on your writing surface, and with a pencil, sketch a 1/2-inch border around the edge.

Write your name or the name of the person whose card you are making in the rectangle in the center.

To decorate the border of the place card, cut 2 strips of wrapping paper, about ½ -inch wide by 1½ -inch long. Cut 2 more strips about ½ -inch wide and 2½ -inches long. You can use all 1 pattern or mix and match. Glue these onto the border area, leaving your name completely visible. If you like, cut the wrapping paper into a 1½ - x 2½ -inch rectangle and glue it to the back of the place card.

Make place cards for everyone in the group, decide where each person will sit, and position the proper card in front of each plate, in the 12 o'clock position.

Before-Dinner Fun: A Veddy Proper Table

SETTING THE TABLE THE TRADITIONAL WAY CAN BE FUN on Gracious Night. Get out a tablecloth and cloth napkins. Use the diagram below for a guide on how to set each place. Space the settings so that everyone is sitting comfortably at the table. If you're feeling very fancy, you can use a service plate when setting the table; this is a plate that is removed when the food is served (on dinner plates) and never seen again. You can also just leave that spot empty until the dinner plates are brought to the table. Some people like to place the napkin in the center of the service plate or in the empty spot. Others place the napkin to the left of the forks. The forks go just to the left of the plate, with the one that will be used first (the salad fork) on the outside, farthest from the plate. The main-course fork (or forks, if you are having both meat and fish) goes to the right of the salad fork (with the fish fork in the middle of the other two, if you're doing all the courses, to be used after the salad fork). Knives and spoons go to the right of the plate: knife closest to the plate, blade facing inward (or if you're using a salad knife, it goes farther from the plate, with the main-course knife right next to the plate). You can place the dessert spoon next to the knife or bring it to the table after dinner, along with the dessert plate. If you're having soup, place the soup spoon next to the dessert spoon, farthest from the plate. Water and wine glasses go to the right of the plate, above the knives and spoons, and a bread plate goes to the left, above the napkin. A coffee cup with a saucer and spoon can go to the right of the glasses if you like.

What's etiquette?

ETIQUETTE IS A SET OF GUIDELINES that help us know how to treat people in all kinds of situations. The word *etiquette* is a French word that originally meant "ticket" or "label." The other meaning came about when the king's gardeners at the Palace of Versailles put up signs—etiquettes—telling people to keep off the grass. Gradually the rules expanded to include other aspects of good manners—which is another term for etiquette. Some people associate etiquette with old-fashioned, even snooty rules, but most etiquette experts disagree. Etiquette expert Elizabeth L. Post wrote this, decades ago: "Etiquette was never intended to be a rigid set of rules. It is, rather, a code of behavior that is based on consideration, kindness and unselfishness—something that should not, and will not, ever change. But manners . . . must change to keep up with the world." For example, at one time, a man was expected to open the door for a woman. Today, women open doors all the time for each other and for men. That's a change in manners. Good etiquette, however, says that it's not right to let a door slam in somebody's face, no matter who that person is.

MONOGRAM CANAPÉS

DON'T WORRY IF YOU DON'T HAVE MONOGRAMMED NAPKINS to use at this fancy dinner; these hors d'oeurves are named by their monograms! The kids will like cutting toasted sandwich bread into fun shapes (each slice should make 4 canapés) and topping the shapes with one or more of the toppings. *PB & J Canapés* are made with everybody's favorite sandwich combo. *J Canapés*, with cheese, grapes, and salami, is so named because my daughter Jessica created the recipe. *SSDB Canapés* are a classic—smoked salmon with dilled butter. You can make any combination of these—or make up your own topping—but be sure to put some initials in its name. It's easier to toast the bread lightly and spread it with whichever spread you like before you apply the cookie cutter.

MAKES 16 CANAPÉS

4 slices sandwich bread, lightly toasted

PB & J Canapé Topping

1 tablespoon creamy peanut butter per slice of bread

2 teaspoons jelly or jam per slice of bread

J Canapé Topping

1½ teaspoons honey mustard per slice of bread, plus more to taste

4 or more pieces shaved Parmesan or Cheddar cheese (¼-to ½-ounce) per slice of bread

1 or 2 thin slices Genoa salami (3 inches in diameter) per slice of bread, cut into bite-sized triangles (optional)

1 red seedless grape per slice of bread, each sliced crosswise into 4 pieces

Toast the bread lightly. Mash the dill with the margarine, if using. When the bread is cool enough to handle, spread the slices with either peanut butter, honey mustard, or dilled butter. (You might want to tackle one at a time, so the ingredients don't get mixed up.)

Cut each slice of bread into 4 pieces, trimming the crusts off, or use a 2- to 3-inch metal cookie cutter to cut out 4 shapes. (Basic shapes like triangles, diamonds, hearts, circles, or flowers are best.)

Place the cut shapes on a work surface and add the toppings: a dab of jelly on the *PB & J*; a slice of cheese and salami on the *J*, topped with a grape slice; and a piece of smoked salmon and a dill sprig, if you like, on the *SSDB*.

SSDB Canapé Topping

½ to 1 tablespoon heart-healthy margarine or softened unsalted butter per slice of bread

1 teaspoon chopped fresh dill per slice of bread plus small dill sprig tips, for garnish

1 ounce smoked salmon per slice of bread, cut into bite-sized pieces

What are hors d'oeuvres?

HORS D'OEUVRES ARE LITTLE SNACKS THAT ARE EATEN BEFORE the meal to satisfy the strongest hunger pangs or whet the appetite. The term is French and translates literally as "outside the work." In this case, the "work" is the meal. Canapés are hors d'oeuvres that you make with pieces of bread or crackers and yummy toppings. They're small enough to hold in your hand and eat in one or two bites.

What's a monogram?

A MONOGRAM IS A DESIGN MADE FROM THE INITIAL OR INITIALS of a name. Some people like to put their monograms on table linen, towels, stationery, silverware, leather goods, and other personal items. Some people save their monogrammed tableware for special occasions. Some people don't use them at all. What does your family do? After dinner, try designing a monogram from your initials.

FANCY-SCHMANCY SALAD WITH CREAMY CAVIAR DRESSING

YOU WON'T WANT TO USE FINE CAVIAR HERE, but the affordable varieties that you can find in most supermarkets will gussy up your salad and provide the kids with an easy, fun introduction to this much-celebrated luxury food. They just might like the popping, crunching sensation in their mouths when they taste it! Be sure to buy a red or gold caviar; the black will taste fine, but it will turn the dressing an unappealing shade of gray. All the traditional accompaniments to caviar are here—hard-cooked egg, sour cream, an oniony element in the form of fresh chives—but they're reconfigured into a salad.

MAKES 4 SERVINGS

Caviar Dressing

¼ cup mayonnaise

¼ cup light cream or fat-free half-and-half

2 tablespoon chopped fresh dill

2 teaspoons red salmon roe, golden whitefish roe, or red lumpfish caviar or other red or golden caviar

Salad

4 cups washed, dried, and torn Boston, Bibb, or butter lettuce

20 grape tomatoes, halved

1 hard-cooked egg, chopped (see page 187)

1 or 2 tablespoons snipped fresh chives, or to taste

To make the dressing, combine the mayonnaise, cream, and dill in a small bowl and mix thoroughly. Gently mix in the caviar until the dressing takes on a pink or golden tint (the shade will depend on which caviar you use). Be careful not to crush the tiny eggs. Spoon into a serving bowl and chill until serving.

Combine the lettuce, tomatoes, crumbled egg, and chive in a salad bowl, and toss to combine. Divide the salad among 4 bowls and pass the dressing at the table.

Simply put, caviar is fish eggs. The finest caviar has traditionally come from Russian or Iranian sturgeon and, depending on the variety, can cost several hundred dollars for an ounce or two. Some sturgeon are endangered species and sales are limited or prohibited. But the eggs, or roe, of several other varieties of fish can be just as tasty, and provide plenty of choices that are affordable, ecologically sound, and perfect for a Friday night dinner with the kids.

To keep the yolks of your hard-cooked eggs a sunny yellow, follow this method for hard-cooking perfect eggs. Bring a pot of water to a rapid boil. Gently submerge the eggs in the water. Set a timer for exactly 12 minutes. Once they have boiled for 12 minutes, remove the pot from the heat and submerge the eggs in cold water to cool them quickly.

TABLE TALK

Can you give some examples of good table manners?

GO AROUND THE TABLE AND LET EVERYONE COME UP WITH ONE. Here are a few time-honored ideas that will make dinner more pleasant for everyone at the table. Can you think of anything to add to this list?

- Sit up straight, facing the table in a comfortable position, elbows off the table. Don't fuss with your hair—you don't want hair in your food! And don't play with your chair—you don't want to fall off!
- Open your napkin in your lap and use it to wipe your face and hands when necessary.
- Wait to start eating until everyone at the table has been served.
- If you want something on the table (say, the salt and pepper) but can't reach it or if you would have to reach over someone to get it, ask the person nearest to the item to hand it to you.
- Chew with your mouth closed, and don't try to talk with food in your mouth.
- Don't forget to say "thank you" when you are served or handed something.
- If you think you won't like something, try to taste just a little bit. You might be surprised. If you really don't want it, remember to say, "No, thank you." Don't make negative comments about the food that someone has taken the time to cook and that others at the table are enjoying.
- Enjoy the meal and make pleasant conversation. Ask the folks at the table how their day has gone—or try out some of the Table Talk ideas in this book. You never know where the conversation will go!
- Stay at the table until everyone has finished eating. It's fun just to chat with everyone. If you must get up and move around, however, it's polite to ask, "May I be excused?"

CURRY CURRY COUSCOUS

A HINT OF CURRY POWDER AND A LITTLE BIT OF DRIED FRUIT give this simple-to-prepare dish an exotic flavor and aroma. You can substitute golden raisins for the apricots if you wish.

MAKES 4 SERVINGS

½ cup dried apricots, chopped in ¼-inch pieces

1 tablespoon olive oil

1 clove garlic, finely chopped

1½ cups plain couscous

1 (14.5-ounce) can chicken stock

¼ teaspoon salt, plus more to taste

¼ teaspoon curry powder

2 tablespoons chopped fresh parsley (optional)

Place the apricots and ¾ cup of water in a microwavable container, and microwave on high power for 1 to 2 minutes, or until slightly softened. Drain the apricots, reserving the liquid.

Heat the oil in a large saucepan set over medium-high heat. When it shimmers, add the garlic, and cook, stirring, for 15 to 30 seconds, or until softened. Add the stock and apricot liquid, and bring to a boil. Add the couscous, apricots, ¼ teaspoon salt, and curry powder, if you like, and stir to combine. Remove from the heat, cover, and let stand for 5 minutes, or until the liquid is absorbed and the couscous is soft and fluffy. Taste and season with salt if necessary; stir well again. Add the parsley, toss to incorporate, and serve.

When couscous first appeared on the contemporary culinary scene, some people mistakenly thought it was a grain. It's actually tiny balls of pasta. Couscous originated centuries ago in the area around the Mediterranean Sea. It's still a staple in North Africa and the Middle East and has spread throughout the world. The variety known as Israeli couscous, also called Levantine couscous, is larger than regular couscous. Traditional couscous requires longer cooking, but the quick-cooking variety available in most supermarkets makes preparation easy.

FINGER-LICKIN' CHICKEN CORDON BLEU

OUR EVER-SO-WELL-MANNERED DINNER PARTY COMPANIONS won't actually lick their fingers over this chicken, but they might have to restrain themselves. True to its name (*cordon bleu* means "blue ribbon"), it's a winner of a dish that will please kids and adults alike.

MAKES 4 SERVINGS

¾ cup all-purpose flour

1 large egg

1 cup unseasoned breadcrumbs

1 teaspoon salt, divided

½ teaspoon dried thyme leaves
(optional)

2 tablespoons heart-healthy margarine
or unsalted butter, melted

2 tablespoons honey mustard

4 skinless, boneless chicken breast
halves (about 1½ pounds)

4 slices deli or packaged ham

4 slices Provolone or other strongly
flavored cheese

1 tablespoon unsalted butter

1½ tablespoons vegetable oil,
plus more if needed

Pour the flour into a shallow bowl. Beat the egg lightly in another shallow bowl.

Pour the breadcrumbs into a third shallow bowl, add ½ teaspoon salt and the thyme, and stir to incorporate. Mix the margarine and honey mustard in a cup until thoroughly combined, and add to the breadcrumbs. Mix with your hands to form coarse crumbs.

Prepare a work surface and line up the bowls next to it, assembly-line style (flour, egg, and crumbs). Place a platter next to the bowl of crumbs.

Place an oven rack in the middle position and preheat the oven to 350°F.

On the work surface, place the chicken breast halves between 2 sheets of waxed paper and pound lightly with a meat mallet to a thickness of about ¼ inch. Remove the paper and season the chicken with the remaining salt. Place a slice of ham on each breast half and top with cheese, making sure to tuck the edges of both ham and cheese in so they don't hang over the edge of the chicken. Fold each breast in half crosswise, and tuck in just about half an inch at both the ends to make a neat bundle.

Dip 1 chicken bundle first into the flour, tapping lightly to remove any excess, then into the egg, and finally into the crumbs, turning to coat and tapping lightly to remove any
(continued on next page)

excess. Re-form the bundles neatly if necessary. Set on a plate and repeat with the remaining chicken.

Place 1 tablespoon butter and the oil into a large ovenproof nonstick or cast iron skillet set over medium-high heat. Melt the butter, but don't let it brown, and swirl to incorporate into the oil.

With tongs, carefully place the chicken into the skillet in a single layer, seam-side down, and cook for 1 to 2 minutes, or just until golden. Turn with tongs and cook for 1 to 2 minutes more. Transfer the skillet to the oven and bake for about 15 minutes, or until the chicken is cooked through and no longer pink. A meat thermometer inserted into the chicken breast meat should read 160°F—and you can also cheat and peek into the rolled chicken to be sure the inside is done. Carefully remove from the oven, remove the chicken from the pan, and place on a paper-towel-lined platter. Cover and let rest for 5 to 10 minutes and serve.

GUSSIED-UP ASPARAGUS WITH ORANGE-SOY SAUCE

I LOVE ASPARAGUS PRETTY MUCH ANY WAY YOU COOK IT—EVEN PLAIN. But some occasions call for a fancier treatment, and this orange-soy sauce fits the bill. The microwave will steam the components of the dish quickly and easily, and cutting the asparagus into small pieces will ensure even cooking.

MAKES 4 SERVINGS

1 pound thin green asparagus spears, with woody ends snapped off and discarded, and spears cut into 1 to 1½-inch pieces

¼ cup orange juice

2 teaspoons soy sauce

1 tablespoon orange marmalade

½ teaspoon arrowroot

Place the asparagus in a shallow microwavable container, add 2 teaspoons of water, and microwave on high power for 4 minutes, or until tender-crisp. (Don't overcook or you'll have a mushy canned-asparagus effect, minus the can!) Remove from the microwave and keep warm.

Meanwhile, pour the orange juice, soy sauce, marmalade, and arrowroot in a small microwavable container, and mix until thoroughly combined. Cover loosely and microwave on high power for about 3 to 6 minutes, or until reduced in volume and slightly syrupy. Let stand for 1 minute to cool, and then remove from the microwave, being careful to avoid burning yourself on the hot steam.

Pour the sauce over the asparagus, toss to coat, and serve.

TABLE TALK

EVERY CULTURE HAS ITS OWN IDEAS ABOUT GOOD MANNERS. People today do so much traveling that it's a good idea to know something about etiquette in far-off places. Take this quiz and see what you know (answers are below):

True or False:

1. In Arab countries, it's good manners to eat only with your right hand.

2. In Italy, the salad is served before the main course, just as it is in the United States.

3. In China, it's good manners to start eating as soon as you are served.

4. In Latin America, dinner is served at 6 p.m.

5. In Japan, it's bad manners to slurp your noodles.

....

DO YOU KNOW ANY OTHER CUSTOMS FROM OTHER COUNTRIES?

If you do, why not make up some true-false questions and see who gets the right answers?

What should you do if you're eating with someone from another country or culture and he or she does something you find unusual?

1. True. The left hand is reserved for hygiene purposes.

2. False. In a traditional Italian meal, the salad is served after the main course.

3. False. Wait until your host starts eating.

4. False. You can expect to sit down to dinner at 9 or 10 p.m. A teatime in the early evening will tide you over.

5. False. In Japan, people slurp noodles to cool them.

CHERRYMISU

TIRAMISU MAKES AN ELEGANT ENDING TO LOVELY MEAL, but with ingredients like brandy and coffee, it's hardly kid-friendly. Here it's retooled, using chocolate syrup, cherries, and cherry juice, as well as the mascarpone and ladyfinger cookies familiar from the original. Look for packaged ladyfingers that are slightly firm to the touch. I don't buy sweetened fruit juice for drinking, but for a dessert recipe, I think it's fair game, as it eliminates the need to add more sugar to the sauce. For the grown-ups, you may drizzle a little chocolate brandy or cassis (currant liqueur) over the top once the desserts are plated.

MAKES 4 SERVINGS

¼ cup chocolate syrup

1 cup sweetened cherry juice

16 to 20 packaged ladyfingers, preferably the harder Italian-style *savoiardi*

8 ounces mascarpone

1 tablespoon granulated sugar, plus more to taste

½ teaspoon unsweetened cocoa powder

1 teaspoon arrowroot

1 (15-ounce) can sweet Bing cherries in syrup, drained, or 2 cups frozen cherries, thawed and drained

Confectioners' sugar, for dusting

Combine the chocolate syrup and cherry juice in a medium-sized microwavable bowl, and stir to mix thoroughly.

In a medium-sized mixing bowl, combine ¼ cup of the cherry-chocolate mixture with the mascarpone and sugar, and mix until thoroughly combined. Taste the mascarpone and add more sugar if necessary. Set aside.

Dip the ladyfingers into the remaining cherry-chocolate mixture just to coat and divide them among 4 dessert plates.

Mix the arrowroot and cocoa into the remaining cherry-chocolate mixture, and microwave on high power for about 2 minutes, or until just slightly thickened. Let cool.

Top the ladyfingers on each plate with one quarter of the mascarpone mixture.

Place the drained cherries into the cooled chocolate-cherry mixture and roll with a spoon to coat. Divide the cherries among the 4 dessert plates. (Don't worry if they don't all fit on top of the ladyfingers; a few scattered around them will make the plate look pretty.) Drizzle one quarter of the remaining chocolate-cherry syrup over each cherrymisu. Dust with confectioners' sugar and serve.

Superheroes to the Rescue!

AT THEIR MOST BASIC, STORIES OF SUPERHEROES BUILD ON THE IDEA OF THE hero who puts community before self. But the superhero story endows these noble souls with fantastical powers that enable them to defend a world where bad things can and do happen. Each age has had its superheroes, whether or not they were called by that name. And why not? Wouldn't it be nice if there really was somebody who could fly around the world and save the day? This dinner gives the superheroes in the house a chance to try out their super powers with appetizers they can see through and a dessert that requires super-strong thumbs.

Menu

X-Ray Vision Summer Rolls

Strong to the Finish Spinach Salad

Real Superheroes Eat Quiche

Muscle-Thumb Thumbprint Cookies

Game Plan

★ If you are making the crust for the Real Superheroes Eat Quiche from scratch, prep the dough and refrigerate it for at least 2 hours. If you are using a frozen crust, prepare according to package directions.

★ When you are ready to prepare the rest of the dinner, if you are making the crust, roll it out, line a pie plate with it, chill for 15 more minutes, and then bake for 20 to 25 minutes.

★ Make (and nibble) the X-Ray Vision Summer Rolls.

★ Get the kids started on the Superhero Comic Book craft.

★ Make the quiche filling. When the crust is ready, fill it and bake for 25 to 30 minutes.

★ Prep one or both (mild or zesty) Tomato Salad Dressings and set aside to pass at the table.

★ Cook the bacon and prep the ingredients for the Strong to the Finish Spinach Salad. Assemble the salad.

★ If time allows, prep the dough for the Muscle-Thumb Thumbprint Cookies and refrigerate for 30 minutes.

★ Never fear; dinner's here!

★ Prep and bake the Muscle-Thumb Thumbprint Cookies.

★ Time for a super-duper dessert!

DINNER PREP IN SMALL BITES:

If you have time the night before or earlier in the day, prep and chill the dough for the quiche crust and cookies—or go ahead and bake one or both. You can also make one or both of the salad dressings.

FRIDAY NIGHT TIME-SAVER:

If time is short, use a store-bought refrigerated pie crust for the quiche—or buy a whole premade quiche. Buy a good-quality tomato-based salad dressing. You can also buy cookie mix or refrigerated ready-to-bake cookie dough and let the kids use their strong thumbs to decorate them before baking.

HERE'S A CHANCE TO DESIGN YOUR OWN SUPERHERO OR SUPERHEROINE! Give him or her any special powers you can think of. Don't limit yourself to the typical leaping over buildings or moving faster than a speeding bullet. How 'bout a superhero who saves the world by giving out green vegetables? Or chocolate? Kids who can write will want to fill in dialogue and word balloons to go with their illustrations, but younger ones can tell the story in pictures alone.

3 (8½ - x 11-inch) sheets white or
  light-colored paper for each person

Stapler

Transparent tape

Pencils

Markers

First think about your superhero. What is his or her name? What are his or her powers? What does his or her costume look like? Design a shield with his or her initial or a pictorial symbol of his or her powers (an "S-D" for Super-Duper Girl, or a "C" for Chocolate Man, or a broccoli flower for Green Vegetable Boy).

Stack your 3 sheets of paper on top of one another, fold in half crosswise, and staple on the inside fold. Fold the pages again and sketch your superhero on the cover of the book. Write his or her name in easy-to-read letters at the top of the page.

Open the book and number the pages, odd numbers on the left and even numbers on the right.

Make up an adventure for your superhero and illustrate it on the pages of the book. You can use the first page to illustrate his or her powers or list them in words.

Put a little bit of the story on each page and plan your story so that it ends on the last page. (If you have more to tell, you can always add pages.) You can use pictures to tell the story, but if you would like to write out what the characters are saying and thinking, leave room at the top of the page for word balloons.

X-RAY VISION SUMMER ROLLS

SUMMER ROLLS, ALSO CALLED SALAD ROLLS, are a Vietnamese treat usually eaten cold, as opposed to their hot, fried cousin, the spring roll. Summer rolls are made with translucent rice wrappers that let you see through to the filling. If that's not a superhero treat, I don't know what is. You can fill these with whatever you like—for instance, cooked chicken, bean sprouts, and broccoli—but the combination below of shrimp, carrots, and water chestnuts makes for a nice mix of richness and crunch, while the fresh basil adds a lively herbaceous note. You can also substitute a tangy peanut sauce for the hoisin if you like.

MAKES 8 ROLLS

Dipping Sauce

2 tablespoons soy sauce

2 tablespoons seasoned rice vinegar

2 tablespoons fresh lime juice

1 clove finely chopped garlic (optional)

Summer Rolls

2 ounces rice sticks (rice vermicelli)

4 tablespoons hoisin sauce, divided, plus more to taste

1 (8-ounce can) sliced water chestnuts, rinsed and drained

8 (8½ - to 9½ -inch) spring roll wrappers

1 large carrot, julienned

16 fresh basil leaves, cut into chiffonade (see page 74 for instructions)

16 medium (31 to 40 count) cooked, shelled, deveined shrimp

To make the dipping sauce, combine the soy sauce, vinegar, and lime juice in a small bowl, add the garlic, and let stand until ready to serve. (If you are not making and eating the rolls right away, strain out and discard the garlic after about 10 minutes.)

Boil a large pot of water and cook the rice sticks in it for about 5 minutes, or until softened. Prepare a bowl of cold water. When the noodles are cooked, rinse in the cold water and drain well. Toss with 3 tablespoons hoisin sauce and set aside.

In another bowl, toss the water chestnuts with the remaining 1 tablespoon hoisin and set aside.

Prepare a large bowl of warm (not boiling) water. Prepare a work surface and lay out each filling ingredient within easy reach. Dip 1 spring roll wrapper into the water and let it soften for a few seconds. With one hand on either side, hold it over the water, let it open back into a circle, and drain it a bit. Then transfer it to your work surface and pull gently to remove any large wrinkles. These wrappers can be difficult to work with, so take your time. Small wrinkles are okay. If your wrapper develops large holes or tears on both sides, discard it and try again. A small tear on one side is okay (but don't tell a real Vietnamese chef!); just position the tear on the work surface so it's on the farthest side from you.

Check the shrimp and remove any shell, including tails, if necessary.

Fill the wrapper, starting on the side of the circle closest to you: Place 2 shrimp end to end, about 1 inch from the edge. Top with about 4 water chestnut slices, 4 or 5 carrot sticks, a pinch of basil chiffonade, and about 1 ½ tablespoons rice sticks. Fold the 1-inch edge over the filling as tightly as you can, fold the sides in over the filling, and then roll up the summer roll. It will seal itself. Repeat with remaining spring rolls.

Serve with the dipping sauce. If you are not serving these immediately, chill until ready to serve.

 *Rice sticks, or rice vermicelli, are extremely thin noodles made of rice flour and* water. They are often sold in packages of 6 or 8 "bricks" of about 2 ounces each. They only need a few minutes to soften in boiling water; then they are quickly rinsed in cold water and drained. They make a wonderful addition to soups and Asian noodle dishes, as well as a tasty filling for summer rolls. Rice papers, also called spring roll wrappers, are likewise made of rice flour and water, but are fashioned into stiff, translucent, paper-thin circles that you need only dip into warm water before using.

★ TABLE TALK

Did you know?

SUPERMAN IS CONSIDERED TO HAVE BEEN the first comic book superhero on the scene, appearing in 1939.

What's a hero? What's a heroine?

SOMETIMES THESE WORDS ARE USED TO DESCRIBE the main characters in a story: the hero is the main man or boy and the heroine is the main woman or girl. But "hero" and "heroine" can also refer to men and women who are courageous and good, and help their friends, families, or communities, sometimes putting themselves at risk to do so.

Can you think of any real-life heroes? Heroines?

STRONG TO THE FINISH SPINACH SALAD

SPINACH IS PACKED WITH IRON, and that's just what a superhero needs to stay strong and healthy. A little bacon, cucumber, and a tangy salad dressing make it interesting. There are two versions of this easy tomato dressing here—one mild and one zesty. Make one or the other or both to suit everyone at the table. If you make both, you might want to reduce the proportions of each, though these dressings will keep, covered, in the refrigerator for 2 to 3 days.

MAKES 4 SERVINGS AND ¾ CUP DRESSING

Salad

6 strips bacon

4 cups baby spinach, washed and dried

½ medium cucumber, cut into thin half-moons (about 1 cup)

Mild Tomato Dressing

½ cup ketchup

2 tablespoons mayonnaise

Place 2 sheets of paper towels on a microwavable platter large enough to hold the bacon strips in a single layer. Place the bacon on it. Cover with 2 more sheets of paper towels and microwave on high power for 4 to 7 minutes, or until crispy. (Check the package instructions for a more exact time.) Remove from the microwave, blot with fresh towels, and when the bacon is cool enough to handle, crumble or chop it. Set aside.

Stir together the dressing ingredients for one or both dressings until thoroughly combined and salmon-colored. Set aside until you are ready to serve.

2 tablespoons light cream or fat-free
  half-and-half

Zesty Tomato Dressing

¼ cup ketchup

¼ cup cocktail sauce

2 tablespoons mayonnaise

2 tablespoons light cream or fat-free
  half-and-half

Combine the spinach, bacon, and cucumber in a salad bowl and toss. When you are ready to serve, divide the salad among 4 bowls and pass one or both dressings at the table.

TABLE TALK

CAN YOU NAME SOME SUPERHEROES AND SUPERHEROINES?

Who are your favorites?

HERE ARE SOME YOU MIGHT LIKE:

Superman

Supergirl

Wonder Woman

Batgirl

Batman and Robin

Spider-Man

The Incredible Hulk

Wonder Pets

The Incredibles

The Legion of Superheroes

The X-Men

The Powerpuff Girls

REAL SUPERHEROES EAT QUICHE

SOME YEARS AGO, THERE WAS A JOKE ABOUT "REAL MEN" NOT EATING QUICHE.
One thing superheroes don't worry about is what other folks think. This quiche is loaded with good-for-you ingredients: apple, eggs, and sour cream. If you have the time, you can make a luscious from-scratch crust, but you need to allow at least 2 hours for the dough to chill in the refrigerator. If the clock is ticking, a store-bought frozen or refrigerated crust works just fine. Look for a 9 or 9½-inch crust (but not a deep-dish one) and prep according to package directions.

MAKES 6 TO 8 SERVINGS

From-scratch Crust (or one (9 or 10-inch) store-bought crust)

1½ cups all-purpose flour

1 stick (½ cup) unsalted butter, softened and cut into chunks

¾ teaspoon salt

2 tablespoons ice water, plus more as needed

Nonstick cooking spray

Filling

3 large eggs

1 cup (8 ounces) sour cream

½ teaspoon salt

1 Gala or Fuji apple, cored, halved, and cut into 1/8-inch slices

8 ounces shredded or grated Monterey Jack, Gruyere or other flavorful cheese

If you are making the crust, combine the flour and salt in a mixing bowl, add the butter, and mash thoroughly with your hands until you have a buttery, crumbly mixture. Add 2 tablespoons water and continue mixing to form a smooth, very pliable dough. Add a little more water if necessary. Roll the dough into a ball, cover, and refrigerate for at least 2 hours or overnight.

When you are ready to bake the quiche, place the oven rack in the middle position and preheat the oven to 450°F.

Remove the dough from the refrigerator and bring to room temperature. Spray a 9 or 9½-inch pie plate (or tart pan) with nonstick cooking spray.

Place the dough on a work surface and form it into a ball, and then, with a rolling pin, roll it into a circle about ¼-inch thick. Roll the dough onto the rolling pin and position it over the prepared pan. Carefully unroll the dough so it covers bottom and side of the pan, letting any excess hang over the side. Use your fingertips to press the dough snugly into the pan. Neatly remove the excess overhanging dough. Set the trimmings aside. Pierce the unbaked pie shell lightly with a fork.

Cover and chill in the refrigerator for about 15 minutes. If you are using a store- bought refrigerated pie crust, unfold it into your pie pan and pierce it lightly with a fork. Trim overhanging dough and reserve.

Place the reserved excess dough on the work surface and roll it to a thickness of ¼ inch. Cut it into ½-inch strips. Set these aside.

Remove from the crust from the refrigerator. Line it with aluminum foil, and fill with dried beans or pie weights (or simply put another pie plate on top of the crust). Bake for 20 to 25 minutes, or until golden and flaky. When cool enough to handle, remove the foil and weights or the pie plate.

If you are using a store-bought, prepare it according to the package directions, pre-baking it if necessary.

To make the filling, beat the eggs in a medium bowl. Reserve about 1 or 2 tablespoons beaten egg in a small cup, for egg wash. Add the salt and sour cream to the remaining egg in the bowl and mix until thoroughly combined.

When the baked crust has cooled slightly, mix the egg reserved in the cup with 1 or 2 tablespoons water to make an egg wash. Brush the crust with the egg wash to seal it.

Arrange the apple slices evenly around the bottom of the crust, trying not to overlap them too much. Scatter the cheese evenly over them. Pour in the egg-sour cream mixture, spreading it around with a spoon to fill any gaps and cover the quiche completely. Arrange the dough scraps on the top of the quiche to form an "S" for superhero. Brush with the egg wash.

Bake for 25 to 30 minutes, or until the quiche is golden on the top and a toothpick inserted into the center comes out clean.

MUSCLE-THUMB THUMBPRINT COOKIES

THEY MIGHT NOT BE ABLE TO BEND STEEL IN THEIR BARE HANDS, but the superheroes and superheroines in your house will have fun using their super-strong thumbs to make these cookies. You can make them plain or dusted with shredded coconut or chopped almonds. If you need to avoid almonds because of a nut allergy, omit the almond extract and use 1 whole teaspoon vanilla extract. Allow at least half an hour for the dough to chill. (It can be made up to two days ahead.) The shortening or margarine in the recipe keeps them from spreading too much and helps maintain the thumbprint shape. They'll likely disappear quickly, but if you freeze them, it's best to freeze them unfilled, as the jam tends to get sticky when frozen.

MAKES 16 COOKIES

6 tablespoons (¾ stick) unsalted butter, at room temperature

4 tablespoons butter-flavored shortening or unsalted margarine

½ cup granulated sugar

1 large egg, separated

¼ teaspoon almond extract (optional)

½ teaspoon pure vanilla extract

2 tablespoons whole milk

1⅔ cup all-purpose flour

⅛ teaspoon salt

2 teaspoons water

1 cup sliced almonds, finely chopped or 1 cup shredded coconut (optional)

½ cup raspberry, strawberry, or other jam, at room temperature

Combine the butter, shortening, and sugar in a large mixing bowl and, with an electric mixer set at low speed, beat for about 2 minutes, or until well combined. Add the egg yolk, almond extract, if using, vanilla, and milk, and beat for 1 more minute, or until well combined.

In another bowl, whisk the flour and salt together.

With the mixer still set at low speed, add the flour to the butter mixture and beat for about 1 minute, or until well combined. The dough should clump together and feel quite pliable.

Shape the dough into a log about 8 inches long, and wrap it well with plastic wrap.

Chill the dough in the refrigerator for at least 30 minutes or up to 2 days.

When you are ready to bake, preheat the oven to 350°F. Line a baking sheet with parchment.

Cut the log of dough into 16 equal pieces. Roll the pieces between your palms to form (1¾-inch) balls.

In a small bowl, mix the egg white and water with a fork to make an egg wash. If you are using the almonds or coconut, pour one or the other into a small bowl. Dip each ball of dough into the egg wash and then into the nuts or coconut. Place it on the prepared baking sheet.

Here's where you'll need your super-strong thumb: With your thumb, make a depression in the middle of the cookie, pressing down hard so there is a distinct indentation. If the cookie dough cracks at the edges, press it together again. (Don't worry if the cookies crack slightly around the edges during baking; that's fine.)

Bake the cookies for 18 to 20 minutes, or until the tops look almost dry, the cookies are beginning to brown, and if you are using the nuts, they look toasted.

Remove the cookies from the parchment with a thin metal spatula. Cool them completely on a wire rack.

Spoon ¼ to ½ teaspoon jam into each cookie.

The Happy Wanderer Picnic

HERE'S A DINNER THAT YOU CAN PACK UP AND TAKE ON A PICNIC,
carry out the back door to dine alfresco on your patio, or enjoy indoors.
The name comes from "The Happy Wanderer," a song that became popular in
the 1950s and 1960s. It starts out, "I love to go a-wandering along the mountain
track . . . " It was written by a German man named Friedrich-Wilhelm Möller in the
1940s. His sister, Edith, ran the Obernkirchen Children's Choir. In 1953, the
children performed the song at a music festival that was broadcast by the BBC.
It became an international sensation and was translated into many languages. If
you know the song, try singing it while you make this dinner . . . or in the car as you
travel to your picnic . . . or while you hike! It perfectly captures the feeling you
get when you go out for a walk on a beautiful day.

Menu

Blue-Sky Eggs

Seared Tuna Po' Boy with Olivey Aioli

End of the Rainbow Lentil Salad

Trail Mix Brownies

Game Plan

★ Make (and nibble or pack up) the Blue-Sky Eggs. ✋

★ Get the kids started on the compass craft.

★ Prep the Trail Mix Brownies, bake for 30 minutes, and let cool for 10 minutes. ✋

★ Cook the lentils for the End of the Rainbow Lentil Salad for about 20 minutes and let cool.

★ Mix up the Olivey Aioli and prep the Po Boy sandwich fixings; prep and sear the tuna and let it rest for 10 minutes.

★ Prep the vegetables for the End of the Rainbow Lentil Salad and toss with the lentils.

★ Gather 'round the picnic blanket; it's time to eat!

★ And now, a dessert worthy of a journey!!

DINNER PREP IN SMALL BITES:

If you have time the night before or earlier in the day, prep and chill the End of the Rainbow Lentil Salad, color the Blue-Sky Eggs, and bake the Trail Mix Brownies. You can also sear the tuna and mix up the Olivey Aioli for the Tuna Po' Boy and refrigerate both, but don't assemble the sandwich until just before your picnic or the bread will get soggy.

FRIDAY NIGHT TIME-SAVER:

If time is short, buy a lentil or other colorful salad at the deli counter. Use a brownie mix and top with trail mix.

Crafty Friday:
MAKE YOUR OWN COMPASS

EVERY HAPPY WANDERER NEEDS TO KNOW WHICH WAY IS WHICH; if you can figure out which way is north and you have good directions or a map, you can probably find out where you should be headed. If you're facing north, you'll find east to your right, west to your left, and south behind you. This "compass" will serve your purposes, even if you don't have a real one. (It requires a bowl of water, so it might be something to do before you get started on your hike. It also requires a fairly strong magnet; the refrigerator magnets that we all have around the house probably won't work. But a cow magnet, which is relatively inexpensive and available in some toy stores (in science kits) or from science equipment Web sites, works beautifully. (A cow magnet is so named because farmers feed them to cows. A cow can pick up a fair amount of iron grazing in the grass and a magnet in the belly attracts the metal and keeps the cow from getting sick. The magnet stays in the cow's belly without harming it.) This is a group project, so you only need one of each item.

1 cow magnet

1 piece of Styrofoam big enough to hold the magnet (a disposable bowl will work)

Transparent or masking tape

1 ceramic or plastic bowl (no metal content) big enough to hold the Styrofoam

Water to fill the bowl

Tape the magnet to the Styrofoam.

Fill the ceramic bowl with water.

Place the magnet into the bowl and watch as it turns to face north.

What's a compass?

A compass is a tool that helps travelers figure out how to get where they want to go. The oldest and most common form, dating back at least 900 years, is the magnetic compass. Magnetism has to do with the way atoms (the tiny particles that make up all things) are attracted to or push away from one another. When a piece of metal becomes magnetized, the electrons (even tinier particles within the atoms) all spin in the same direction. Only a few metals make useful magnets: iron, steel (which is mostly made of iron), nickel, cobalt, and one that's a tongue twister—neodymium (pronounced "nee-oh-DIE-me-um"). In early times, the needle of a compass was made of lodestone, an iron-based mineral that's naturally magnetic. Today, magnets are made of magnetized steel.

A magnetic compass makes use of the very strong magnetic fields that are generated deep inside the Earth. The Earth's magnetic fields are strongest near the North and South Poles, in spots called Magnetic North and Magnetic South. (For more information on the poles, see Table Talk, page 123.)

A magnetic compass consists of a base, usually round. In the center is a magnetized needle mounted on a stem called a pivot, which allows the needle to spin around in different directions. One end will be red or pointed like an arrow, and that end points to the nearest pole. In the Northern Hemisphere, it points north. No matter which way the person holding it is facing, if the compass is held properly, the needle will always turn and point to the nearest magnetic pole.

Today, most ship captains, airplane pilots, and adventurers use GPS, referring to the Global Positioning System, a completely different kind of navigation system, based on satellites that orbit the Earth and receive and transmit information about the user's current location and destination. But smart GPS users still keep a trusty magnetic compass as a backup—just in case their GPS device's satellite communication fails.

BLUE-SKY EGGS

HARD-COOKED EGGS ARE TRADITIONAL PICNIC FARE; they're easy to transport and easy to eat. All your picnickers will like these colorful eggs, which call to mind blue skies and white clouds on the outside and a yellow sun on the inside. They're a cross between Easter eggs and tea eggs, a traditional Chinese treat. To make tea eggs, you prepare hard-cooked eggs and crack the shells all over without removing them. Then you steep the eggs in seasoned tea, which creates a mottled, marbled pattern on the white of the egg inside. For this recipe, instead of tea, we use the blue dye from an Easter egg kit or some blue food coloring. We only want blue skies for a picnic! You might want to spread some newspapers under your work area to make cleanup easier and avoid stains.

MAKES 4 EGGS

4 large eggs

1 teaspoon blue food coloring gel or 1 blue egg dye pellet

White vinegar as directed in the egg coloring instructions (optional)

Coarse-grained salt for serving (optional)

Mayonnaise for serving (optional)

Bring a large pot of water to a boil; the water should be deep enough to cover the eggs. Prepare a large bowl of cold water for an ice bath.

Carefully lower the eggs into the boiling water and boil for 12 minutes. With a spoon, remove the eggs from the hot water and carefully transfer to the cold water. Allow to cool for a few minutes. Reserve the cooking pot and hot water.

Place the eggs on a work surface and press gently but firmly to make lots of tiny cracks all over the shell. Try not to let the shell come off, and avoid pressing so hard that the cooked egg breaks inside the shell. (If either of these things happen, don't worry; the recipe will still work.)

Prepare the dye and vinegar, if using, with hot water as directed on the package and soak the eggs in the colored water for 4 to 5 minutes, or until the egg white inside takes on a swirly blue and white appearance. (You'll be able to see it, somewhat, through the cracks.) You might have to turn the eggs once or twice with a spoon. Carefully remove the eggs from the dye and drain on a paper plate until dry.

When the eggs are dry, remove the shells to reveal a blue-sky-and-clouds effect. Just before you are ready to eat, cut the eggs in half lengthwise to let the sun come out. Season with salt and serve with mayonnaise.

TUNA PO' BOY WITH OLIVEY AIOLI

THIS TUNA AND AIOLI COMBINATION IS GOOD HOT OR COLD, so you can cook and eat these flavorful sandwiches right away, or you can make the aioli and tuna steaks ahead, refrigerate them, and assemble the sandwiches just before you eat. If you go the cold route, don't preassemble the sandwiches, as the crusty Italian bread will be nicer if it isn't chilled. The salt, pepper, and garlic make an easy, tasty crust on the fish. If you don't have a coarse-grained salt, then just season the fish lightly with regular table salt to taste; don't use the 2 tablespoons called for here or it will be way too salty.

MAKES 4 SANDWICHES

Aioli

¾ cup mayonnaise

2 tablespoons extra-virgin olive oil

10 pitted kalamata olives, coarsely chopped

2 sun-dried tomato slices, coarsely chopped

⅛ teaspoon dried oregano

Tuna

4 (4-ounce) ahi or other tuna steaks

2 tablespoons coarse-grained salt such as sea salt or kosher salt

1 tablespoon freshly ground black pepper, plus more as needed (optional)

To make the aioli, combine the mayonnaise, olive oil, olives, sun-dried tomatoes, and oregano in a food processor or mini-chopper fitted with a metal blade and process until the olives and tomatoes are finely chopped and the mayonnaise is pink in color. Set aside.

Combine the salt and pepper in a shallow bowl, and put the finely chopped garlic into another shallow bowl.

Dip a tuna steak into the salt and pepper to lightly coat both sides, evening it out with your fingertips if necessary. Dip just 1 side into the garlic. Place on a platter and repeat with the remaining steaks.

Heat the oil in a large nonstick skillet set over medium-high heat. When it sizzles, carefully place the tuna into it, in a single layer, garlic-side down, working in batches if necessary. Cook for about 30 seconds, turn with tongs, and cook for 1 to 3 minutes more, or until the tuna is golden-brown and cooked to the

(continued on the next page)

2 cloves garlic, finely chopped

2 tablespoons olive oil, plus more as needed

4 to 8 crisp Romaine lettuce leaves, trimmed and washed

1 large vine-ripened tomato, cored and thinly sliced

1 loaf Italian bread (about 1 pound)

desired degree of doneness. You will be able to see the degree of doneness by looking at the side of the steak and watching the color change from deep pink to light pink to beige (for well-done). Reduce the heat if necessary to prevent the tuna from burning, but don't return it to the garlic side, as garlic burns easily. Remove from the skillet, place on a platter, and let rest for 10 minutes. Once the fish has rested, you can make the sandwich immediately or chill and serve later.

When you are ready to make your sandwich, slice the bread lengthwise, spread both halves with the aioli, distribute the lettuce and tomato evenly over the bread, and top with the tuna steaks. Close up the sandwich, cut into 4 pieces, and serve.

A po' boy, or poorboy, is a sandwich that originated in New Orleans in the early twentieth century. When brothers Benny and Clovis Martin came to the city, they found work as streetcar conductors. After a few years, they opened a sandwich shop together, but they remained friends with their fellow streetcar workers. When the streetcar workers went on strike in 1929, the Martins gave out free sandwiches to the strikers. The name of the sandwich arose because when a striker entered the shop, one of them would call out, "Here's another poor boy." The key to a po' boy is the bread—a crusty roll or French or Italian loaf that is the same width from end to end.

Aioli is a mayonnaise sauce that originated in southern France. It's like regular mayonnaise in that it's made with vegetable oil, egg yolks, and lemon juice or vinegar, but traditional aioli requires the addition of garlic as a seasoning. It's generally made with olive oil, which gives it a lovely, almost fruity flavor. In this version, I've taken the liberty of skipping the garlic, which can be quite strong, and substituting olives and sun-dried tomatoes. I use good-quality jarred mayonnaise as a base, as it's pasteurized, which eliminates any worry about raw eggs. But if you prefer to make your own mayonnaise, it will be delicious.

END OF THE RAINBOW LENTIL SALAD

LEGEND HAS IT THAT IF YOU FOLLOW A LEPRECHAUN to the end of the rainbow, you'll find a pot o' gold . . . but gold isn't any good for eating. Here's a rainbow-colored pot o' salad that will keep you from going hungry while you're out wandering. You can make it ahead of time and chill it, but if you make it just before you head out, the frozen veggies will cool down the freshly cooked lentils nicely; they also add color and save you chopping time! If you have the time to chop and chill, you can use all fresh veggies if you prefer.

MAKES ABOUT 4 TO 6 SERVINGS

2 cups vegetable stock

1 cup dried lentils, preferably black or a multicolored mixture

1 cup frozen mixed vegetables (peas, carrots, and corn are good, but any colorful mix will do), rinsed but not thawed

2 stalks celery, chopped in $\frac{1}{4}$-inch pieces (about $\frac{2}{3}$ cup)

1 red bell pepper, seeds and membrane removed, chopped in $\frac{1}{4}$-inch pieces (about $\frac{2}{3}$ cup)

2 or 3 scallions, thinly sliced

$\frac{1}{4}$ cup seasoned rice vinegar

Salt and freshly ground black pepper to taste (optional)

Bring the stock to a boil in a medium saucepan. Examine the lentils, picking out any small stones or debris. Then rinse and drain them in a fine-mesh sieve.

When the stock is boiling, add the lentils. Return to a boil and boil for 3 minutes. Then reduce the heat and simmer for about 20 minutes, or until the stock is absorbed and the lentils are tender but not mushy. (If the lentils are still tough to the bite, add a little water and cook for a few more minutes.)

Transfer the lentils to a bowl and add the frozen vegetables, celery, pepper, scallions, and rice vinegar, and toss gently until all the ingredients are thoroughly mixed. Taste, season with salt and pepper if necessary, and toss gently again. The frozen vegetables should cool the lentils, but you can chill the salad in the refrigerator until serving.

Lentils—small round, flat seeds—belong to the legume family. They are dried when they are harvested, but unlike other legumes, do not require a long soaking before they can be cooked. Lentils originated in South Asia and are a staple protein there. They come in many colors: brown, green, yellow, white, black, and orange-red. They are sold in single colors or in multicolored packages. Typically used in soups, stews, salads, or in Indian *daal,* they cook fairly quickly.

TABLE TALK

WHAT ARE SOME SAFETY TIPS TO THINK ABOUT before you set out for a wanderer's picnic? What should you bring with you?

Here are a few ideas to get you started:

- Find out something about the area you'll be wandering in. Does it require strenuous hiking or is it appropriate for all ages and skill levels? Does it require a permit? Can you build a fire there? Are there rest stations if you need them? Pick a safe area whose terrain will suit all members of your family and has all the amenities you'll need.

- Get a guide to poisonous plants that might grow in your path and give everyone a good look before you set out—so they know what *not* to step on or touch.

- To keep your picnic from spoiling in the heat, throw a cold-pack into your (lightweight) cooler, or freeze your juice boxes or water bottles the night before. They'll be thawed by the time you eat and will keep the food cool.

- Pack a few essentials to ensure that your trip goes smoothly. Sunscreen, hats, sunglasses, insect repellent, cell phone, maps, compass, first aid kit, a sweater or lightweight rain poncho in case the weather changes, and a flashlight are useful items.

- A trash bag is a good idea, so you don't leave litter behind, and it can make a good rain poncho if necessary.

- A pocket field guide that will help you identify local plants and animals can add to your fun.

TRAIL MIX BROWNIES

TRAIL MIX—A CONCOCTION OF NUTS, DRIED FRUIT, and sometimes bits of candy—is a tasty, easy-to-carry pick-me-up for a day of hiking and picnicking. These brownies turn the trail mix concept into a full-fledged dessert that is still easy to pack up. I like trail mix made with a variety of nuts, but if someone at your picnic blanket has a nut allergy, use a variety made with seeds, dried fruits, and candies—or better yet, mix up your own.

MAKES 16 BROWNIES

Nonstick cooking spray

½ cup (3 ounces) semisweet chocolate pieces

4 ounces (1 stick) unsalted butter

1 cup granulated sugar

2 large eggs

½ teaspoon pure vanilla extract

⅔ cup all-purpose flour

½ teaspoon salt

½ teaspoon baking powder

1 (6- to 8-ounce) package trail mix or 1 cup mixed nuts, seeds, bite-sized pieces of raisins or other dried fruits, and small candies

Place an oven rack in the middle position and preheat the oven to 350°F. Spray an 8- or 9-inch square nonstick baking pan with nonstick cooking spray.

Put the chocolate, butter, and sugar into a microwave-safe container and microwave on medium (50 percent) power for 1½ to 2 minutes, or until the butter is nearly melted and the chocolate glistens. Remove from the microwave and stir until the chocolate is melted and all the ingredients are thoroughly combined.

In a medium mixing bowl, lightly beat the eggs and vanilla until combined. Add the chocolate mixture.

Mix the flour, salt, and baking powder in a small bowl. Add to the chocolate mixture and stir until all the ingredients are thoroughly incorporated. With a spatula, scrape the batter into the prepared pan. Sprinkle the trail mix evenly over the top and bake for about 30 minutes, or until a toothpick inserted into the center comes out clean or with just a few crumbs on it. Cool in the pan for 10 minutes and cut into squares.

After-Dinner Fun: Nature Scavenger Hunt

WHETHER YOU HAVE PACKED UP THIS DINNER and taken it to a concert or the park, dined al fresco on the patio, or stayed put at the kitchen table, you can finish the evening with this amped-up nature walk. Before you start out, review the safety rules. I always say that nobody picks up things found along the way; instead, everyone gets a small notebook in which to sketch them. This way, nature stays just the way we found it. My daughter and her friends love carrying their field notebooks on the scavenger hunt and checking off the items as they find them.

Gather some small palm-sized notebooks and pencils for all your happy wanderers. On the first page of each book, make a list of the items to be "scavenged." You can use the same list for everyone, or make individual lists geared to the ages of the participants. Draw in little check boxes next to each item; kids love to check off each thing they find.

Here are some suggestions for items to put on the list:

THINGS TO LOOK FOR:

- Something blue (or each wanderer's favorite color.)

- Something that starts with the letter B (or that begins with the first letter of the wanderer's name.)

- Three different kinds of insects

- An animal or bird

- An animal, bird, or insect's home (Look but don't touch!)

- A cloud that's shaped like something

- Negative and positive signs that people taken this path before you (tell the kids how important it is not to litter, to prevent forest fires, and to take care of the Earth.)

THINGS TO LISTEN FOR:

- Bird call (Can you imitate it?)

- Other animal sound (How many can you think of?)

- Other nature sounds (running water, cracking ice, chirping crickets, or scampering animals)

THINGS TO SMELL

Ask the kids to notice any odors, pleasant or stinky, as they walk.

- Flowers

- Grasses

- Leaves or rotting trees

- Animal habitats

- Mossy or swampy areas

Poetry Slam

HERE'S A DINNER THAT'S HARD TO BEAT.

It's got lots of rhymes and good things to eat.

A poetry slam is a kind of a show

Where poetry's recited, wouldn't you know?

So just for tonight, work in rhyme.

You'll get the hang of it in no time!

Then pick a poem—maybe one you've read,

Or make one up right out of your head.

Recite with a smile, never a frown.

Deliver your poem and then sit down.

Snap, snap, snap to show what you like

Rhymes and good eats will set the night right!

Menu

Edamame Salami

Fish Delish

Nice Rice Pilaf

Easy Snow Peasy

Cool Strawberry-Orange Fool

Game Plan

★ Make (and nibble) the Edamame Salami. ✋

★ Get the kids started on the Concrete Poetry craft.

★ Prep the Nice Rice Pilaf and microwave for 15 to 20 minutes or bake in the oven for 30 to 40 minutes.

★ Prep and cook the Fish Delish and sauce and keep warm.

★ Prep and microwave the Easy Snow Peasy.

★ Dinner's up! Time to sup!

★ Prep the Cool Strawberry-Orange Fool. ✋

★ Now for a sweet that can't be beat!

DINNER PREP IN SMALL BITES:
If you have time the night before or earlier in the day, make the Edamame Salami, the Nice Rice Pilaf, and the Cool Strawberry-Orange Fool.

FRIDAY NIGHT TIME-SAVER:
If time is short, use precooked, lightly breaded fish fillets for the Fish Delish (you can make the sauce or not, but it's worth the few minutes it takes) and prepared whipped topping for Cool Orange Fool.

Crafty Friday:
CONCRETE POETRY

THERE ARE LOTS OF WAYS TO ENJOY POEMS. We can make them up and write them down. Or we can read other people's poems, either silently to ourselves or aloud to others. Sometimes we memorize them. Most poetry is made up of words, but there's a kind of poetry made with pictures—or shaped printed words, at any rate—that's called concrete poetry or visual poetry. In this kind of poetry, written words are formed into shapes that make pictures, so that you get the meaning of the poem from reading the words and seeing the pictures they make.

For example, a concrete poem about brushing your teeth might look like this:

BrushbrushbrushBrushbrushbrushBrushbrushbrushBrushbrushbrush
Brushbrushbrush
Brushbrushbrush
Brushbrushbrush

And   don't
   Stop   'til
     Every tooth
     Sparkles.

Plain white paper

Pencils

Erasers

Colored markers

Computer, computer paper, printer, safety scissors, and glue sticks (optional)

In this craft, you'll try your hand at concrete poetry. You can write out your poem or use a computer to print the words, and then cut them out and glue them to another piece of paper in a visual pattern. Try making a concrete poetry alphabet, picking a word for each letter and then arranging that word in a pattern that gives a visual image of its meaning. For *(continued on the next page)*

A, you might use the word "apple":

app

apple apple apple apple apple

apple apple apple apple apple apple

apple apple apple apple apple apple

crunch crunch apple apple app

apple apple apple apple apple apple

ple apple apple apple apple ap

yum yum yum yum yum yum

yum yum yum

yum

Try some other letters and see what you come up with. Pick something you love, like ice cream, and write a concrete poem about a cool, creamy treat. The sky's the limit.

What's a poem?

A POEM IS A GROUP OF WORDS THAT makes you feel something. Many, but not all, poems make use of rhyme and rhythm. The poet's choice of words usually helps you see a picture in your mind more vividly than regular writing or speech. Sometimes poems rhyme, which means the words' ending sounds are the same. In the title of this book, "night" and "bite" rhyme. Rhyming poems have a distinct rhythm: some sounds are emphasized and others are not as they flow, one after the other. If you want to hear the rhythm of a poem or song or group of words, try clapping it out.

EDAMAME SALAMI

BECAUSE MORE AND MORE FAMILIES ARE DISCOVERING ready-to-eat edamame as a yummy, nutritious snack, I wanted to include them in this book. At first I dismissed the possibility of putting them into this chapter; after all, edamame's only rhyming counterpart is *salami*. But then I decided to try it. You'll be as surprised as I was to discover this delightful pairing. The salami jazzes up the edamame nicely, and makes an edible poem for an appetizer or anytime snack.

MAKES 4 SERVINGS

2 ounces Genoa salami

8 or 9 ounces ready-to-eat shelled soybeans (edamame)

Chop the salami very finely or pulse in a mini-chopper to make small pieces. Transfer to a microwavable container and microwave on high power for 45 seconds to 1 minute, or until crispy.

Pour the edamame into a serving bowl, and when the salami is cool enough to handle, pour it in and toss to mix well. Serve with plenty of napkins.

Edamame is the Japanese word for fresh, young, green soybeans that are picked while they are still tender. They are typically partially boiled immediately on picking to preserve their character. They can be used as snacks or in vegetable dishes, soups, and even desserts. They come in pods but are increasingly sold pre-shelled, fresh or frozen. If you can't find the ready-to-eat edamame, buy shelled soybeans, cook according to package directions, and chill to room temperature.

DELISH FISH

THIS IS A VERY SIMPLE YET APPROACHABLE WAY to get the family to love mild white fish such as tilapia. It's based on the classic French *meunière,* but with a twist . . . of orange. You can serve it right out of the pan, without the sauce and just a squeeze of lemon, if you like. But the sauce is quick, easy, and tasty. Judge the amount of fish you cook by the folks at your table. Hearty eaters might want two fillets, while smaller appetites might be satisfied with just one. If you make just four fillets, reduce the other ingredients listed.

MAKES 4 SERVINGS

½ cup all-purpose flour

1 teaspoon salt, plus more to taste

6 (7- to 8-ounce) tilapia or other mild, boneless, skinless fish fillets

1½ tablespoons unsalted butter

1½ tablespoons olive oil

¾ cup orange juice

½ cup chicken stock, plus more as needed

Freshly ground black pepper (optional)

Fresh chopped parsley for garnish, (optional)

Pour the flour into a shallow bowl or plate. Season both sides of the tilapia fillets with salt, and dip them into the flour, coating both sides and tapping off any excess.

Heat the butter and oil in a nonstick skillet set over medium-high heat until the butter is melted. Swirl to incorporate it into the oil, and place the fillets in the pan in a single layer, working in batches if necessary. Cook for 1 to 2 minutes, or until golden in color; then turn with a spatula and cook for 1 to 3 minutes longer, or until completely white and opaque and cooked through. (The cooking time will depend on the thickness of the fillet.) If the skillet seems too dry, add a little more butter and oil. Transfer the cooked fillets to a platter and keep warm.

Add the orange juice and stock to the skillet and cook, stirring, for about 6 minutes, or until you can "draw" a line in the bottom of the pan with a spoon. Taste and season with salt and pepper if necessary. If the sauce is too sweet, add a little more stock. Stir to incorporate and cook for 1 minute longer, or until the sauce is thickened again and nice and hot. Place the fillets on individual dinner plates, divide the sauce among them, sprinkle with parsley if you like, and serve.

Fish makes a wonderfully healthful meal; it contains good-quality protein and fats that can help prevent heart disease. But the headlines are often full of news about endangered species of seafood or health alerts due to contamination of certain waters. To find out what's good to eat, check out the Monterey Bay Aquarium's online Seafood Watch, which has up-to-date information on which fish to avoid and which to seek out. Sometimes the same species will appear in both categories depending on how and where it is caught!

TABLE TALK

RAP IS MUSIC, BUT IT'S ALSO POETRY. Can you make up a rap?

NICE RICE PILAF

I MUCH PREFER RICE PILAF to plain old boiled rice. A little stock and some seasonings transform the humble grains into something fragrant and elegant. You can cook your pilaf on the stove, but I like to make it in the microwave or the oven because then the stovetop is available for other things and I don't have to monitor the rice pot.

MAKES 4 SERVINGS

2 tablespoons olive oil

1 medium onion, finely chopped

1 clove garlic, finely chopped

1 cup basmati or jasmine rice, rinsed and drained

½ cup slivered almonds (optional)

1 to 2 tablespoons raisins or dried currants

2 cups warm chicken stock

Salt and freshly ground black pepper to taste

If you are using the oven, preheat it to 350°F.

Heat the olive oil in a casserole or skillet that can go from stovetop to microwave (or oven, if you prefer). Add the onion and cook, stirring and shaking the pan, for about 3 to 4 minutes, or until very soft and translucent. Add the garlic and cook for 30 seconds, or until softened. Add the rice, the almonds, if using, and the raisins, and stir to coat. Cook for about 1 minute. If you need to, transfer to an ovenproof or microwavable casserole, add the stock and cover.

If you are using the microwave, place the pot into it and microwave on high power for 15 to 20 minutes, or until the liquid is absorbed and the rice is tender. Remove from the
(continued on the next page)

microwave. If you are using the oven, bake for 30 to 40 minutes or until the liquid is absorbed and the rice is tender. Remove from the oven.

Taste, season with salt and pepper if necessary, and stir to incorporate. Serve hot.

 A pilaf is a Middle Eastern dish of rice or bulgur wheat that is cooked first in oil and then in stock, a technique that keeps the individual grains separate. A pilaf can be seasoned with spices, as well as legumes, meat, nuts, or dried fruit. The dish originated in the Middle East but migrated along with the population throughout Central Asia, where it is known by various names: *pilav, pilau, pulao,* and so on.

TABLE TALK

What's haiku?

Haiku is a form of poetry that originated in Japan. It consists of three lines; the first has five syllables, the second has seven, and the third has five. It does not rhyme. Haiku often concerns nature. Here's an example of a haiku:

How pleasant it is
To share a good meal and talk
With my loved ones now.

Do you know any haiku? Can you make one up?

EASY SNOW PEASY

SNOW PEAS ARE TYPICALLY A COMPONENT OF A STIR-FRY or other Asian recipe, but here they stand alone, their natural sweetness complemented by a mild salty-sour lemon-butter sauce. I like my snow peas al dente—crisp to the bite—and a quick turn in the microwave is perfect for cooking them that way. For a softer texture, microwave them for a little longer, until done to your liking. You can use the easy lemon-butter sauce for pretty much any steamed veggie; adjust the cooking time of the vegetable accordingly.

MAKES 4 SERVINGS

2 tablespoons unsalted butter

1 tablespoon fresh lemon juice

½ teaspoon salt

1 pound snow peas, trimmed (see note, below) and halved

Combine the butter, lemon juice, and salt in a large shallow microwavable container that is big enough to hold all the snow peas. Microwave on high power for 30 to 45 seconds, or until most of the butter is melted. Carefully remove from the oven and stir to incorporate thoroughly. Add the snow peas and toss well to coat. Return to the microwave and cook on high power for 1 to 1½ minutes, or until tender-crisp.

Snow peas originated in Asia and are prized for their tender, edible pods. Buy them crisp, not soft or wrinkled. To trim, just snap off the tiny hard ends. You can remove the strings if you like, but they are entirely edible. If you stir-fry them, they'll cook in about a minute.

COOL STRAWBERRY-ORANGE FOOL

A FOOL IS A TRADITIONAL ENGLISH DESSERT THAT, in its simplest form, consists of puréed or mashed fruit and whipped cream. Kids will love the name, but it's got nothing to do with being silly; the term "fool" is believed to have come from the French word *fouler*, "to mash." A fool is often made with gooseberries or other slightly tart fruit. You can also use just strawberries; if so, increase the quantity of fruit to about 3 cups and add more sugar to taste.

MAKES 4 SERVINGS

1 cup frozen strawberries, just slightly thawed

3 tablespoons confectioners' sugar, divided, plus more to taste

2 cups heavy cream

1 (15-ounce) can mandarin oranges, preferably in water, drained

Pour the strawberries and 1 tablespoon sugar into a food processor fitted with a metal blade, and process until smooth and creamy. Taste and if the berries are very tart, add a little more sugar. Pulse to combine, and set aside.

To make the whipped cream, pour the cream into a mixing bowl, add 2 tablespoons sugar, and whip with a whisk or beat with an electric mixer set at low to medium speed until soft peaks form. (The peaks will rise when you lift the beaters from the mixture but will fall immediately.)

Fold the strawberry purée into the whipped cream and mix gently but thoroughly; then fold in the orange sections and mix gently to distribute them throughout. Spoon into dessert bowls and serve.

"There once was a man from Dublin. . ."

A LIMERICK IS A FIVE-LINE RHYME that originated in Ireland. Typically, limericks are funny little poems. The first two lines end with words that rhyme, the next two end with a new rhyme, and the final line reverts to the first rhyme. It's written in a rhythm called an anapest, which consist of three beats, the third of which is emphasized. Say "Better *yet,*" and you'll hear what an anapest sounds like.

Here's an example of a limerick:

There once was a dinner for rhymers,
And they were all jolly-old-timers.
In an awfully good mood,
They cooked up some food,
After which, they were sleepy bed-climbers.

Do you know any limericks? Can you make one up?

After-Dinner Fun: Family Poetry Slam

TRY WRITING A FAMILY POEM. Agree on a topic and then work on the poem together, line by line, writing it down so all can see (on a chalkboard, a dry-erase board, or even a big pad). You can try rapping, limericks, haiku, or a simple rhyme. When you're done, recite it together. Or, if the kids are old enough, have each person make up a poem and then read all the poems aloud to one another. If you know any poems by heart, you can add those to the program. Or gather your favorite poetry books together and read out loud.

Dino Dinner

THEY LOOK A LITTLE LIKE MONSTERS, BUT THEY'RE TOTALLY, thoroughly real. They lived long ago—comfortably long enough not to be a threat to us humans. Finding their bones can be kind of like going on a treasure hunt. Is it any wonder that kids find tales of dinosaurs and other prehistoric creatures so intriguing? Here's a soup-salad-sandwich dinner that builds on that intrigue, with food to please adults and kids alike. And don't even think of skipping the Chocolate Dinoturtles for dessert!

Menu

Fossil Breadsticks

Primordial Soup

Saber-Toothed Salad

Quesadillasaurus

Chocolate Dinoturtles

Game Plan

★ Make (and nibble) the Fossil Breadsticks. ✋

★ Get the kids started on the Elbones Fossil craft.

★ Prep and cook the Primordial Soup and keep warm.

★ Prep the Quesadillasauruses and bake for 15 minutes. ✋

★ Prep the Saber-Toothed Salad and toss with the dressing.

★ The Dinnerzoic Era has begun! Serve the soup and salad first, and assemble the Quesadillasauruses at the table.

★ Prep the Chocolate Dinoturtles. ✋

★ Everyone knows that the Dinnerzoic Era was followed by dessert!

DINNER PREP IN SMALL BITES:

If you have time the night before or earlier in the day, make the Fossil Breadsticks and the Chocolate Dinoturtles.

Because this dinner is relatively quick and easy and conducive to help from little hands, you might want to save the Crafty Friday Elbones Fossil for after dinner.

FRIDAY NIGHT TIME-SAVER:

If time is short, use a good-quality prepared vegetable soup.

Crafty Friday:
ELBONES FOSSILS

WHAT KIND OF FOSSIL IS AN ELBONES FOSSIL? One that's made from the remains of the infamous Elbow Noodlesaurus, of course. When you stand the noodles end to end or side to side with the round side up, you've got what looks (with a little imagination) like a skeleton. Add a bit of sand around the "bones," and you've stumbled upon the remains of a prehistoric creature, jutting out of the sand after having been buried for millions of years. You can buy a jar or two of colored craft sand, but because you don't need all that much, you can also use any craft sand that's left over from another project, if you have it. (Or if this is an impromptu pantry project, you can skip the sand altogether.) If you don't care to get glue on your fingers, use a plastic paintbrush to spread it; find an old one that you can toss in the trash when the project is done.

½ to 1 cup dry elbow pasta

1 (9- x 13-inch) sheet construction paper per person

1 or more small paintbrushes, for spreading the glue

Craft glue

Colored craft sand

Other dry pasta (optional)

Plan your dinosaur fossil first, by arranging the elbow noodles on the construction paper without any glue. Place them with the flat, cut ends touching on the paper, so they stand with curved "elbow" sides facing up and it looks like the tops of the bones are just peeking out of the ground.

To make a fossil that looks like the dinosaur is face down, place some noodles end to end for a backbone, tail, legs, and claws. To make a rib cage, place 1 noodle on either side of the backbone at a 90° angle to it, leaving about a quarter-inch of space between backbone and rib; repeat the configuration six or more times, depending on the size of your dinosaur—just be sure the tail extends beyond the rib cage. For a head, place some noodles side by side on the other end of the dinosaur. Or, if you wish, use another pasta shape for the head. Use elbows or other pasta shapes to make 4 legs, 2 on either side of the rib cage.

To make a fossil that looks like the side view of a dinosaur, use the noodles, cut side down and round side up as before, to outline the shape of the dinosaur's body. (Littler children might find this idea easier to comprehend.)

When you have a design that you like, remove all the noodles from the construction paper, and with a brush or your fingers, spread a thin layer of glue roughly covering a 6-inch square or circle in the center of the paper. Working carefully, pour some sand all over the glue, tilting the paper gently to spread it evenly until the glue is covered. Re-create the dinosaur design that you planned, pressing the noodles gently into the sticky sand, so that they adhere. Let dry.

What happened to the dinosaurs?

DINOSAURS LIVED ON EARTH LONG, LONG BEFORE THE FIRST HUMANS, between 248 and 65 million years ago, in a period of time called the Mesozoic Era. There were all kinds of dinosaurs; some were as big 127 feet long and 50 feet tall, while some were only as big as a turkey. Some ate plants; others ate meat. They laid eggs from which baby dinosaurs were born. Some walked on two legs, others on four. Some might have been covered in feathers, although they didn't fly. (Back then, there were flying reptiles called pterosaurs, but scientists don't consider these to have been dinosaurs. There were also giant reptiles that swam in the sea, called plesiosaurs and ichthyosaurs.)

Dinosaurs were the main animal on Earth for about 160 million years. The name *dinosaur* comes from the Greek words for "terrible lizard" or "powerful lizard," because the scientist who named them thought they probably resembled the lizards of recent times. But nobody really knows exactly what they looked like, because they became extinct—they died out completely—well before any human ever lived. Some scientists think the dinosaurs died out because the Earth's climate changed and dinosaurs couldn't live under the new conditions; others believe a giant asteroid hit the Earth and made massive dust clouds that blocked sunlight and oxygen that the dinosaurs, as well as other plants and animals of that time, needed to live.

Nobody knows for sure why dinosaurs died out, but we do know that they were followed by other kinds of animals, and eventually, by humans. What we know about dinosaurs comes from studying fossils. (See Table Talk, page 231, to find out a little about fossils.)

FOSSIL BREADSTICKS

THESE WHIMSICAL BREADSTICKS MIGHT GIVE THE BUDDING PALEONTOLOGISTS at your table an idea of how fossils were embedded in sedimentary rock. You can make them sweet and pretend that your fossils are full of tiny prehistoric sea creatures (actually granola) and bone fragments (banana chips), or make them savory and imagine that you've got some fossilized leaves (fresh sage). Or make some of both and reduce the amount of each topping proportionately.

MAKES 12 BREADSTICKS

1 (12-piece) package refrigerated breadstick dough

Savory Topping

2 cloves garlic, finely chopped

¼ teaspoon salt

1 tablespoon unsalted butter or heart-healthy margarine

4 to 6 chopped sage leaves (optional)

24 fresh sage leaves

Sweet Topping

1 tablespoon unsalted butter or heart-healthy margarine

24 dried banana chips

1 tablespoon granola, plus more to taste

Place an oven rack in the middle position and preheat the oven to 375°F. Open the package of dough, separate it into 12 pieces, and place them on a baking sheet. (They won't spread much at all, so you can squeeze them onto 1 sheet.)

To make the savory topping, place the garlic in a small microwavable bowl and cover with the salt. Add the butter and microwave on high power for 30 to 45 seconds, or until the butter is melted. Let cool slightly.

Brush about ¼ teaspoon butter onto each breadstick. You can strain out the garlic, or, for a more intense garlic flavor, sprinkle a little of the garlic on each. For an intense herbal flavor, sprinkle a little chopped sage on each.

Place 2 whole sage leaves end to end on each breadstick and press down on them well, in the center and at the edges, so that they are embedded in the dough.

To make the sweet topping, place the butter into a microwavable bowl and microwave on high power for 30 to 45 seconds, or until melted. Let cool slightly.

Brush about ¼ teaspoon butter onto each breadstick.

Sprinkle each with about ¼ teaspoon granola, and place 2 banana chips end to end on each breadstick. Press down on them well, in the center and at the edges, so that they are embedded in the dough.

Bake for 11 to 15 minutes, or until the breadsticks are golden and baked through. Remove from the oven, let cool a bit and serve. (If any of the toppings curl up or fall off, you can point out that not every leaf or bone became a fossil!)

TABLE TALK

FOSSILS ARE THE REMAINS OR TRACES OF LIVING THINGS that existed on Earth long, long ago. We might think of dinosaur bones when we think of fossils, but fossils can also be the remains—or even imprints—of plants, tiny sea creatures, and other animals that lived before and after dinosaurs walked the Earth. The oldest known fossils are about 3.5 billion years old!

Fossils have been found in the form of bones, teeth, shells, footprints, "body" prints, leaf prints, and even underground burrows dug by these living things. When these long-ago creatures died, they were covered over with layers of fine soil called sediment, which was in turn covered with more soil and rock, until the weight of the sediment caused the outline, or imprint, of the creature to be molded into the rock. Often the actual remains of the animal or plant often turned to dust, leaving just the imprint, but sometimes the remains stayed tightly sealed in the sediment. In other cases, water dripped through the sediment and the traces of mineral in the water turned to stone, creating a different kind of imprint. In still other cases, the remains of prehistoric creatures were preserved in a gooey material on or near the surface of the Earth called a tar pit. It's important to remember that very few of the plants and animals that lived back then ever became fossils; most got eaten up by scavenging animals; other remains were crushed or washed away by water or wind.

PRIMORDIAL SOUP

WHEN SCIENTISTS TALK ABOUT PRIMORDIAL SOUP, they mean the bodies of water full of different kinds of materials that came together to form the first life on Earth. The primordial soup we're cooking here is full of several different kinds of ingredients that will help sustain life—for this dinner, at least. Inspired by *caldo verde,* Portuguese kale soup, it's warm, flavorful, and hearty enough to serve as a meal in itself—or as an accompaniment to the tasty quesadillas in this Dino Dinner. Portuguese cooks typically use a spicy chorizo sausage made of pork in their soup; I use turkey kielbasa because it has less fat than pork sausage but still has plenty of flavor. If your crowd likes their soup spicy, try turkey chorizo. If not, almost any flavorful sausage will work nicely. Likewise, the traditional Portuguese soup calls for a local cabbage, but kale or Swiss chard are delicious substitutes.

MAKES 4 TO 6 SERVINGS

3 to 4 tablespoons olive oil, divided

12 to 16 ounces turkey kielbasa, or other flavorful precooked turkey sausage, cut in ¼ -inch rounds

2 large or 3 medium leeks, washed well (see note, next page), trimmed and cut in ½ -inch pieces

1 (1 pound) bunch kale, washed, trimmed, and cut into chiffonade (see note, page 74)

1½ quarts chicken stock

Heat 2 tablespoons oil in a large saucepan set over medium-high heat. Add the kielbasa and cook, stirring, for 2 to 3 minutes, or until golden-brown on both sides.

Remove the pan from the heat, transfer the kielbasa to a plate, add 1 tablespoon oil and the leeks to the pan, and return the pan to the heat. Cook the leeks, stirring, for about 2 to 3 minutes, or until softened and translucent.

Add the kale and cook for 1 to 2 minutes, or just until all the pieces are wilted and brilliant green in color, adding a little more oil if necessary. Return the kielbasa to the pan, add the stock, and simmer for about 5 minutes, or until the stock is heated through. Keep warm until ready to serve.

The leek, with its long leaves and a bulb at the root, is a cousin of the onion, but with a milder flavor. It absorbs lots of sand and soil as it grows, so it must be washed very, very well before you can begin to cook. Here's how many chefs do it: First trim off the hard, papery outer green leaves; cut off the top, down to the pale green part, and then peel off any below that point that look too hard to eat. Then place the leek on a work surface, hold it at the root end, and with a sharp knife, make a lengthwise cut, starting about an inch from the root and extending the full length of the leek. Rotate the leek 90 degrees and make another lengthwise cut. Still holding the root, wash each section carefully under running water, letting the water get in between each layer until the leek is entirely clean. Rinse your work surface as well and place the leek back on it. Trim off any remaining hard leaves. Gather the sections of the leek back together and slice crosswise in ½-inch pieces. Discard the root.

Kale, a member of the cabbage family, is a wonderfully nutritious green, full of vitamins A and C, calcium, folic acid, iron, and disease-fighting antioxidants. Look for a bunch with crisp, not limp, leaves. To trim and slice, first remove and discard the hard stems. Then working with 1 leaf at a time, fold the leaves in half and cut out the stem from within the leaves. You can then cut it as you wish; for chiffonade, place a few leaves on top of each other, roll lengthwise into a cylinder, and slice crosswise ¼-inch pieces. Let the leaves unravel and repeat with the remaining leaves.

TABLE TALK

What's a paleontologist?

SCIENTISTS CALLED PALEONTOLOGISTS STUDY FOSSILS and rocks to learn what the Earth was like long ago and how its changes in the past might affect life in the future. Paleontologists spend part of their time carefully digging up fossils and the rest of their time restoring them in their labs and studying the science of the past. How do they know where to dig? Often, fossils are found by builders or farmers or just regular folks who come across them while digging up the soil or walking in the wild. When they find something that looks interesting, they call in the scientists!

In the Beginning

"PRIMORDIAL" MEANS SOMETHING THAT CAME BEFORE ANYTHING ELSE—first. Some 3.9 billion years ago, most of the Earth's surface was covered with water, and that water was full of many kinds of elements—scientists have called it a soup, although nobody ate this particular chowder! These elements somehow came together to create tiny, primitive life forms. (These early life forms were similar to bacteria-like organisms—called Archaea—that are still around today.) With time, life became more and more complex. About 440 million years ago, the first fish appeared. Then, 360 million years ago, the first amphibians evolved from fish, and crawled up on land. Amphibians are still with us today, in the form of frogs and salamanders. But amphibians, then and now, have to return to water to lay their eggs. By 300 million years ago, the first reptiles—which could live out their lives entirely on land—appeared. Still, these early lizards weren't dinosaurs. True dinosaurs would have to wait another 40 million years (that would be 260 million years ago!) before making their appearance. Dinosaurs roamed the Earth until about 65 million years ago. And scientists believe that even as the world was changing and dinosaurs were dying out because they could not adapt to the changes, they were evolving into the birds of today.

SABER-TOOTHED SALAD

THIS SALAD IS NAMED FOR THE LONG, SHARP TEETH OF THE SABERTOOTH CATS that developed on Earth about 34 million years ago. Technically, they came after the dinosaurs, but they're still pre-historic, so they're appropriate for this dinner. Use your imagination, and baby corn can look a bit like a long, sharp tooth—a sabertooth. Add a handful of cashews (salted or not according to your preference) for sharp fangs, and you've got the full set of choppers. But these "teeth" won't hurt anybody at your table; *you* bite them. If anybody at your table is allergic to nuts, just omit them.

MAKES 4 SERVINGS

1 tablespoon fresh lime juice

1 tablespoon hickory-flavored
  barbecue sauce

3 tablespoons extra-virgin olive oil

¼ teaspoon salt, plus more to taste

Freshly ground black pepper to taste
  (optional)

Canned baby corn, rinsed and drained,
  plus more to taste

1 (5- or 7-ounce bag) mixed greens,
  washed and dried

¼ to ½ cup salted or unsalted cashews

1 tablespoon snipped fresh chives

Mix the lime juice, barbecue sauce, oil, salt, and pepper, if using, in a shallow container. Place the corn into the container and roll to coat. Set aside.

Just before you are ready to serve, place the greens, cashews, if you are using them, and chives into a bowl. Add the corn and all of the dressing from the container. Toss gently to coat the greens. Divide among 4 salad bowls, making sure that each has at least 2 corn cobs. You can stick the pointy end of the corns up out of the salad if you like.

QUESADILLASAURUS

AS BEFITTING A DINOSAUR, WHEN THE QUESADILLASAURUS IS ASSEMBLED and garnished, it likely won't fit on an average dinner plate. The solution? Just for tonight, instead of plates, use sheets of parchment paper instead. If you think any of the folks at your table will want more than one Quesadillasaurus, add the required number of tortillas and increase the filling ingredients proportionately. Scallions and grape tomatoes serve as the neck, head, tail, and legs, but if you wish, you can substitute other ingredients that your personal paleontologists might prefer.

MAKES 4 SERVINGS

2 cups shredded Cheddar or Mexican-blend cheese

1 scallion, trimmed and finely chopped, plus 4 more scallions, halved crosswise, divided

2 grape tomatoes, chopped, plus 6 grape tomatoes, halved lengthwise, divided

4 best-quality (8-inch) flour tortillas

Place an oven rack in the middle position and preheat the oven to 450°F. Prepare 4 (10- x 12-inch) sheets of aluminum foil or parchment paper.

Combine the cheese, chopped scallion, and chopped tomato in a small bowl, and toss to distribute the vegetables evenly throughout the cheese. Place 1 sheet of foil on a work surface, and center 1 tortilla on it. Arrange about ½ cup of the cheese mixture on one half of the tortilla, leaving the other half empty so that you can fold it over the cheese; leave a border of about ½-inch around the cheese, so that it does not ooze out as it melts. Fold the "empty" half of the tortilla over the cheese and press lightly. Make a foil packet by folding the foil over the quesadilla on all sides. Make 3 more quesadillas in foil with the remaining ingredients. Place the quesadillas on a baking sheet and bake for 15 minutes, or until the cheese is melted and the tortillas are slightly crispy. (You can open a packet and check if you're not sure.)

Meanwhile, prepare 4 sheets of parchment paper, about 16 by 10 inches. Place the halved scallions and grape tomatoes on a serving platter and set aside.

When they are done, remove the quesadillas from the oven and allow to cool slightly. Place on a serving platter. When you are ready to serve, place 1 parchment sheet at each person's place at the table. Place a quesadilla on the parchment sheet, curved side facing away from you. Make a neck by placing the tip of a scallion half on one side of the quesadilla and position the scallion so it extends like a long neck. Place a half tomato at the end for the head. Make a tail by placing the other scallion half at the other side of the quesadilla and letting it extend out like a tail. Place 4 tomato halves at the bottom of the quesadilla to make legs. Eat up!

TABLE TALK — Why do many dinosaurs have "saurus" in their names?

In 1842, Sir Richard Owen, an English scientist, gave the dinosaur its name, using Greek words. *Sauros* means lizard, which is what the dinosaurs looked like to those early scientists. (The "dino" part is based on the Greek word, *deinos*, which means terrible or powerful.) When scientists realized that there were many kinds of dinosaurs, they gave them individual names, and some of them have "saurus" in them, like tyrannosaurus and stegosaurus. There were hundreds of kinds of dinosaurs, and scientists have given names to all whose fossils have been discovered.

Can you think of any other dinosaurs by name?

If you were a scientist and you had to name a dinosaur, what would you call it?

CHOCOLATE DINOTURTLES

KIDS LOVE CHOCOLATE TURTLES; here we go back in time and visit their prehistoric ancestor, the Dinoturtle, which looks a bit like a stegosaurus, with pointy plates and spikes running down its back and tail. For this recipe you will need a Silpat or other nonstick baking sheet insert or foil, or a lightly oiled nonstick baking sheet. The bowl you use to melt the chocolate must be clean and absolutely dry. Even tiny amounts of liquid can make the chocolate seize and become grainy. Use a medium-sized or large bowl so the chocolate will melt evenly. Milk or dark chocolate or chocolate chips are fine for this recipe; use whichever you prefer.

MAKES 12 DINOSAURS

Nonstick cooking spray, as needed

24 soft caramels (about 6 ounces)

1 cup (about 4 ounces) pecan halves, cut in half lengthwise (substitute almond slivers)

1½ cups (about 9 ounces) milk or dark chocolate, finely chopped (or chocolate chips)

12 sesame seeds or tiny candies, for eyes (optional)

Line a baking sheet with a nonstick insert sheet or spray a nonstick baking sheet lightly with nonstick cooking spray.

Working with a few at a time, place the unwrapped caramels on a microwavable plate, and microwave on medium power for 10 to 15 seconds, or until pliable. Work carefully, as sugar doesn't always absorb microwaves evenly and there can be hot spots; feel each caramel before letting children handle them.

With your hands, roll 2 caramels together to form a smooth log. Shape the caramel log into a dinosaur (imagine a stegosaurus shape) by elongating one end into a neck and head and the other into a tail. Flatten the middle a bit, but keep it nice and round. At the bottom of the middle, make two small pinches and stretch the caramel down to form short legs. You should now have a shape that resembles a dinosaur!). Repeat with the remaining caramels.

Place them on the prepared baking sheet. Starting at the top rounded edge of a dinosaur (where its backbone would be), place pieces of nut under the edge of the caramel to form spikes. Use large pieces for the back and progressively smaller pieces along the tail. Don't worry if they don't adhere completely at this point, as the chocolate will hold them to the candies.

Place the chocolate into a perfectly dry microwavable bowl, and microwave at medium power for 1 minute. Stir it with a dry spoon or spatula. Microwave for another 30 seconds and then stir again. Continue microwaving 30 seconds at a time, then stirring, until the chocolate is almost melted, which should take about 2 to 3 minutes in all.

Scoop about 1 tablespoon of the melted chocolate onto the dinosaur's back. With a small butter knife, pastry brush, or the wooden stick that comes in some caramel bags, quickly smooth the chocolate over the candy, letting some chocolate run onto the nuts where they are attached to the caramel.

If you like, place a sesame seed or candy or a very small piece of nut on the head where the eye would be. Let the chocolate harden at room temperature.

When you are melting chocolate, it can seize—that is, it can become grainy and clump up. Not very palatable, but you can smooth it out by adding solid vegetable shortening such as Crisco. Add 1 tablespoon at a time, microwave for 10 to 20 seconds, and stir. Repeat until the mixture is smooth. This mixture will not set up as firmly as plain chocolate; nor will it taste as good. But it can still be used for the candies if you don't want to start over with more chocolate. Another way to loosen seized chocolate is to add butter or cream in the same manner as the vegetable shortening. This mixture, however, will be too thin to firm up on the candies. It can be stored in the refrigerator or the freezer for another use, such as a dessert sauce or an addition to frosting.

TABLE TALK

After-Dinner Fun: Virtual Museum Visit

WE DON'T KNOW EXACTLY WHAT DINOSAURS LOOKED LIKE, because they became extinct long before the first human beings were born. But fossils can give us an idea of what dinosaurs looked like. When a number of fossilized bones are found in one place, scientists try to figure out how they went together inside the dinosaur's skin, and then they try to reconnect them, using wires and tools. Many museums that specialize in natural history own fossils, either individual bones or groups of bones that scientists have put back together. You can visit these museums online. Here are just a few with major exhibits on the prehistoric world. After dinner, pick one or two and take a journey back in time! And if you live near one of these museums, plan a family outing there. There's nothing quite like standing next to a dinosaur fossil that's as big as your house!

• The Academy of Natural Sciences, Philadelphia, PA (www.ansp.org/)

• The American Museum of Natural History, New York City, NY (www.amnh.org/)

• The Field Museum of Natural History, Chicago, IL (www.fieldmuseum.org/)

• The Florida Museum of Natural History, Gainesville, FL (www.flmnh.ufl.edu/)

• The Hooper Natural History Museum at the Ottawa-Carleton Geoscience Centre, Ottawa (http://hoopermuseum.earthsci.carleton.ca//index.html)

• The Museum of Paleontology at the University of California at Berkeley, Berkeley, CA www.ucmp.berkeley.edu/)

• The New Mexico Museum of Natural History and Science, Albuquerque, NM (www.nmnaturalhistory.org/)

• The Smithsonian Institution's National Museum of Natural History, Washington, DC (http://www.mnh.si.edu/)

• The University of Michigan Museum of Paleontology, Ann Arbor, MI (www.paleontology.lsa.umich.edu/)

• The University of Nebraska State Museum's Division of Vertebrate Paleontology, Lincoln, NE (www-museum.unl.edu/research/vertpaleo/vertpaleo.html)

• Yale University's Peabody Museum of Natural History, New Haven, CT (www.peabody.yale.edu/)

Thanksgiving Anytime

HOW LUCKY WE ARE TO HAVE ENOUGH TO EAT—AND SUCH DELICIOUS THINGS, at that! How lucky we are to have each other! When my day has been less than perfect, I try to remember all the things I can be thankful for—I make a mental list, and it always cheers me up. In a world where some are overly focused on getting more and more and still more stuff, while others don't have enough, this is what I want to teach my child; let's be thankful for what we have, for what is most important, and let's make time to enjoy the important things together. I guess that's what *Friday Night Bites* is really all about.

Menu

Seeds of Gratitude

Turkey Cutlets with Cover-All-Bases
Cornbread-Cranberry-Sweet Potato Stuffing

Harvest Festival Green Beans with Pancetta

Yumpkin Pudding Parfait

Game Plan

★ Make and nibble the Seeds of Gratitude. ✋

★ Get the kids started on their Cornucopias of Thanks. ✋

★ Prep and microwave the vanilla and pumpkin puddings for the Yumpkin Pudding Parfait and refrigerate.

★ Prep the Cover-All-Bases Cornbread-Cranberry-Sweet Potato Stuffing.

★ Prep and cook the Turkey Cutlets, and heat with the stuffing in the oven for 15 minutes.

★ Make the Harvest Festival Green Beans with Pancetta.

★ Give thanks for dinner!

★ Mix the graham cracker crumbles and assemble the umpkin Pudding Parfaits.

★ And give thanks again, for dessert!

DINNER PREP IN SMALL BITES:

If you have time the night before or earlier in the day, bake up some Sunshine Cornbread (page 38) for the Cover-All-Bases Cornbread-Cranberry-Sweet Potato Stuffing. (Or use a simple cornbread mix if you wish.) If you wish to bake the sweet potatoes instead of using canned, you may do so the night before or earlier in the day. Peel and cube them when ready to cook the stuffing.

FRIDAY NIGHT TIME-SAVER:

If time is short, use store-bought corn muffins or prepared cornbread stuffing mix as a base for the stuffing, but if you use the preseasoned stuffing mix, omit the salt and poultry seasoning specified in the recipe. The microwave Yumpkin Pudding Parfait comes together quickly, but if you're really tight on time, you can use ready-made vanilla pudding and just make the pumpkin pudding and Graham Cracker Crumbles, or skip the pumpkin pudding altogether and just do vanilla pudding and crumbles.

Crafty Friday:
A CORNUCOPIA OF THANKS

HERE'S A PROJECT THAT WILL PUT YOU IN A THANKFUL MOOD. It yields a pretty little craft and gets you thinking about some important stuff at the same time.

1 (9- x 13-inch) sheet brown construction paper per person

Safety Scissors

2 (9- x 13-inch) sheets red construction paper, plus more as needed

2 (9- x 13-inch) sheets yellow construction paper, plus more as needed

2 (9- x 13-inch) sheets orange construction paper, plus more as needed

2 (9- x 13-inch) sheets green construction paper, plus more as needed

Construction paper in other colors (optional)

Transparent tape

Markers or pens

Fold your brown construction paper in half crosswise. Cut into the fold, making 5 ($3\frac{1}{2}$-inch) slits perpendicular to the fold. (Start about $1\frac{1}{2}$ inches from the edge of the paper and space the slits about an inch apart.)

Set 1 sheet each of red, yellow, orange, and green construction paper aside. Cut the remaining colored construction paper sheets crosswise into 1-inch-wide strips. (Depending on how many cornucopias you make, you might not use every strip; save leftovers for another craft project.)

Unfold the brown paper and weave the colored strips into it crosswise, weave the first strip under and over the slits, and the next over and under, and so on, alternating the colors.

When you are finished weaving, fold the woven sheet crosswise into a cone and tape it securely.

Cut each sheet of the remaining colored construction paper into enough sections so that every person has a piece of each color. (If there are 4 people, cut each piece into 4.) Cut the paper into the shapes of vegetables and fruits: red tomatoes and/or apples, yellow bananas and/or lemons, green cucumbers and/or grapes, and, if you like, other fruits and vegetables in other colors, using more construction paper if you need to.

(continued on the next page)

Think about the things you are thankful for, and write the name of one on each fruit or vegetable. Younger kids who can't write can draw small pictures. The things you are thankful for might be the same as the paper fruits and vegetables you've created—you can write "apples" on the apple shape, for example. Or they might be other foods—maybe mac-and-cheese or chocolate. Or they might be things or people that have nothing to do with food, such as Mom and Dad, sisters and brothers, grandparents, aunts, uncles, cousins, friends, pets, a house to live in, toys—whatever you are thankful for.

TABLE TALK

What's a cornucopia?

A CORNUCOPIA IS A HORN-SHAPED CONTAINER that symbolizes an abundant harvest. Sometimes called a horn of plenty, the cornucopia originated in a Greek myth. As the story goes, a goat took care of Zeus, the king of the gods, when he was a baby. The goat's horn broke off, and it magically filled with fruit. Horn-shaped baskets filled with fruit, flowers, and vegetables are a common symbol of Thanksgiving.

Pepita, the Spanish word for seed, is the term that Mexican cooks use for the seeds of pumpkins and other varieties of squash. A common ingredient in Mexican mole and pipian sauces, pepitas also make a yummy and healthful snack. They are sold hulled or in their shells, roasted or raw, and salted or unsalted. For this recipe, you are doing the roasting and seasoning, so buy the hulled, raw, unsalted variety.

If you are lucky enough to have a fresh pumpkin around, don't waste the seeds. Cut out the circle around the stem as if you were going to carve a jack o' lantern (perhaps you will?), and scoop out the seeds. They'll be full of pumpkin goo, so place them into a large fine-mesh sieve and rinse them well with water. Try to get all the goo and membrane off; pull the big clumps off with your hands. Then toast them as described in this recipe.

SEEDS OF GRATITUDE

RAW GREEN PUMPKIN SEEDS are good just eaten out of hand, but this recipe makes them a sweet-salty flavor extravaganza. Use your favorite seasoned salt or grilling spice blend, or if you wish, mix up your own blend. If anyone at your table is sensitive to such things, read the labels carefully and avoid the blends that contain hot pepper flakes.

MAKES 2 CUPS

2 cups hulled, raw, unsalted pumpkin seeds (pepitas)

1 tablespoon vegetable oil

1 tablespoon packed light brown sugar

1 tablespoon seasoned salt or grilling spice blend

Place an oven rack in the middle position and preheat the oven to 350°F. Line a baking sheet with parchment paper.

Combine the seeds and oil in a medium-sized bowl. Combine the brown sugar and seasoned salt in a cup, and stir to blend well. Pour the sugar-salt mixture over the seeds, and toss gently until every seed is lightly coated.

Pour the pumpkin seeds onto the prepared baking sheet; spread as much as possible into a single layer. Bake for 7 minutes, stir, and bake for another 5 to 8 minutes, or until the seeds are golden and nearly dry. Cool slightly before eating.

TURKEY CUTLETS WITH COVER-ALL-BASES CORNBREAD-CRANBERRY-SWEET POTATO STUFFING

THERE'S AN ABBREVIATED THANKSGIVING MEAL IN THIS DISH. Quick-cooking turkey cutlets are matched with a traditional fresh cornbread stuffing that is flavored with two more traditional Turkey Day elements: cranberries and sweet potatoes. To make this dish easy to put together at any time of year, the cranberries are dried. And to make it easy to do without long prep time, the sweet potatoes are canned. (If you have the time, roast 2 medium-sized sweet potatoes, pierced all over with the tines of a fork, in a 400°F oven about 45 minutes, depending on the size, or until they can be easily pierced with a knife. However, a can of sweet potatoes or yams gives you a taste of fresh with no pre-cooking, and they're good with all other stuffing ingredients.) If you do have the time, you can bake the Sunshine Cornbread (page 38), but if not, store-bought cornbread or corn muffins will work very nicely. If someone at your table has a big appetite, you might want to make an extra cutlet for him or her. While the turkey and stuffing finish cooking in the oven, you can make the pan gravy.

MAKES 4 SERVINGS

Stuffing

4 cups (½-inch) cubes Sunshine Cornbread or store-bought cornbread or 2 large corn muffins, cut into ½-inch cubes)

2 tablespoons olive oil

2 cups chopped onion (about 1 large onion)

1 cup chopped celery (about 3 medium stalks)

Place an oven rack in the middle position and preheat the oven to 400°F. Arrange the cornbread cubes in a roasting pan in a single layer, and roast for 10 minutes.

Heat the oil in a large, nonstick skillet set over medium-high heat, and when it shimmers, add the onion and celery, and cook, stirring and shaking the pan, for 3 minutes. Add the garlic and cook, stirring, for about 1½ minutes longer, or until the onion, celery, and garlic are softened, translucent, and beginning to brown. Add the cranberries and toss. Remove from the heat, add the yams, and toss to combine.

Remove the cornbread from the oven, and add the vegetables

2 cloves garlic, chopped, or to taste

¼ cup dried cranberries

1 (15-ounce) can yams or sweet
  potatoes, drained and cut into
  ½-inch pieces

8 ounces chicken stock

1 tablespoon melted unsalted butter

1 teaspoon salt

½ teaspoon poultry seasoning

Turkey

½ cup all-purpose flour

1 teaspoon salt, plus more to taste

4 (4- to 5-ounce) turkey cutlets

1½ tablespoons olive oil

Gravy

8 ounces chicken stock

1 teaspoon arrowroot

Freshly ground black pepper (optional)

to it in the roasting pan, reserving the skillet and its juices for cooking the turkey. In another container, combine the chicken stock, melted butter, salt, and poultry seasoning, and stir to incorporate. Pour over the stuffing, and mix until the liquid is distributed throughout. Set aside.

Mix the flour and salt in a shallow bowl. On the work surface, place the turkey cutlets between 2 sheets of waxed paper, and pound lightly with a meat mallet to a thickness of about ¼ inch.

Dip the cutlets into the flour to coat both sides, and tap off any excess. Heat the oil in the skillet you used for cooking the vegetables over medium-high heat. Place the turkey cutlets into it in a single layer, working in batches if necessary, and cook for 3 minutes, or until just golden. Turn with tongs and cook for 3 minutes longer.

Reduce the oven temperature to 350°F. With tongs, transfer the cutlets to the stuffing in the roasting pan, nestling the cutlets into the stuffing and spooning some stuffing over them. Reserve the skillet and its juices. Place the stuffing and cutlets into the oven, and bake for 15 to 17 minutes, or until the turkey is cooked through and no longer pink inside. Remove from the oven and let rest, covered, for 10 minutes.

To make a light gravy, set the reserved skillet over medium heat. Add the chicken stock and arrowroot and cook, stirring to loosen any flavorful brown bits on the bottom of the skillet, for 3 to 4 minutes, or until the sauce thickens slightly. Season to taste with black pepper, if you wish, and transfer to a serving bowl or gravy boat.

Place a turkey cutlet and some stuffing on each of 4 dinner plates. Pass the gravy at the table.

Why do we celebrate Thanksgiving?

YOU HAVE PROBABLY HEARD THE STORY OF THE FIRST THANKSGIVING. Nearly 400 years ago, in 1620, a group of about 100 English citizens sailed across the Atlantic Ocean and landed at a spot in what is now the state of Massachusetts. There they established a community that they called the Plymouth Plantation. The group came to be known as the Pilgrims. The word *pilgrim* means traveler, and often refers to someone on a religious journey. The Pilgrims came to the New World because they wanted to be free to practice their religion as they pleased.

When they arrived, they were greeted by a Native American tribe, the Wampanoags, who helped them get through their first difficult year in the New World. The Pilgrims had to learn about their new land while building shelter from the harsh winter and growing, hunting, and gathering all their food. Many in the group did not live through the first year. The following fall, in 1621, when the crops were harvested, the Pilgrims shared a feast of thanksgiving with the Wampanoags. This was not the first, nor the last, Thanksgiving feast in the New World; many Native American tribes celebrated Thanksgiving, as did other groups of European settlers. But it is the one we remember best, and the one on which the contemporary holiday is based.

More than 200 years later, long after the English colonists had declared their independence and set up the United States of America, President Abraham Lincoln declared that Thanksgiving would be celebrated each year on the fourth Thursday of November. Congress made it official in the 1940s.

HARVEST FESTIVAL GREEN BEANS WITH PANCETTA

YES, YOUR AUNT SUE WAS FAMOUS FOR HER GREEN BEAN CASSEROLE made with canned soup and French fried onions, but for Thanksgiving Anytime, why not try something different? Here the beans get jazzed up with a little pancetta and rosemary in a quick and easy preparation.

MAKES 4 SERVINGS

4 thin slices pancetta , roughly chopped

2 sprigs fresh rosemary, divided

1 tablespoon olive oil

1¼ pounds green beans, trimmed and cut into 1½ -inch pieces

Place the pancetta into a microwavable bowl or container large enough to hold the beans (but don't add the beans yet), nestle 1 sprig rosemary into it, and microwave on high power for 2 to 3 minutes, or until crispy. Remove from the microwave and carefully transfer the pancetta to a small plate, reserving the bowl. When the pancetta is cool enough to handle, crumble it finely. Discard the rosemary.

Meanwhile, drain all but 2 teaspoons pancetta fat from the reserved bowl (you might not get much more, but it will depend on the fattiness of the pancetta). Add the olive oil to the fat, and stir to combine. Add the beans, toss to coat them all, nestle the remaining rosemary sprig into them, and microwave for 6 to 7 minutes, or until tender.

When the beans are cooked, remove the rosemary sprig and discard. Add the crumbled pancetta to the beans and toss to incorporate. Keep warm until ready to serve.

Pancetta is a flavorful Italian bacon that is cured but not smoked. It is often rolled up, sausage style, and sliced. Italian cooks like to use it to flavor sauces and stews.

YUMPKIN PUDDING PARFAIT

OF COURSE, PUMPKIN PIE IS THE TRADITIONAL THANKSGIVING TREAT, but this half-pumpkin, half-vanilla microwave pudding gives you a taste of tradition in a quick and easy form. Your house will fill with the tantalizing aromas of vanilla and cinnamon. You only need half a cup of canned pumpkin purée, but you can freeze the rest for another time. Alternate layers of pudding with buttery-sweet Graham Cracker Crumbles (the makings for a graham cracker crust, without the pie plate), dig in, and you'll see why I call it "yumpkin!"

MAKES 4 SERVINGS

Vanilla Pudding

2½ cups whole milk

¼ cup cornstarch

¼ cup granulated sugar

⅛ teaspoon salt

1 tablespoon unsalted butter

2 teaspoons pure vanilla extract

Pumpkin Pudding

2 cups whole milk

3½ tablespoons cornstarch

½ teaspoon ground cinnamon

½ cup canned plain pumpkin purée

½ cup granulated sugar

1 teaspoon pure vanilla extract

⅛ teaspoon salt

To make the vanilla pudding, combine the milk and cornstarch in a measuring cup or small bowl and stir to dissolve. If there are any stubborn lumps that won't dissolve, strain through a fine-mesh sieve. Pour the mixture into a microwavable container with a lid, and stir in the sugar and salt until dissolved. Cover and microwave on high power for 1½ minutes, stir, cover again, and repeat the process twice more, for a total of 4½ minutes; then add the butter and stir in the vanilla, cover, and microwave for 1½ minutes. Stir to blend, cover, and microwave for 30 seconds. The pudding should be thickened and creamy and the butter should be completely melted and incorporated thoroughly. (Microwave ovens can vary in power, and some cook unevenly, so if by chance it is not pudding consistency, cover and microwave for an additional 30 seconds.) Remove from the microwave, let cool a bit, and refrigerate until ready to serve.

To make the pumpkin pudding, combine the milk, cornstarch, and cinnamon in a small bowl and stir to dissolve. If there are any stubborn lumps that won't dissolve, strain through a fine-mesh sieve. Pour the mixture into a clean

Graham Cracker Crumbles

8 graham crackers

½ cup packed brown sugar

2 ounces (½ stick) unsalted butter, melted

microwavable container with a lid and stir in the pumpkin, sugar, vanilla, and salt until dissolved. Cover and microwave on high power for 1½ minutes, stir, cover again, and repeat the process 3 times, for a total of 6 minutes; then stir again, cover, and microwave for 30 seconds. Remove from the microwave, let cool a bit, and refrigerate until ready to serve.

To make the crumbles, combine the graham crackers, brown sugar, and butter in a food processor and pulse to coarse crumbs. Set aside.

To serve, spoon about 1 tablespoon of the crumbles into each of 4 parfait glasses or deep wine glasses (not the balloon shape). Top with ¼ cup vanilla pudding, another tablespoon of crumbles, and ¼ cup pumpkin pudding. Repeat, dividing the crumbles and puddings evenly among the 4 glasses, and alternating between vanilla and pumpkin. Top with a dusting of crumbles and serve.

TABLE TALK

WHY SHOULDN'T WE WASTE FOOD? Does everyone have enough to eat? What can we do to help people who are hungry?

After Dinner Fun: A Thanksgiving Anytime List

EVERYONE CAN GO AROUND THE TABLE AND THANK SOMEONE for a nice thing he or she did. Then everyone can empty their cornucopias and tell what they're thankful for. Give everyone a chance to speak a few times and acknowledge them for the thoughtful things they do.

Index